DOCUMENTS IN EARLY
CHRISTIAN THOUGHT

Maurice Wiles has written: *The Spiritual Gospel* (Cambridge University Press, 1960), *The Christian Fathers* (Hodder and Stoughton, 1966), *The Divine Apostle* (Cambridge University Press, 1967), *The Making of Christian Doctrine* (Cambridge University Press, 1967), *The Remaking of Christian Doctrine* (S.C.M. Press, 1974).

Mark Santer was a contributor to *The Phenomenon of Christian Belief*, ed. G. W. H. Lampe (Mowbray, 1970).

DOCUMENTS IN EARLY CHRISTIAN THOUGHT

Edited by

MAURICE WILES
Regius Professor of Divinity, University of Oxford

MARK SANTER
Principal of Westcott House, Cambridge

CAMBRIDGE UNIVERSITY PRESS

CAMBRIDGE

LONDON · NEW YORK · MELBOURNE

Published by the Syndics of the Cambridge University Press
The Pitt Building, Trumpington Street, Cambridge CB2 1RP
Bentley House, 200 Euston Road, London NW1 2DB
32 East 57th Street, New York, NY 10022, USA
296 Beaconsfield Parade, Middle Park, Melbourne 3206, Australia

First published 1975
First paperback edition 1977
Reprinted 1979

Printed in Great Britain
at the University Press, Cambridge

Library of Congress Cataloguing in Publication Data
Main entry under title:
Documents in early Christian thought.
1.   Christian literature, Early – Collected works.
2.   Theology – Collected works – Early church, ca. 30–600.
I.   Wiles, Maurice F.   II.   Santer, Mark.
BR60.A62D62   281′.1   74–31807
ISBN 0 521 20669 3 hard covers
ISBN 0 521 09915 3 paperback

CONTENTS

Contents

Contents

ACKNOWLEDGEMENTS

The translations are those of the editors with a small number of adaptations of existing translations. The publisher and editors acknowledge the kind permission of the following for the revision of their translations:

Mrs J. M. Shapland for an extract from C. R. B. Shapland, *The Letters of Saint Athanasius Concerning the Holy Spirit* (§ 19);

Longman Group Ltd and The Newman Press for an extract from J. N. D. Kelly's translation of *Rufinus: A Commentary on the Apostle's Creed* (§ 54);

SCM Press Ltd and The Westminster Press for extracts from *The Library of Christian Classics* (§§ 6, 9, 18, 20, 26, 34).

The publisher and editors also acknowledge the kind permission of the Revd Dr J. K. Downing and Harvard University Archives for the use of Dr Downing's text of Gregory of Nyssa's sermon on 1 Corinthians 15: 28 (§ 56).

ABBREVIATIONS

ACO   Acta Conciliorum Oecumenicorum, edited by E. Schwartz (Strasbourg and Berlin, 1914–40)

CCL   *Corpus Christianorum*. Series Latina (Turnhout and Paris, 1953–)

CSEL   *Corpus Scriptorum Ecclesiasticorum Latinorum* (Vienna, 1866–)

GCS   *Die griechischen christlichen Schriftsteller der ersten drei Jahrhunderte* (Leipzig and Berlin, 1897–)

JTS   *Journal of Theological Studies* (London, 1899–)

LCC   *Library of Christian Classics* (London and Philadelphia, 1953–)

LS   H. G. Liddell and R. Scott, *A Greek–English Lexicon*, new edition (9th) by H. Stuart Jones and R. McKenzie (Oxford, 1925–40)

LXX   Septuagint

PG   J. P. Migne, ed., *Patrologia Graeca* (Paris, 1857–66)

PL   J. P. Migne, ed., *Patrologia Latina* (Paris, 1844–64)

SC   *Sources chrétiennes* (Paris, 1941–)

x

INTRODUCTION

The aim of this book is easier to describe than to achieve. Its purpose is to bring within the compass of a single volume a representative selection of extracts from the writings of the early Christian Fathers covering all the main areas of Christian thought. The importance of the Fathers as those who gave a distinctive and lasting shape to Christian theology is universally recognized. Those who have the time and the skill to read the writings of the Fathers *in extenso* and in the original will have no need of this volume. But we believe that there are an increasing number, not only of theological students, who would welcome a book which will introduce them to the thought of the Fathers at first hand. It is for such people that this book is designed.

The extracts are arranged topically. We have tried to select passages which make their point in a sufficiently self-contained manner to make sense when removed from their wider context, which are long enough not merely to declare a conclusion but to illustrate the kind of reasoning which leads up to it, and yet short enough to allow us to cover all the main areas of thought. The period is most renowned for its determination of 'orthodox' belief and denunciation of 'heresy'. Some of the passages given come from directly polemical writings of this kind. But the Fathers did not indulge only in polemics. They preached, they taught, they wrote letters, they wrote commentaries on the Bible. Passages have deliberately been chosen from all these different types of writing.

Introductory material and annotation has been kept to a minimum. There is a short introduction to each section, placing the extracts that follow in their particular context within the development of Christian thought. At the head of each passage we have indicated what edition of the text we have used in making the translation. Most of the translations are our own. Where we have used an existing translation, this has always been checked with the original and revised. Biblical references are given in the case of direct allusions. Notes have been restricted to three types: cases where in translation we have deviated from the the text being followed, points in argument which are likely to be obscure without some explanation, and significant cross-references to other passages translated in this book. It should be noted that biblical quotations are often given by patristic authors in a Greek or Latin version differing not only from the Hebrew but also from the usual text of the Septuagint and the Greek New Testament. Such deviations are explicitly referred to only in particularly unusual or puzzling cases.

We have not included any detailed account of the various writers or of the history and thought of the period. This is readily accessible elsewhere. For factual information about the Fathers and their writings, see B. Altaner, *Patrology* (Freiburg and London, 1960) or J. Quasten, *Patrology*, vols. I–III (Utrecht, 1950–60). For an outline of the history of the period see Henry Chadwick, *The Early Church* (Harmondsworth, 1967) or W. H. C. Frend, *The Early Church* (London 1965). For a general account of the doctrine of the period, see Maurice Wiles, *The Christian Fathers* (London, 1966), or, more fully, J. N. D. Kelly, *Early Christian Doctrines* (London, 1968⁴).

1 God

The conception of God is both the most fundamental and the most difficult part of any scheme of religious thought. The Fathers were heirs to two traditions – the anthropomorphic accounts of God's loving activity in the Bible and the philosophical reflection on the changeless source of all being in Hellenistic thought. In the work of the Eastern Fathers in particular we see the interaction of these two traditions upon one another. The first four extracts chosen all come from the Eastern Church and illustrate that interaction.

Clement of Alexandria, writing towards the end of the second century, seeks to show how, on the one hand, poets and philosophers (above all Plato) and, on the other, Scripture point alike to the ineffability of God. In doing so he draws on the writings of Platonists of his own time. Origen held similar convictions, but the extensive nature of his expository and homiletic use of Scripture required him to work out their implications in more detail. The extract given here shows this concern leading him into an interesting discussion of the nature of religious language.

Basil's letter belongs to a more directly polemical context. The later Arians had claimed that it was logically impossible for the same God to be both essentially unknowable and yet known in Christian revelation. Basil meets the objection by drawing a distinction between God's essence and his attributes.

The passage from his brother Gregory of Nyssa shows the strongly religious character of this approach. Gregory, like his pagan Neoplatonist contemporaries, had a profoundly spiritual notion of the human intellect. Nevertheless, in his view the knowledge of God transcends not only the senses but even the intellect itself. He uses the scriptural story of Moses meeting with God in the darkness of Mount Sinai and develops the paradoxical notion of the vision of God in darkness.

In the final passage of this section, we see another form of the interweaving of the languages of devotion and of philosophical reflection. Augustine too was deeply influenced by Neoplatonism. As he expounds the praises of God in the Psalms,

3

regularly used in the worship of the Church, he reflects on the relation between God who is absolute goodness and being in himself and the created goods that he has made.

1   Clement of Alexandria
    Miscellanies 5, xii, 78–82
    [*GCS* 15, 377–81]

78. 'To discover the father and maker of this universe is a hard task; and having discovered him it is impossible to declare him to all men ... for it is something which cannot be expressed in words like other subjects of knowledge.'* So says Plato, that lover of truth. He had clearly heard how the most wise Moses when going up into the mountain (going up, that is, to the highest point of the intelligible order for holy contemplation) had to give orders that the whole people were not to go up with him. And when Scripture says, 'Moses entered the darkness where God was' [Exod. 20: 21],† that is an indication for those able to grasp it that God is both invisible and ineffable, and that the unbelief and ignorance of the majority of mankind is indeed a darkness obstructing the passage of the light-rays of the truth. Orpheus too, that teacher about God, drew on the same source. After saying: 'There is One, complete in himself, and from this One everything is derived' (or 'born', which is an alternative reading), he continues: 'No mortal has seen him but he himself sees all men'; and more explicitly still: 'Him I do not see; around him a cloud is fixed. For mortal men have only little mortal pupils in their eyes, natural growths of flesh and bone.' ‡

79. The apostle provides us with a further witness when he says 'I know a man in Christ caught up into the third heaven' and from there 'to Paradise, who heard ineffable words which man has no power to speak' [2 Cor. 12: 2, 4]. This is his way of indicating the ineffability of God; when he uses the words 'no power' he is not

---

* Plato, *Timaeus* 28 C; *Epistle* vii 341 C. Clement also combines these two quotations in *Protrepticus* vi, 68, 1. Both were standard quotations, much used in the contemporary Middle Platonism. See J. Daniélou, *Gospel Message and Hellenistic Culture* (ET London and Philadelphia, 1973), pp. 108–14.

† For a fuller development of this interpretation of Moses' ascent of Mount Sinai, see Gregory of Nyssa, *Life of Moses*, pp. 12–17 below.

‡ Orpheus, fragment 5, 9–11; 15–17 (ed. E. Abel, *Orphica* [Leipzig and Prague, 1885], p. 146).

referring to any law or fear of disobeying some command but is declaring that it is not within human capacity to give expression to the divine, even though such expression may quite properly begin to be possible beyond the third heaven on the part of those whose task is to instruct elect souls in the higher mysteries there. I know a passage where Plato also considers the question of a multiplicity of heavens. (My plan in this writing is, as I undertook at the beginning, to defer the many examples that could be drawn from non-Greek teaching to an appropriate point later on.) In the *Timaeus* the problem is raised whether one should think of many worlds or just this one – the exact terms are not significant as 'world' and 'heaven' are treated as synonymous – and the text reads: 'Have we been right to talk of one heaven or would it have been more correct to speak of many, countless heavens? We must say one, if we are to hold that it was made in accordance with its pattern.' *

80. And in the epistle of the Romans to the Corinthians we also read of 'the ocean which no man can pass and the worlds beyond it'. †

In similar vein the noble apostle speaks of 'the depth of the riches and wisdom and knowledge of God' [Rom. 11: 33]. Was this not also the prophet's hidden meaning when he ordered the making of unleavened 'griddle' cakes [Exod. 12: 39]? ‡ Was that not an indication that the truly sacred and mystic word about the unbegotten and his powers needed to be hidden in 'riddles'? This is confirmed by what the apostle explicitly says in his letter to the Corinthians: 'We speak wisdom among the perfect, not the wisdom of this age or of the rulers of this age who are passing way – but we speak the wisdom of God in a mystery, the wisdom which is hidden' [1 Cor. 2: 6–7]. Elsewhere he speaks of the 'knowledge of the mystery of God in Christ in whom all the treasures of wisdom and knowledge are hidden' [Col. 2: 2–3].

This is still further confirmed by the words of our Saviour himself: 'To you it is given to know the mystery of the kingdom of heaven' [Matt. 13: 11]. Again the gospel declares that our Saviour spoke the word to the apostles in a mystery; for it is of him that the prophecy says: 'He will open his mouth in parables and will utter things that from the beginning of the world have been hidden' [Matt. 13: 35 (Ps. 78: 2)]. And then the Lord himself indicates concealment by means of the parable of the leaven: 'The kingdom of heaven', he says, 'is like leaven which a woman took and hid in

---

* *Timaeus* 31 A.   † 1 Clement 20, 8.
‡ Clement plays on the word ἐγκρυφίας as Philo had done (*de Sacr. Ab. et Caini* 60).

three measures of meal until the whole was leavened' [Matt. 13: 33]. This indicates either that the tripartite soul achieves the saving way of obedience through the spiritual power hidden in it by faith or that the strong and effective power of the word which has been granted to us draws to itself in a hidden and invisible way anyone who accepts it and takes it into his own being, and brings all aspects of his life into unity.

81. Solon thus said very profoundly of God: 'It is very hard to grasp the invisible measure of the mind, which alone possesses the ultimate bounds of all things.'* For, in the words of the poet of Agrigentum, the divine 'cannot be approached with our eyes or grasped with our hands – and that is the greatest way of persuasion leading to the minds of men.' †

Again John the apostle writes: 'No one has seen God at any time; the only-begotten God, who is in the bosom of the Father, he has declared him' [John 1: 18]. He uses the name 'bosom' of God to refer to his invisibility and ineffability; for this reason some people have used the name 'depth' to indicate that he is inaccessible and incomprehensible but embraces and enfolds all things.‡

This is the hardest part of the discussion about God. The first cause of anything is hard to discover. It is therefore particularly hard to describe the first and original cause, which is the source of the existence of everything else which is or has been. For how is one to speak about that which is neither a genus nor a differentia nor a species nor an individuality nor a number – in other words which is neither any kind of accidental property nor the subject of any accidental property? Nor can one properly speak of him as a 'whole', for a whole is a matter of size and he is 'Father of the whole universe'. Nor can one speak of him as having parts, for that which is 'One' is indivisible and therefore also infinite – infinite not in the sense of measureless extension but in the sense of being without dimensions or boundaries [82], and therefore without shape or name. §

* Solon, fragment 16 (ed. E. Diehl, *Anthologia Lyrica Graeca* [3rd edition, Leipzig, 1949], 1, 37).

† Empedocles, fragment 133 (ed. H. Diels, *Die Fragmente der Vorsokratiker* [7th edition, Berlin, 1954], 1, 365).

‡ 'Bythos' or 'depth' is the name of the primary aion in Valentinian Gnosticism with which Clement was familiar. See Irenaeus, *Against the Heresies* 1, 1, 1.

§ Albinus, *Epitome* 10, 4, has striking similarities to this passage and Clement may be dependent on it. At the very least it shows how very close he was to the Middle Platonist tradition with its use of Aristotelian categories within a Platonist framework.

If we do give it a name, we cannot do so in the strict sense of the word: whether we call it 'One', 'the good', 'mind', 'absolute being', 'Father', 'God', 'Creator', or 'Lord', it is not a case of producing its actual name; in our *impasse* we avail ourselves of certain good names so that the mind may have the support of those names and not be led astray in other directions. For taken individually none of these names is expressive of God but taken together they collectively point to the power of the Almighty.

Ordinarily names given are derived either from the properties of things themselves or from their mutual relations; but neither of these can be applied to God. Nor is the demonstrative reason any more help, because this always rests on prior and better known facts and there is nothing prior to the Unbegotten. So it remains that we can only apprehend the unknown by divine grace and by the Word that proceeds from him. This is just what Luke in the Acts of the Apostles records Paul as saying: 'Men of Athens, I see that you are in all things scrupulously religious. For going around and looking at your altars, I found an altar with this inscription: "To God unknown". He whom you worship in ignorance is the one whom I am declaring to you' [Acts 17: 22–3].

2 Origen
Homilies on Jeremiah 18, 6 (on Jeremiah 18: 7–10)
[*GCS* 6, 157–60]

'An end* will I declare concerning a nation or even a kingdom.'

The text appears to speak of an end without any qualification. But in fact it does say what kind of an end. The 'end' which 'I will declare concerning a nation or kingdom' is of this kind: to the first nation the end that is spoken is 'I will overthrow you' and to the second nation it is 'I will build you up'. And again to the first group it is said 'I will root you out' and to the second group 'I will plant you'. Does the fact that the end has been spoken mean that that end must happen? God who is not one who changes his mind or repents is said by Scripture to do so. Let us look carefully at this passage to see if we can explain in what way these things are said there and so accept the saying.

The text reads: 'An end will I declare concerning a nation or a

* πέρας in the LXX is presumably intended to be understood adverbially (as רֶגַע in the Hebrew) but is treated by Origen as a noun.

kingdom to remove them and to destroy them; but if that nation turns away from those evils of which I have spoken concerning it, I also will repent of the evils which I had intended to do to them. And an end will I declare concerning a nation or a kingdom to build it up or plant it; but if they act wickedly in my sight, not obeying my voice, I also will repent of the good things that I said I would do to them.'

'The repentance of God' demands some explanation from us. Repenting seems to be something reprehensible and unworthy, not merely in the case of God but even in that of a wise man. I do not envisage a wise man repenting, because in the customary meaning of the term, one who repents does so where his previous decisions have been badly made. But God, who foreknows the future, cannot have made bad decisions and repent on that score.

I have not yet shown the way in which Scripture introduces God as saying 'I will repent'. It does so in the book of Kings, where it is stated 'I repent that I anointed Saul as king' [1 Sam. 15: 11]. It is also said of him in general terms 'and repenting of the evil' [Joel 2: 13].

Consider the general teaching we are given about God. 'God is not like a man that he should be deceived nor like a son of man that he should be moved by threats' [Num. 23: 19] – from this passage we learn that God is not like a man. But there are other passages which claim that God is like a man – 'the Lord your God disciplined you as a man disciplines his son' [Deut. 8: 5] and 'he bore your ways as a man does with his son' [Deut. 1: 31]. Thus when the Scriptures are speaking about God as he is in himself and are not concerned with his involvement in the affairs of men, they say that he is not like a man; for example, 'there is no end of his greatness' [Ps. 145: 3], 'he is to be feared above all gods' [Ps. 96: 4] and 'praise him, all God's angels, praise him all his powers, praise him sun and moon, praise him all stars and light' [Ps. 148: 2–3]. And you could find thousands of other examples from the holy Scriptures which would illustrate the principle that 'God is not like a man'.

But when it is is a matter of that dispensation by which God is involved with the affairs of men, then he takes on the mind, the ways and the speech of a man. When we talk to a two-year-old, we use baby language for the child's sake, because if we were to keep to proper adult speech and talk to children without coming down to their way of speaking they would not be able to understand. Imagine something very like that to be true in the case of God when he has dealings with the human race, and especially with those who are still infants. Observe how we adults even change the names of things in speaking to very small children. We give 'bread' a different name in talking to them and we have a special word to refer to 'drink'. We do not use the adult language we use in speaking to our peers, but a different childish or babyish form of speech. In referring to clothes with children, we give them different names, making up some sort of childish name for them. Does that mean that we are not grown-up? If anyone were to hear us talking to children, would they say 'that old man has gone out of his mind' or 'that man has forgotten his beard, forgotten how old he is'? Or is it accepted that one needs to adapt oneself in communicating with a child and therefore does not use the language of the elderly or of the fully grown but that of the child? God too is speaking to children – 'Behold, I and the children whom God has given me' [Isa. 8: 18; Heb. 2: 13] is what the Saviour says. One might say to an old man speaking to a child in a childish manner (or – to put the point more forcefully – in a babyish manner) that 'you have borne the ways of your son, you have borne the ways of a baby and have adopted his condition'. It is in this sense that you should understand Scripture also when it says: 'The Lord your God bore your ways as a man might bear the ways of his son' [Deut. 1: 31]. It seems that those who translated from the Hebrew did not find a word readily available in Greek and therefore coined one as they did in several other places too, and wrote 'the Lord your God bore your ways as a man might bear the ways of his son' (as in the example I have just given).*

So since we repent, God addresses us as people who repent and says 'I repent'. When he threatens us he acts as if he had no foreknowledge; he addresses us like little children and threatens us. He acts as if he did not foreknow 'everything before it happens' [Susanna 42], but acting the part of a little child, if I may so put it, pretends that he does not know the future. He threatens a nation for its sins and says 'If the nation repents, I will also repent'. God, did you not know when you made the threat whether or not the nation would repent? Did you not know, when you made the promise, whether or not the man or nation to whom the word was directed would remain worthy of receiving the promises? But God acts as if he did not.

You can find many examples of a similarly human kind in Scripture.

* The usual LXX reading has the word τροφοφορέω, meaning 'to provide nourishment' or 'to sustain'. Origen reads τροποφορέω, which means 'to bear someone's ways' in the sense of 'to put up with his manners', but can easily be given a secondary sense of 'to adopt someone's ways'.

In the passage: 'Speak to the children of Israel; perhaps they will hear and will repent' [Jer. 26: 2–3 (LXX 33: 2–3)], God does not say, 'perhaps they will hear', as if he were in doubt about it. God is never in doubt and that cannot be the reason for his saying 'perhaps they will hear and will repent'; the reason is to make your freedom of choice stand out as clearly as possible and to prevent your saying: 'If he foreknows my loss then I am bound to be lost and if he foreknows my salvation then I am quite certain to be saved'. Thus he acts as if he did not know the future in your case, in order to preserve your freedom of choice by not anticipating or foreknowing whether you will repent or not. So he says to the prophet: 'Speak; perhaps they will repent'.

You will find many more similar examples of God bearing the ways of man. If you hear of God's anger and his wrath, do not think of wrath and anger as emotions experienced by God. Accommodations of the use of language like that are designed for the correction and improvement of the little child. We too put on a severe face for children not because that is our true feeling but because we are accommodating ourselves to their level. If we let our kindly feelings towards the child show in our face and allow our affection for it to be clearly seen, if we don't distort our real selves and make some sort of change for the purpose of its correction, we spoil the child and make it worse. So God is said to be wrathful and declares that he is angry in order that you may be corrected and improved. But God is not really wrathful or angry. Yet you will experience the effects of wrath and anger, through finding yourself in trouble that can scarcely be borne on account of your wickedness, when you are being disciplined by the so-called wrath of God.

3   Basil

Letter 234

[Ed. Y. Courtonne, *Saint Basile: Lettres* (Paris, 1957–66), 3, 41–4]

1. 'Do you worship what you know or what you do not know?' If we answer 'We worship something that we know', they retort immediately, 'What is the essence of what you worship?' Then, if we admit that we do not know its essence, they turn round and say, 'Then you worship what you do not know.' Our answer to this is that the word 'to know' has a variety of meanings. For what we say we know is God's greatness, his power, his wisdom, his goodness, his providential care for us, and the justice of his judgement; but

not his actual essence. Their question is thus captious. To deny that one knows the essence of God is not to admit that one has no knowledge of him. The many attributes that we have just enumerated provide a basis on which we form our conception of God.

'But God is simple', we are then told, 'and so every one of the attributes which you have enumerated as knowable must refer to his essence.' That argument is sophistry and the absurdities it involves are innumerable. All these attributes which we have enumerated – do they all of them denote one single essence? Is his attribute of inspiring awe identical with his mercy, with his justice, or with his creative power? Is his foreknowledge identical with his power to reward or to punish? Or his majesty with his providence? And does the mention of any one of those attributes disclose his essence? Now if they say that it does, they should not be asking us whether we know God's essence; they should be inquiring whether we know God as awe-inspiring, as just, or as merciful. And these are things which we confess that we do know. If on the other hand they say that God's essence is something different from these attributes, they must not produce spurious arguments against us on the basis of the simplicity of that essence. For in that case they have themselves admitted that his essence is something different from every one of his attributes. His activities are various, but his essence is simple. Our position is that it is from his activities that we come to know our God, while we do not claim to come anywhere near his actual essence. For his activities reach down to us, but his essence remains inaccessible.

2. 'But', they say, 'if you are ignorant of his essence, you are ignorant of him.' Your answer to this must be, 'If you say you know his essence, you have no knowledge of him.' A man who has been bitten by a mad dog may see the dog on his plate. But in fact he sees no more than the healthy see, and he is to be pitied for thinking he can see what he cannot see. You must not admire him for his assertion, but pity him for his derangement. So recognize the voice of the mockers in the words, 'If you are ignorant of the essence, you are worshipping what you do not know.' *That* God exists, I do know. But *what* his essence is, I regard as beyond my understanding. How then am I saved? By faith. Faith is sufficient for the knowledge *that* God is, not of *what* he is – and of the fact that he rewards those who seek him [see Heb. 11: 6]. So knowledge of the divine essence consists in the perception of his incomprehensibility. What we worship is not that of which we comprehend the essence, but that of which we comprehend that the essence exists.

3. And we can put the following counter-question. 'No man has seen God at any time; the only-begotten Son, he who is in the

bosom of the Father, he has revealed him' [John 1: 18]. What is it of the Father that the only-begotten has revealed? His essence or his power? If it is his power, then we know as much as he has revealed to us. If it is his essence, tell us where he said that the Father's essence consisted in his being unbegotten?*

When did Abraham worship? Was it not when he believed? And when did he believe? Was it not when he was called? Where in this case is there any scriptural testimony to Abraham's having comprehended? And the disciples – when did they worship him? Was it not when they saw creation subject to him? From the obedience of the sea and the winds to him they came to the knowledge of his divinity. Accordingly, his activities are the basis of knowledge and knowledge is the basis of worship. 'Do you believe that I can do this? "I believe, Lord"; and he worshipped him' [See Matt. 9: 28 and John 9: 38]. Thus worship is consequent on faith and faith is grounded on God's power. You say that the believer has knowledge as well as faith. Yes, but his knowledge has the same basis as his faith, and conversely faith has the same basis as knowledge. We know God from his power. Thus we believe in him of whom we have knowledge, and we worship him in whom we have faith.

4   Gregory of Nyssa
The Life of Moses II, 152–69
[*SC* 1 (3rd edition, 1968), 202–16]

152. There follows in the text the account of an ascent, which leads our minds on to the higher ranges of virtue. The man who has been strengthened with nourishment, who has shown his prowess in the struggle with his adversaries and has been victorious over his opponents is now brought to the ineffable knowledge of God.†
Hereby we are taught the manner and the extent to which a man's life must first be set in order before he may dare to approach the mountain of the knowledge of God, to listen to the sound of the trumpets, to enter the darkness where God is and to engrave on tablets the writing of God and, should these be broken through any

---

*Basil's Arian opponents believed that the term 'unbegotten' (ἀγέννητος) precisely denoted God's essence.

† The immediately preceding sections of *The Life of Moses* deal with the provision of manna and the victory over Amalek. In this section Gregory deals with Moses' ascent of Mount Sinai described in Exodus 19–20.

fault, to present to God further tablets, cut by hand, and engrave on them anew with the finger of God the writing that had been spoiled on the first tablets.

153. But it will be best to follow the order of the historical narrative and to relate the spiritual meaning to it as we proceed. The man who follows Moses and the cloud (which together show the way to those who are progressing in virtue, Moses representing the commandments of the law and the guiding cloud its inner meaning) first has his mind cleansed * at the crossing of the water where he puts to death and rids himself of everything foreign. Then he tastes the waters of Marah, that is a life separated from pleasure – something that at first tasting seems bitter and unpleasant but produces a sensation of sweetness in those who accept the wood [see Exod. 15: 22–5].† Then he enjoys the beauties of the palm-trees and springs of the gospels [see Exod. 15: 27]. He is filled with the living water, namely the rock [see Exod. 17: 1–7; 1 Cor. 10: 4]. He eats the heavenly bread [see Exod. 16]. He acts with bravery against the foreigners, owing his victory to the stretching out of the law-giver's hands – a foreshowing of the mystery of the cross [see Exod. 17: 8–13]. Then at length he approaches the vision of the transcendent nature.

154. His road to this knowledge is purity, not only of the body which is to be sanctified by sprinkling, but also of the clothes which are to be washed clean of every stain by water [see Exod. 19: 10]. That means that the man who seeks to approach the vision of intelligible reality ‡ needs total purification. He must be pure and without stain both in soul and body, washed clean of defilement in both alike; he must be pure in the eyes of him who sees in secret and his outward appearance must match his inward disposition.

155. So before his ascent of the mountain he washes his clothes in accordance with the divine command; the clothes are a figurative representation of a respectable habit of life. No one would say that the fact of dirty clothes in a literal sense was any impediment for those who are mounting up to God; but I think that 'clothes' is an appropriate designation for the exterior habits of a man's life.

156. When this has been done and the herd of irrational animals

* The manuscript evidence is confused and no printed text satisfactory. We have read: (...νεφέλη δὲ ἡ προκαθηγουμένη ἡ τοῦ νόμου διάνοια), ὁ διανοίᾳ κεκαθαρμένῃ...
† The wood thrown into the waters of Marah foreshadows the wood of the cross.
‡ Reading νοητῶν with Musurillo in *Gregorii Nysseni Opera* VII, i (ed. W. Jaeger), 83.

has been driven as far as possible from the mountain [see Exod. 19: 13],* he approaches the ascent to higher thoughts. The fact that no animal is permitted to appear on the mountain indicates, in our judgement, that in the vision of intelligible reality one is passing beyond knowledge derived from sense experience. For the distinctive characteristic of animal nature is that it functions entirely at the level of the senses to the exclusion of reason. Animals are normally guided by their sight and impelled by their hearing towards some particular objective. All the other things that activate sensation play a similarly large part in animals.

157. The vision of God however is not achieved in the realm of sight or of hearing nor is it acquired by any of the ordinary processes of apprehension; for eye has not seen, ear has not heard, nor is it one of those things that ordinarily enters into the heart of man [see 1 Cor. 2: 9]. The man who sets out to climb the heights of contemplation must first purify his conduct of all irrational influence coming from the senses; he must wash his mind clean from every opinion derived from past experience, he must withdraw from normal intercourse with his own spouse [see Exod. 19: 15] – that is, from sense-experience which is a kind of spouse and consort to our nature. Thus purified he may dare to attempt the mountain.

158. This mountain – for such indeed is the knowledge of God – is steep and hard of access, and the majority of people scarcely even reach the foot of it. But a real Moses as he ascends will hear the sound of the trumpets, which, the story says, got progressively louder and louder [see Exod. 19: 19]. For the proclamation of the divine nature is a veritable trumpet filling its hearers with alarm. It was great in its impact on its hearers even in its earliest manifestation, but greater still in its later stages.

159. The law and the prophets trumpeted out the divine mystery of the incarnation, but those first sounds were too weak to penetrate unresponsive ears. The hardness of Jewish ears failed to take in the sound of the trumpets. But as they continued, the text says, the trumpets got louder. The final utterances came with the preaching of the gospel and these did reach men's ears. The Spirit expressing itself through various instruments made the sound successively more impressive and more forceful. For prophets and apostles were all instruments giving utterance to one spiritual sound. It was of them that the Psalmist declares: 'Their sound is gone out into all the world and their words to the ends of the earth' [Ps. 19: 4].

160. The multitude could not hear the voice from above but left it to Moses to learn for himself the hidden secrets and to teach the

* The Greek word for 'animal' is ἄλογον, literally 'irrational being'.

people whatever divine truths he might acquire through the teaching coming from above. The same is true in the ordering of the Church. It is not for everyone to push themselves forward to try to comprehend the mysteries. They should select one of their number who is able to grasp divine truth; then they should give careful attention to him and accept as trustworthy whatever they learn from the man who has been initiated into divine truth.

161. It is written, 'Not all are apostles, not all are prophets' [1 Cor. 12: 29], but there are a great many churches nowadays in which this is not observed. Many who still need cleansing from their earlier way of life, some even whose present way of life defiles them like unwashed clothing, dare to attempt the divine ascent with no more help than that of the irrational senses. But they are stoned to death by their own arguments. For heretical ideas are like stones which cause the death of the very man who invented their evil teaching.

162. What is the significance of the fact that Moses went right into the darkness and saw God there? At first sight the account of this vision of God seems to contradict the earlier one. For whereas on that occasion the divine was seen in light, this time he is seen in darkness.* But we should not regard this as involving any inconsistency at the level of the mystical meaning which concerns us. Through it the Word is teaching us that in the initial stages religious knowledge comes to men as illumination. So what we recognize as contrary to religion is darkness, and escape from that darkness is achieved by participation in the light. From there the mind moves forward; by its ever increasing and more perfect attention it forms an idea of the apprehension of reality. The closer it approaches the vision of God the more it recognizes the invisible character of the divine nature.

163. The realm of phenomena is left behind entirely, not merely what is apprehended by the senses but also what is believed to be observed by the eyes of the intellect. So the mind presses on with its journey to the interior, until its persistent search enables it to penetrate to the unseeable and the incomprehensible; there it sees God. For herein lies the true knowledge of the goal of our search and the seeing of it: precisely in not seeing. For the goal of our search is beyond all knowledge; it is surrounded on all sides by a wall of incomprehensibility like a kind of darkness. And that is why the sublime John, who himself had penetrated this brilliant darkness, writes that 'no one has seen God at any time' [John 1: 18]. By that

* A reference to God's appearing to Moses in the burning bush, discussed by Gregory earlier in the *Life of Moses*. See II, 19–26.

negation he declares knowledge of the divine nature to be inaccessible not only to men but to every created intelligence.

164. So it was when Moses had progressed in the knowledge of God that he claimed to see God in darkness; in other words he had come to know that in its nature the deity is that which surpasses all knowledge and comprehension. 'Moses', says the text, 'entered into the darkness where God was' [Exod. 20: 21]. What God? He who 'made darkness his covering around him' [Ps. 18: 11] according to David who himself was initiated into hidden mysteries within that darkness.

165. Having arrived there, the teaching which he had received in a preparatory way through the medium of the darkness was repeated through the medium of words. The intention, I believe, was to impress this basic dogma about God more firmly upon us, by having it explicitly affirmed by the divine voice. So the very first commandment of God is that the divine is not to be likened to anything within the range of human knowledge. This means that any idea that thought or imagination may frame about the divine nature in a form which the mind can grasp can only provide us with an image of God and not actually disclose God himself.

166. Religion can be divided into two halves, one part being concerned directly with God, the other with the establishment of good conduct (for purity of conduct is also a part of religion). First a man must learn what he needs to know about God; and that knowledge consists in knowing nothing about him in the realm of the knowledge that is based on ordinary human apprehension. Then the second part is taught and he learns the kind of practices which go to make up the good life.

167. After that he reaches the tent not made with hands [see Exod. 25: 9; Heb. 9: 11]. Who will follow him as he leads the way on such a journey and elevates his mind to such great heights, moving from one peak to another and always in his ascent of the heights ending up higher than he was before? First he has to leave the foot of the mountain, being separated out from all the others who were not fit enough to attempt the ascent. Then as he mounts higher with the progress of the ascent, he hears the sound of the trumpets. Further on still he penetrates the impenetrable, the invisible sanctuary of the knowledge of God. Even that is not his resting place, for he goes on to the tent not made with hands. That indeed is the final goal of the man who has mounted by such a series of ascents.

168. But I think there is also another sense in which the heavenly trumpet can be regarded as an instructor of the man who climbs the path leading to the realm not made with hands. The marvellous

fabric of the heavens proclaims the wisdom of God to be found there. Through the visible order it declares his great glory; as the psalm has it: 'The heavens declare the glory of God' [Ps. 19: 1]. All this is a loud-sounding trumpet of clear and harmonious teaching: as one of the prophets puts it, 'Heaven has trumpeted from on high' [see Ecclus. 46: 17].

169. The man whose inward ears are purified and alert will hear this sound (by which I mean the sound heard through the contemplation of the universe, leading to knowledge of the divine power) and it will lead him on to penetrate in mind to the very place where God is. And this place is called by Scripture 'darkness'. That, as we have already said, signifies its unknowable and invisible character; and the man who reaches it sees there the tent not made with hands, which he can only show to those below through the medium of a material imitation.

5 Augustine
On the Psalms 134, 3–6 (on Psalm 135: 3)
[*CCL* 40, 1939–42]

3. What reason am I to give you for praising him? 'Because the Lord is good' [Ps. 135: 3]. In one brief word the praises* of the Lord our God are set forth: 'The Lord is good'; but good, not in the way that the things that he has made are good. Indeed, God made all things very good; not only good, but also very good [see Gen. 1:31]. Heaven and earth and all that is in them – he made them good, and he made them very good. If all these things that he made are good, what is he who made them like? Although he made them good and he who made them is much better than the things he made, yet no better word can be found to describe him than 'The Lord is good'; good, that is, in the sense of that real good from which all other goods are derived. He it was who made all things good; but the good which he is was made by no one. He is good in virtue of his own goodness, not by participation in any other goodness. He is good in virtue of the goodness which he himself is, not through cleaving to some other good. 'But for me it is good to cleave to God' [Ps. 73: 28]. He needed no one to make him good, but other things needed him to make them good.

* *Laus* denotes both the activity of praising and the praiseworthiness of that which is praised.

Do you wish to hear how uniquely good he is? It was the Lord, when asked, who said: 'No one is good but God alone' [Mark 10: 18]. The uniqueness of his goodness is something that I am reluctant to pass over quickly but am incapable of praising fitly. If I move on rapidly, I am afraid I shall appear ungrateful. But if I do undertake to expound it, I am afraid of becoming exhausted by the vast burden of the Lord's praises. Even so, my brothers, accept my praise of him, unfit though I am to utter it, so that, even if his praises be not fully unfolded, the zeal of him who utters them may at least be accepted. May God himself approve my intention and pardon my failure.

4. I am filled with ineffable delight when I hear: 'The Lord is good'. I consider and survey all that I see outside me: it all comes from him. And since these things please me, I turn to him from whom they come, and so understand that 'the Lord is good'. Or again, when I travel inwards, so far as I can, towards him, I find that he is both deeper and higher than I can reach. The goodness of the Lord is such that he has no need of these things to make him good. In a word, I do not praise these things apart from him; but him I find to be perfect without them. Untouched by want or change, nowhere does he look for any good which may increase him, nowhere does he fear any evil that may diminish him.

What more is there for me to say? In the creation I find that the sky is good, the sun is good, the moon is good, the stars are good; that the earth is good and that whatever germinates and roots itself in the earth is good; that whatever walks and moves is good; that whatever flies in the air and swims in the water is good. I say too that man is good; for 'a good man out of the good treasure of his heart brings forth good' [Matt. 12: 35]. I say too that any angel is good who has not fallen through pride and so become a devil, but clings in obedience to his maker. All these things I call good, but only with reference to their particular names – good sky, good angel, good man. But when I turn to God, I can think of nothing better to call him than simply 'good'. The Lord Jesus Christ himself spoke of 'a good man', but he also said: 'No one is good but God alone' [Mark 10: 18]. Does not that encourage us to inquire into the difference between the good that is good by virtue of some other good, and the good that is good in itself?

How good is that good from which all goods are derived! No good whatsoever can be discovered whose goodness is not derived from that good. That good which makes things good is truly good, just as it truly 'is'. It is not the case that the things he has made have no being; or rather, it is an insult to him to say of the things he has made that they have no being. Why should he have made them, if what he made has no being? And what was it that he made, if what he made has no being? So the things that he made do have being, and so can after all be compared with him. Yet the words, 'I AM WHO AM' and 'You shall say to the children of Israel, "HE WHO IS has sent me to you"' [Exod. 3: 14], sound as if he alone has being. He did not say, 'The Lord God, the Almighty, the merciful, the just', though if he had done so, he would certainly have been speaking the truth. His answer excludes everything that could be predicated of God or said about him, and says that 'being itself' is what he is called. 'This is what you shall say to them,' he said, 'HE WHO IS has sent me to you' – as if that were his name. His being is such that, in comparison with him, the things that are made have no being. When not compared with him, they have being; for they derive their being from him. But when compared with him, they have no being, for true being is immutable being; and that is his alone. For what is, is; just as the good of goods, is good.

Reflect and consider. Whatever else you praise, you praise it because it is good. Only a madman praises what is not good. If you praise an unjust man on account of his injustice, will not you also be unjust? If you praise a thief because he is a thief, will not you also be his accomplice? If you praise a just man on account of his justice, will not you also have a share in his justice through praising him? Now you would not praise him if you did not love him; and you would not love him if you had no share in his justice. So then, whatever else we praise, we praise because it is good; and you can have no greater, better or surer reason for praising God than that he is good. Therefore, 'praise the Lord, for he is good'.

5. How much more can we say about his goodness? Whose heart can conceive or comprehend how good the Lord is? But let us return to ourselves and acknowledge him there; let us praise the maker in his works; for we are not fit to behold him in himself. One day perhaps we shall be fit to behold him, when our heart has been so cleansed by faith that at last it may rejoice in truth. But now, since we cannot look on him, let us look at his works instead, lest we should fail to praise him. That is why I said: 'Praise the Lord, for he is good; sing to his name, for he is sweet' [Ps. 135: 3]. He would perhaps have been good but not sweet, had he not made you capable of tasting him. However, he has revealed himself to men as one who has also sent bread from heaven, by giving his coequal Son, who is what he is, to be made man and to be put to death for men; so that by means of what you are, you may be able to taste what you are not.

For to taste the sweetness of the Lord was too great a thing for you; it was too high and remote, and you were too low and cast down into the depths. It was to bridge this great gulf that the mediator was sent. You, as man, could not reach God; God was made man. You cannot reach God, but you can reach man; and now you can come to God through man. Thus there was made a 'mediator between God and man, the man Christ Jesus' [1 Tim. 2: 5]. If he were man alone, you would be following what you are, and so you would never arrive. If he were God alone, you would fail to comprehend what you are not, and so you would never arrive. God was made man, so that by following a man, which you can do, you may arrive at God, which you could not do.

He is the mediator, and so was made sweet. What is sweeter than the bread of angels? How can the Lord not be sweet, when man has eaten the bread of angels [see Ps. 78: 25]? For men and angels do not live on different food. This food is the truth, the wisdom and power of God; but you cannot enjoy it as the angels do. How do the angels enjoy him? As he is: 'In the beginning was the Word, and the Word was with God, and the Word, through whom all things were made, was God' [John 1: 1, 3]. And how do you have contact with him? Because 'the Word was made flesh and dwelt among us' [John 1: 14]. It was in order that man might eat the bread of angels that the creator of angels was made man. Therefore, 'sing to his name, for he is sweet'. If you have tasted, then sing. If you have tasted how sweet the Lord is [Ps. 34: 8], then sing. If what you have tasted tastes good, then praise him. Who is so ungrateful that, if he is pleased by some dish, he does not express his thanks to the cook or to his host by praising what he tastes? If we are not silent about things like that, shall we be silent about him who has given us all things? 'Sing to his name, for he is sweet.'

6. And now hear about his works. You have perhaps been straining to see the good of all goods, the good from which are derived all other goods, the good without which nothing else is good, the good which, without anything else, is good. You have been straining to see, and in thus straining your mental sight have perhaps failed and fallen back. I suppose this, because this is my own experience. But if, as is possible – indeed, very well possible – anyone's mental sight is stronger than mine and he can keep the gaze of his heart fixed on him who is, then let him give praise as he is able; let him give praise as we are not able. But thanks be to him who in this psalm has so tempered his praises as to enable both strong and weak to praise him.

The same is also true of that passage in which he commissioned his servant Moses. He said: 'I AM WHO AM', and 'You shall say to the children of Israel, "HE WHO IS has sent me to you"' [Exod. 3: 14]. But because true being is hard for the human mind to grasp and a man was being sent to men, though not by man, God immediately tempered his praises by saying something else about himself that could be grasped with ease. He did not wish to remain at a level of praise which could not be reached by those who would praise him. 'Go,' he said, 'say to the children of Israel, "The God of Abraham, the God of Isaac and the God of Jacob has sent me to you"; this is my name for ever' [Exod. 3: 15]. Surely, Lord, you have that earlier name: you yourself said: 'I AM; HE WHO IS has sent me to you.' Why have you changed your name? Why are you now saying: 'The God of Abraham, the God of Isaac and the God of Jacob'? Is it not reasonable to answer by saying: 'The words "I AM WHO AM" are true, but you cannot grasp them; the words "I am the God of Abraham, the God of Isaac and the God of Jacob" are true, and you can grasp them. "I AM WHO AM" – that relates to me; but "I am the God of Abraham, the God of Isaac and the God of Jacob" – that relates to you. If you fail at what I am to myself, you can grasp what I am to you.'

No one should suppose that God's words, 'I AM WHO AM' and 'HE WHO IS has sent me to you', are his only eternal name, and that his other words, 'I am the God of Abraham, the God of Isaac and the God of Jacob', are a temporal name. When God said, 'I AM WHO AM' and 'HE WHO IS has sent me to you', he did not need to say that this was his name for ever; for that would be understood, even without his saying it. For he is, and he really is; and by the fact that he really is, he is without beginning and without end. But in the case of what he is for man's sake ('I am the God of Abraham, the God of Isaac and the God of Jacob'), he has forestalled any human anxiety that this might be temporal and not eternal, by assuring us that he is leading us out of what is temporal to life eternal. 'This', he says, 'is my name for ever', not because Abraham or Isaac or Jacob is eternal, but because God makes them eternal hereafter without end. Indeed they had a beginning; but they will not have an end.

2 Trinity

The Christian understanding of God involved not only the integration of anthropomorphism and mystery as illustrated in our first section. There was also the need to combine belief in the unity of God with the ascription of divinity to Christ, and also to the Holy Spirit.

The first passage is part of the transcript of a discussion between Origen and a bishop, Heraclides, whose orthodoxy had been called in question. Its discussion form helps to illustrate the nature of the problem as it was experienced not only by a sophisticated theologian but also by an ordinary bishop. We cannot be certain where or when the discussion took place; it is most likely that it was in Arabia towards the end of Origen's life (c. A.D. 244–9). The account is part of a papyrus found in Egypt in 1941.

The issue came to a head in the fourth century with the outbreak of the Arian controversy. Our second extract shows Athanasius dealing with one particular Arian argument – namely that the concept of God as the one unoriginated source of all being rules out the possibility of ascribing full divinity to the Word or Son.

But more was needed than simply to show that the full divinity of the Son was not an absurd concept. The Church needed to develop a positive way of understanding that divinity in relation to her continuing conviction of the unity of God. This was the work particularly of the Cappadocian Fathers (Basil, his friend Gregory of Nazianzus and his younger brother Gregory of Nyssa). The third passage shows the way in which they developed the terms *ousia* and *hypostasis* to refer respectively to the one substance and the three persons of the godhead in a way that was to become standard for all later theology. Although traditionally printed among the letters of Basil, it is in fact a work of Gregory of Nyssa, written in about 380.

Augustine wrote his long work on the Trinity some thirty years later. His aim is not primarily to argue for the truth of the doctrine or to develop a technical terminology for its expression. He is concerned to deepen men's imaginative and devotional grasp upon it. This he does by seeking images of it in the interior life of man in the light of his conviction that man, being in the image of God, must reflect God's trinitarian character. In the passage here given he is reflecting on the nature of the mind, its knowledge of itself and its love of itself.

6   Origen
Dialogue with Heraclides 1–4
[SC 67, 52–62]
Translation of H. Chadwick in *LCC* 3, 437–40: revised.

After the bishops present had raised questions concerning the faith of the bishop Heraclides, that he might confess before all the faith which he held, and after each one had said what he thought and asked questions, Heraclides said:

I also believe what the sacred Scriptures say: 'In the beginning was the Word, and the Word was with God, and the Word was God. He was in the beginning with God. All things were made by him, and without him nothing was made' [John 1: 1–3]. Accordingly, we hold the same faith that is taught in these words, and we believe that Christ took flesh, that he was born, that he went up to heaven in the flesh in which he rose again, that he is sitting at the right hand of the Father, and that thence he shall come and judge the living and the dead, being God and man.

Origen said: Since once an inquiry has begun it is proper to say something upon the subject of the inquiry, I will speak. The whole Church is present and listening. It is not right that there should be any difference in knowledge between one church and another, for you are not the false church.

I charge you, father Heraclides: By 'God' we mean the almighty, the uncreated, he who is supreme and made all things. Do you hold this doctrine?

Heracl.: I do. That is what I also believe.

Origen: Christ Jesus who was in the form of God [Phil. 2: 6], being other than the God in whose form he existed, was he God before he came into the body or not?

Heracl.: He was God before.

Origen: Was he God before he came into the body or not?

Heracl.: Yes, he was.

Origen: Was he God distinct from this God in whose form he existed?

Heracl.: Obviously he was distinct from another being and, since he was in the form of him who created all things, he was distinct from him.

Origen: Is it then true that the Son of God, the only-begotten of God, the firstborn of all creation, was God, and that we need have no fear of saying that in one sense there are two Gods, while in another there is one God?

Heracl.: What you say is evident. But our affirmation is this: the almighty, God without beginning and without end, containing all things, and not contained by anything, he is God; and his Word is Son of the living God, God and man, through whom all things were made, God according to the spirit, man in as much as he was born of Mary.

Origen: You do not appear to have answered my question. Explain what you mean. For perhaps I failed to follow you. Is the Father God?

Heracl.: Assuredly.

Origen: Is the Son distinct from the Father?

Heracl.: Of course. How can he be Son if he is also Father?

Origen: While being distinct from the Father is the Son himself also God?

Heracl.: He himself is also God.

Origen: Then the unity is a unity of two Gods?

Heracl.: Yes.

Origen: Do we confess two Gods?

Heracl.: Yes. The power is one.

Origen: But as our brethren take offence at the statement that there are two Gods, we must formulate the doctrine carefully, and show in what sense they are two and in what sense the two are one God. Also the holy Scriptures have taught that several things which are two are one. And not only things which are two, for they have also taught that in some instances more than two, or even a very much larger number of things, are one. Our present task is not to broach a problematic subject only to pass it by and deal cursorily with the matter, but for the sake of the simple folk to chew up, so to speak, the meat, and little by little to instil the doctrine in the ears of our hearers.

Well then, there are many things which are two that are said in the Scriptures to be one. What passages of Scripture? Adam is one person, his wife another. Adam is distinct from his wife, and his wife is distinct from her husband. Yet it is said in the story of the creation of the world that they two are one: 'For the two shall be one flesh' [Gen. 2: 24; Matt. 19: 5]. Therefore, sometimes two beings can become one flesh. Notice, however, that in the case of Adam and Eve it is not said that the two shall become one spirit, nor that the two shall become one soul, but that they shall become one flesh. Again, the righteous man is distinct from Christ; but he is said by the apostle to be one with Christ: 'For he that is joined to the Lord is one spirit' [1 Cor. 6: 17]. But is it not the case that the man is of a subordinate or low and inferior nature, while Christ is of a more divine, glorious and blessed nature? In that case are they no longer two? Well, the man and his wife are 'no longer two but one flesh' [Matt. 19: 6]; the righteous man and Christ are 'one spirit'. Similarly our Saviour and Lord in his relation to the Father and God of the universe is not one flesh, nor one spirit, but something higher than flesh and spirit, namely, one God. The appropriate word when human beings are joined to one another is flesh. The appropriate word when a righteous man is joined to Christ is spirit. But the word when Christ is united to the Father is not flesh, nor spirit, but more honourable than these – God. This then is the sense in which we should understand 'I and the Father are one' [John 10: 30].

In our prayers we must take care both to preserve the duality and to bring in the unity. This will enable us, first, to avoid falling into the opinion of those who have been separated from the Church and have turned to the illusory notion of monarchy, who abolish the Son as distinct from the Father and virtually abolish the Father also; secondly, we avoid falling into the other blasphemous doctrine which denies the deity of Christ. What then do the divine Scriptures mean when they say: 'Beside me there is no other God, and there shall be none after me' [Isa. 43: 10], and 'I am and there is no God but me' [Deut. 32: 39]? In these utterances we are not to think that the unity applies to the God of the universe . . . * in separation from Christ, and certainly not to Christ in separation from God. Let us rather say that the sense is the same as that of Jesus' saying, 'I and my Father are one.'

It is necessary to study these doctrines because there has been much disturbance in this church. Often people write and demand a signature of the bishop and of those they suspect, asking that they should give their signatures in the presence of all the people, that there may be no further disturbance or dispute about this question. Accordingly, with the permission of God and secondly of the bishops, thirdly of the presbyters, and also of the people, I will again say what I think on this subject. Offering is universally made to

* The unintelligible words τῷ ἀχράντῳ are, with Scherer and Chadwick, left untranslated.

Almighty God through Jesus Christ in as much as, in respect of his deity, he is akin to the Father. Let there be no double offering, but an offering to God through God.

7 Athanasius
Against the Arians I, 30–4
[Ed. W. Bright (Oxford, 1873), pp. 31–5]

30. These considerations are an encouragement to the faithful, but to the heretics they bring only dismay, for in them they see their heresy confuted. The dishonesty of their opinions, their deceit and their craftiness are shown up once again by their next question, 'Is the unoriginate one or two?'* This question is not motivated by any desire to honour the Father; its purpose rather is to dishonour the Word. Suppose that someone who is unaware of their subtlety gives them the answer, 'The unoriginate is one'; then they immediately vomit up their poison and reply, 'Then the Son must belong to the order of things originated; we were quite right to say, "Before his generation he was not".' They will create any kind of confusion and muddle, as long as it will help them to sunder the Word from the Father and to put the creator of the universe into the category of the things that are created.

The first reason for condemning them is this. They find fault with the bishops at Nicaea for using unscriptural expressions (expressions which, far from being improper or irreverent, are effective weapons against their own impiety). Yet they have incurred the same charge themselves by their own use of unscriptural language – and their use of it, by contrast, is designed to revile the Lord, for they understand 'neither what they are saying nor the things about which they make their assertions' [1 Tim. 1: 7].

They should take their questions to the Greeks who taught them – for it was they, not the Scriptures, who invented the term *ageneton*. If they do this, they will discover that the term has all sorts of meanings; and that will make them realize that, even on ground of their own choosing, they do not know how to frame their questions properly. I have acquainted myself on their account with the various

---

* The text here reads ἀγέννητον; throughout the rest of the passage it reads ἀγένητον. The manuscript evidence is divided. It appears that Athanasius himself spells the word indifferently with one ν or with two νν. See G. L. Prestige, 'ΑΓΕΝ[Ν]ΗΤΟΣ and cognate words in Athanasius', *JTS* xxxiv (1933), 258–65.

meanings of the word.* First, *ageneton* can be predicated of 'that which has not yet undergone a process of becoming but could do so' – for example, wood which has not yet become a boat but certainly could become one. Secondly, *ageneton* can be predicated of 'that which neither has undergone a process of becoming nor ever could do so', such as a triangle becoming four-sided or an even number becoming odd. For a triangle never has nor ever could become four-sided, and an even number never has nor ever could become odd. Again, *ageneton* can be used of 'that which exists but did not originate from any source and is thus quite fatherless'. Finally, there is another meaning produced by that unprincipled sophist Asterius, the apologist of this heresy. In his *Syntagmation* † he uses *ageneton* of 'what is not made but always is'. So if they want to ask this question, they ought to make it clear in what sense they are taking the word 'unoriginate' (*ageneton*). Then those whom they question will be able to answer them rightly.

31. But if they still think they are putting a proper question when they ask, 'Are there one or two unoriginate beings (*ageneta*)?', then we must deal with them as the ignorant men they are and tell them that, in one sense of the word, there are many *ageneta* and, in another, there are none at all. There are very many *ageneta* in the sense of things 'which could undergo a process of becoming', but none at all in the sense of things 'which could not undergo a process of becoming'. This we have already shown. If, on the other hand, in putting the question they are using the word in Asterius' sense of 'what is not made but always is', then they must be told, and told again, that in this sense the Son can properly be called unoriginate. He does not belong to the order of things originated or made, but he coexists with the Father eternally. We have already shown that this is the case, and it remains so however many shifts of position they adopt – all with the aim of being able to abuse the Son with 'He is from non-being' and 'Before his generation he was not'.‡

Then finally if, after failure on every other line, they decide to employ the remaining meaning of 'that which exists but is without origin from any source and thus fatherless', then we must of course say that this sense of 'unoriginate' is applicable only to the Father, and to him alone. But getting this answer out of us will get them no

---

* The common characteristic of these four definitions of *ageneton* is the fact of not having undergone a process of change. *LS* defines the 'radical sense' of γένεσθαι as 'to come into a new state of being'.

† This work, written after the Council of Nicaea, is lost except for fragments preserved in the writings of Athanasius and Marcellus.

‡ Arian propositions condemned at Nicaea.

further. Speaking of the Father as in this sense unoriginate does not prove the Son to be originated; as our previous arguments have clearly shown, the Word must be such as is he who has begotten him. Thus if God is unoriginate (*agenetos*), his image (which is his Word and Wisdom) will not be something that has come into being (*genetos*); rather it will be his offspring, something begotten (*gennema*). For what likeness can there be between something that has come into being and something unoriginate? (We must not grow weary of repeating things we have said before.) If they argue that the originated being is like (*homoion*) the unoriginate and that consequently to look on the former is to behold the latter, they will soon be saying that the unoriginated itself is an image of its creatures. The end of this will be utter confusion. Things which have come into being are put on a level with the unoriginate, and the unoriginate is brought down to the rank of things created. The object of it all is of course to reduce the Son to the level of the created order.

32. However, I do not imagine that even they will want to go as far as this – not at any rate, if they listen to that sophist Asterius. He is indeed a zealous advocate of the Arian heresy and maintains that 'the unoriginate is one'. He nonetheless contradicts these words by speaking of God's wisdom as something unoriginate and unbegun. This is an extract from his writings: 'The blessed Paul did not speak of himself as preaching Christ *the* power of God or *the* wisdom of God but, without the article, God's power and wisdom [1 Cor. 1: 24]. Paul was thus speaking of Christ as a power distinct from the proper power of God himself, which is innate in him and coexists with him unoriginately (*agenetōs*).' A little further he continues: 'The eternal power and wisdom of God, which true reasoning clearly declares must be unbegun and unoriginate, must always be one and the same.' *

Asterius of course misunderstands the apostle in supposing that there are two wisdoms.† But even so, in speaking of an unoriginate wisdom coexistent with God, he is no longer saying that 'the unoriginate is one', but is speaking of the existence with God of a second unoriginate being. For the notion of coexistence implies coexistence with a being other than oneself. They should then do

* Translating ἡ αὐτή in place of αὐτή. See *De Synodis* 18.
† Arius himself had also spoken of two wisdoms (see Athanasius, *Against the Arians* 1, 5). The idea derives from a distinction in Hellenistic philosophy between ideas in the mind of God and ideas as entities distinguishable from God himself. Thus Philo speaks of wisdom both as an eternal property of God and as an incorporeal being created by God.

one of two things. If they want to follow Asterius, they must stop asking, 'Is the unoriginate one or two?' Otherwise they will find themselves arguing against him. If, on the other hand, they decide that they differ from him, they must stop making use of his *Syntagmation*. For 'if they bite one another they will find themselves destroyed by one another' [Gal. 5: 15].

So much for their ignorance. But what words are sufficient for their deceit and lack of principle? Are we not right to detest them for raving as they do? They have discovered that they are no longer free to say 'From non-being' or 'Before his generation he was not', and so they have thought up for themselves this expression 'unoriginate'. This was to enable them to speak of the Son in the hearing of the simple as 'originated' and so once again to convey the sense of 'From non-being' and 'Once he was not'. For what those phrases signify is precisely beings that are originated and created.

33. If they have any confidence in their opinions, they ought to stick by them and not keep shifting about. Why will they not do this? Because of an idea that success will be easy as long as they can shelter their heresy behind their use of the word 'unoriginate'. Now, in spite of all their fuss, the meaning of this word 'unoriginate', as applied to God, has nothing to do with any reference to the Son. Its meaning is found in reference to the things that are originated. The same holds for the expressions 'Almighty' and 'Lord of the powers'.* The power and lordship over all things which is denoted by these expressions are exercised by the Father through the Word. As Word and image of the Father, the Son wields the Father's kingship and holds power over all things. This makes it plain enough that the use of the word 'Almighty' does not mean the inclusion of the Son among the 'all things'. It is not with reference to the Son that God is called 'Almighty' and 'Lord', but with reference to the things which have come into being through the Son and over which he exercises his power and lordship through the Word. Thus too 'unoriginate' draws its significance not from reference to the Son, but from reference to those things which have come into being (*genomena*) through the Son. This is a proper use of language, for God is not in the same category as things originated. Rather he is their creator and maker through the Son.

Now just as 'unoriginate' has significance with reference to things originated, so too 'Father' plainly points to the Son. If one predicates the words 'maker', 'creator' and 'unoriginate' of God, one plainly has the created and originated order in mind. But if one calls God

* παντοκράτωρ and κύριος τῶν δυνάμεων are alternative renderings, both found in the LXX, of the Hebrew *Yahweh Sebaoth*.

'Father', then the Son is immediately brought into view. One can only marvel at this combination of obstinacy and impiety on the part of the heretics. This word 'unoriginate' has the perfectly good sense which we have indicated and can be used with propriety. And yet they only bring it out in a sense which suits their own heresy, in order to dishonour the Son. They clearly have not read that he who honours the Son honours the Father and 'he who dishonours the Son dishonours the Father' [John 5: 23]. If they were really concerned for the worship and honour due to the Father, they would do very much better indeed to acknowledge God as 'Father' and to speak of him as such, than to call him by this other name. For as we have pointed out, in calling God 'unoriginate', which relates to the things which have been originated, they are calling him no more than creator and maker. Their idea in using this terminology is that it will enable them to do what they want and give the Word the status of a creature. But if one calls God 'Father', one is describing him in relation to the Son, fully aware that the existence of a Son necessarily implies that the whole originated order was created through the Son. Our opponents, in calling God 'unoriginate', are describing him only in relation to his works. Thus they reveal that they are as ignorant of the Son as the Greeks are. Those who, by contrast, call God 'Father', are describing him in relation to the Word. And to acknowledge the Word is to acknowledge him as maker, and to understand that 'through him all things came into being' [John 1: 3].

34. Piety and truth are therefore better served by describing God in relation to the Son and calling him 'Father' than by naming him in relation to his works alone and calling him 'unoriginate'. For, as we have seen, the only reference of this latter term is to all the works, both individually and as a whole, which have come into being by the will of God through the Word. 'Father', however, has significance and meaning only in relation to the Son. The difference between the Word and the originated order is the measure, though an inadequate one, of the difference between calling God 'Father' and calling him 'unoriginate'.

Furthermore, 'unoriginate' is not only unscriptural; one must also be careful of its perplexing variety of meaning. 'Father', on the other hand, has one plain meaning, it is scriptural, it is more accurate, and it refers only to the Son. 'Unoriginate' is an invention of the Greeks, who have no knowledge of the Son; 'Father' was used and given us by our Lord. He himself knew whose Son he was when he said, 'I am in the Father and the Father is in me' [John 14: 10], and 'He who has seen me has seen the Father' [John 14: 9] and 'I and the Father are one' [John 10: 30]. Nowhere do we find him calling the Father 'unoriginate'. In teaching us to pray he did not say, 'When you pray, say: "God unoriginate"'. What he said was, 'When you pray say: "Our Father who art in heaven"'. The summary of our faith used in baptism was also intended to make the same point. For he commanded us to be baptized not into the name of unoriginate and originate, not into the name of creator and creature, but 'into the name of Father, Son and Holy Spirit'. In this initiation, creatures though we are, we are made adopted sons. We use the word 'Father'; and by our use of that word we acknowledge not only the Father, but also him who is in the Father himself – the Word.

This argument from the term 'unoriginate' is thus demonstrably worthless and quite without substance.

8 Gregory of Nyssa
On the difference between ousia *and* hypostasis *1–4*
[Ed. Y. Courtonne, *Saint Basile, Lettres* (Paris, 1957), 1, 81–7] *

1. There are many who, in discussing the doctrine of the divine mystery, make no distinction between the concept of *ousia*, which is general, and that of *hypostasis*. They treat them as identical notions and see no difference between using *ousia* and using *hypostasis*. Where people accept this kind of thing uncritically, we find those who speak of a single *ousia* speaking of a single *hypostasis* as well, while conversely those who accept the three *hypostaseis* feel that by this acceptance they are committed to the assertion of a threefold division of *ousiai*. It is to save you from falling into similar errors that I have composed, as a memorandum for you, this short discussion of the subject. To put the matter as briefly as I can, the meaning of these terms is as follows.

2. All nouns can be divided into two classes. There are those which refer to a plurality of numerically distinct subjects and therefore have a more general meaning. An example is 'man'. The use of this word signifies a common nature; it does not mark off and specify any one particular man. For 'man' does not apply to Peter any more than to Andrew, John and James. The general category applies equally to everyone who comes within the range of meaning

---

* This work has been preserved as No. 38 among the letters of Basil. On its authorship and attribution to Gregory of Nyssa see A. Cavallin, *Studia zu den Briefen des hl. Basilius* (Lund, 1944), pp. 71–81.

of the one noun. If we are to understand not just man in general but Peter or John in particular, some further distinction is required.

Other nouns have a more particular meaning. Their purpose is not the indication of a shared nature but the specification of a particular object. Inasmuch as they characterize the particular, they exclude the general features shared with all other objects of the same class. Examples are 'Paul' or 'Timothy'. In using such words we are no longer referring to a common nature. Rather we are isolating particular specified objects from their comprehensive categories in order with the aid of these nouns to be able to make those objects stand out clearly. If we take two or more similar objects – Paul, Silvanus and Timothy, for instance – and try to give an account of the *ousia* of these men, we shall not give one account of the *ousia* applying to Paul, another applying to Silvanus, and yet another to Timothy. Rather, whatever terms indicate the *ousia* of Paul will also fit the others. Since their *ousiai* can be described in identical terms, they are of one *ousia* (*homoousioi*) with each other. If, however, after discovering what two objects have in common, we then turn our attention to the particular features which distinguish them from one another, we shall find that the account which characterizes the one will no longer be identical with the account which describes the other – even if there are points at which our account of one is found to include elements common to both.

3. We can now say this. What is predicated of an object in its particularity is indicated by the term *hypostasis*. If we say 'man', we produce in our hearers a somewhat diffuse concept because of the indefinite character of the word's meaning. This noun indicates a nature; it does not signify any object as an actual existent (*hyphestos*) which is thereby specifically denoted. But if we say 'Paul', then we signify this nature as actually existent (*hyphestōsa*) in the object specifically denoted by that noun. This, then, is what *hypostasis* is. It is not an indefinite notion, like *ousia*, the general character of whose meaning excludes concrete existence (*stasis*); rather it gives particular and specified existence to what is general and unspecified as it occurs in a particular object with the help of the particular characteristics to be observed in that object.

Scripture itself is accustomed to proceed in this way. One out of many possible examples is in the story of Job. There, at the very beginning of the narrative, it begins by mentioning the general and saying 'man'. But this is immediately delimited by the particular, by the addition of 'a certain' [Job 1: 1].* The description of the *ousia* is passed over in silence, since this has nothing to contribute

---

* The book of Job begins ἄνθρωπός τις . . .

to the intended purpose of the tale. But the expression 'a certain' is given definition by means of the subject's particular characteristics, mention being made of the place, the marks of his character and all the external adjuncts which will help to differentiate him and mark him off from the general notion of 'man'. Name, place, qualities of mind and externally observable particulars – all serve to produce a clear description of the subject of the story. But suppose that an account of Job's *ousia* had been given. Such a description of his nature would have included none of those items. The same account would have done for Baldad the Sauchite, for Sophar the Minaean, and for each of the other men mentioned in the story.

You have seen how this principle of differentiation between *ousia* and *hypostasis* applies on the human level. Apply this now to the doctrine of God, and you will not go wrong. Whatever conception you may adopt of what the being of the Father is like (and in the light of the conviction that this 'being' is superior to all concepts, there clearly cannot be any definitive concept to direct the mind to), this you must also apply to the case of the Son, and similarly in turn to the Holy Spirit. The notion of uncreatedness and incomprehensibility applies in exactly the same way to the Father, to the Son, and to the Holy Spirit. No one of them is either more or less incomprehensible or uncreated than either of the others. Now in the case of the Trinity it is essential to keep the distinctions free from all confusion with the help of the particularizing characteristics. So in deciding what is particular to each, we shall leave out of account everything which the three are observed to have in common, such as being uncreated and being beyond comprehension. We shall look only for those things which allow us clearly and without confusion to distinguish our conception of each of the three individually from our conception of the three considered together.

4. It seems to me therefore a good idea to press on with our inquiry along these lines. Every good thing which comes to us from the divine power is, we say, the working of the grace which works all in all; as the apostle says, 'All these things are the work of the one same Spirit distributing them separately to each man as he wills' [1 Cor. 12: 11]. But if we inquire whether this supply of good things which thus comes to those worthy of them has its origin with the Holy Spirit alone, we are led once again by Scripture to the belief that this supply of good things which are worked in us through the Spirit has its origin and cause in the only-begotten God. For, so we are taught by holy Scripture, it is through him that all things came into being [John 1: 3] and in him that they hold together [Col. 1: 17]. Then when we have been enabled to attain to this

conception, once again divinely inspired guidance leads us on to learn that while he is indeed the power through which all things are brought from non-being into being, nevertheless he is not their ultimate origin. For there is yet another power which exists without generation or origin; and this power is the cause of the cause of everything that is. So the Father is the source from whom comes the Son, the one through whom all things exist, and it is possible to conceive of the Son only in inseparable conjunction with the Holy Spirit; for no notion of the Son is possible unless one is first enlightened by the Spirit.

Thus the Spirit, who is the source of the entire supply of good things which flows forth upon creation, is linked to the Son in that the two are known in a single act of apprehension, and is dependent on the Father as the cause from which his being derives and the source from which he proceeds. Here then is the mark which characterizes him in his particular *hypostasis*: that he is known after the Son and together with him, and that his existence springs from the Father. The Son is he who through himself and together with himself makes known the Spirit who proceeds from the Father; and he alone has shone forth as only-begotten from the unbegotten light. Thus in his particular characteristics he has nothing in common either with the Father or with the Holy Spirit; the marks of which we have spoken apply to him alone. As for God who is over all, his *hypostasis* has the special characteristic, which is his alone, that he is Father and that his existence springs from no other cause. This then is the mark by which he too is known in his particularity.

We therefore affirm that while they share *ousia* in common there are characteristics to be seen in the Trinity which are incompatible and not held in common; these constitute the particular character of the persons (*prosōpa*) of whom the faith has taught us. Each of them is apprehended separately in virtue of his own characteristics and thus, with the aid of the marks of which we have spoken, we can discover the distinction of the *hypostaseis*. But as to all such qualities as infinity, incomprehensibility, uncreatedness, and that of being uncircumscribed in space – as far as these are concerned, there is no distinction at all within the life-giving nature (by which I mean the Father, the Son and the Holy Spirit). What we see here is a sort of continuous and indivisible community. Whatever the concepts are which enable you to form an idea of the majesty of any one of the members of the Holy Trinity in whom we believe, these will bring you without distinction to Father, to Son and to Holy Spirit, and to a vision of their glory. Your mind will not lose itself in any void between Father, Son and Holy Spirit. For there is nothing which intrudes itself between them, neither any subsistent object in addition to the divine nature, which would introduce a division into that nature by its insertion of something alien to it, nor any empty gap, something without subsistence, which would sunder the inner coherence of the divine nature and create a separation in its continuity by the insertion of a void. No, to have a notion of the Father means not only that one has a notion of him individually but also that one has already got an idea in one's mind of the Son; and the idea of the Son is inseparable from that of the Spirit. So one will have reproduced within oneself, successively as far as their order is concerned but unitedly as far as their nature is concerned, that faith which is a blending of the three in one.

Thus if one speaks of the Spirit alone, one necessarily includes in this confession him whose Spirit he is. And since the Spirit is Christ's, he is also from God, as Paul says [see Rom. 8: 9; 1 Cor. 2: 12]. If you take hold of one end of a chain, you will pull the other end with it; in the same way if (in the words of the prophet [see Ps. 119: 131 (LXX)]) * you draw the Spirit, you will also draw through him the Son and the Father as well. Again, if you have really grasped the Son, you will have hold of him on both sides. On the one side he will bring his Father with him, and on the other his own Spirit. He can never be cut off from the Father, for he is always in the Father; and he can never be sundered from his own Spirit, in whom he works all things. Similarly yet again, if you have acknowledged the Father, you will have acknowledged together with the divine power the Son and the Spirit as well. It is impossible to conceive of any kind of severance or disjunction which would enable one to think of the Son without the Father or to sunder the Spirit from the Son. Rather one apprehends in them an ineffable and inconceivable kind of both community and distinction. The difference of the *hypostaseis* does not disintegrate the continuity of the nature, nor does the community of the *ousia* confuse the particularity of the individual characteristics. If we speak of the same thing as both joined and separate, this must not astonish you. Nor must you be surprised if, as if speaking in riddles, we produce the new and paradoxical conception of a united separation and a separated union.

* 'I opened my mouth and drew breath (*pneuma*).'

9   Augustine
On the Trinity IX, i, 1–v, 8
[*CCL* 50, 292–301]
Translation of J. Burnaby in *LCC* 8, 57–63: revised.

1. The object of our present inquiry is Trinity – not *a* Trinity, but *the* Trinity which is God – the true, supreme, and only God. The reader then must be patient: we are still inquiring, and such inquiry deserves no censure, provided that our search for what must baffle knowledge and expression be made in unshaken faith. Affirmation indeed calls at once and rightly for censure from any who may see and instruct to better purpose. 'Seek the Lord, and your soul shall live' [Ps. 69: 32]; but we are warned against any rash boast of having already attained: 'Seek his face always' [Ps. 105: 4]. 'If anyone thinks that he knows something, he does not yet know as he ought to know. But if one loves God, one is known by him' [1 Cor. 8: 2–3]. He does not say 'has known him', which would be dangerous presumption, but 'is known by him'. So elsewhere, after saying, 'now that you have come to know God', he at once corrects himself: 'rather are known by God' [Gal. 4: 9]; and most emphatic is that other passage: 'Brethren, I do not consider that I have attained; but one thing I do, forgetting what lies behind and reaching out to what lies ahead, I am intent to follow after the prize of the upward call of God in Christ Jesus. Therefore let those of us who are perfect be thus minded' [Phil. 3: 13–15]. By perfection in this life he understands nothing but to forget the things which lie behind, and to reach out intently after the things which lie ahead. The safest intention is that of seeking continually until the goal of all our effort and our reaching out be attained. The intent is rightly directed only if it sets out from faith. A sure faith is itself a beginning of knowledge; but sure knowledge will not be perfected till after this life when we shall see face to face. Let us then be thus minded, convinced that the temper of the truth-seeker is safer than that of rashly taking the unknown for known. Let us seek as expecting to find, and let us find as expecting still to seek. For 'when a man has finished, he is just beginning' [Ecclus. 18: 7]. Let us shun all doubt concerning matters of faith, let us refuse all hasty affirmation concerning matters of understanding: in the one, holding to authority, in the other, seeking out the truth.

As for our present inquiry, let us believe that Father, Son, and Holy Spirit are one God, maker and ruler of the whole creation:

that Father is not Son, nor Holy Spirit Father or Son; but a Trinity of mutually related Persons, and a unity of equal essence. And let us seek to understand this truth, praying for the help of him whom we would understand, and to set forth what we are enabled to understand with such careful reverence as to speak nothing unworthily, even if we sometimes speak mistakenly. Let us endeavour, for example, that if we say of the Father what properly does not belong to him, it may belong to the Son or to the Holy Spirit, or to the whole Trinity; that if we say something of the Son which does not properly apply to the Son, it may at least apply to the Father, or to the Holy Spirit, or to the whole Trinity; that if we say something of the Holy Spirit indicating a property which is not peculiarly his, then it should not be foreign to the Father or to the Son, or to the one God which is the Trinity itself. Thus we may desire to see whether the Holy Spirit be properly that most excellent gift of charity. If he is not, then either the Father is charity, or the Son, or the whole Trinity; since we may not oppose the certainty of faith and most mighty authority of the Scripture which says 'God is charity'. But we must never let the error of impiety so lead us astray that we ascribe to the Trinity anything that belongs not to the Creator but to the creature, or is the result of baseless speculation.

2. In view of all this let us consider those three things to which our inquiry has brought us. We are not yet concerned with things in heaven, not yet with God, Father, Son, and Holy Spirit; but with this image, inferior but still an image, which is man – so much more familiar and less difficult for the infirmity of our mind to study. I, the inquirer, present in my love for anything three things: myself, what I love, and love itself. I cannot love love without loving a lover; for there is no love where nothing is loved. Lover, the loved, and love: these are three. But suppose my love's object be myself; then the three become two – the object of love, and love. For when the lover loves himself, subject and object are the same; just as loving and being loved are in the love of self the same thing: there is no difference between the statements 'he loves himself', and 'he is loved by himself'. In that case, to love and to be loved are not two things, any more than are the lover and the beloved two persons. But still the love and its object remain two. For the subject of self-love can be identical with love only if love itself be the object of love. But to love oneself and to love one's love are not the same thing, since love which is loved must already have its object, else it is no love. In self-love, then, there are two things present, love and what is loved: the lover and the loved being one. From which it appears that a triad is not necessarily implied in the existence of love.

Let us abstract from our present consideration all the other elements of which human nature is composed; and in order to find what we are looking for in as clear a form as the matter permits, let us take the mind in isolation. In the mind's love for itself, two things are displayed – mind and love. Self-love is the will to be at one's own disposal for self-enjoyment. If the mind wills to be no more and no less than what it is, then will corresponds to mind and love is equal to lover. If love is a really existing thing, it is not body but spirit. The same is true of the mind; yet the mind and its love are not two spirits, but one spirit, not two essences but one. In other words two objects are one, lover and love, or (if you prefer to put it so) love and love's object. And these two are mutually related terms; lover being related to love and love to lover; for the lover loves in virtue of a particular love and love is the activity of a particular lover. Mind and spirit, on the other hand, are not relative terms but denote the essence in itself; it is not the fact that mind and spirit belong to a particular man that constitutes them as mind and spirit. Remove that element, the addition of which constitutes a man, i.e. the body, and mind and spirit will still remain. But remove the lover and there will be no love; remove the love and there will be no lover. Thus as mutually related terms, they are two: in themselves, each is spirit, and both together are one spirit; each is mind, and both together are one mind. Where then is there a trinity? Let us apply all our powers to the question, invoking the everlasting Light to illuminate our darkness, that we may see in ourselves as may be permitted to us the image of God.

3. The mind cannot love itself unless it also knows itself. That it should love what it does not know is impossible. It would be folly to allege that the mind forms either a general or a specific concept from its experience of other minds, believes itself to belong to the same class of being and on that basis loves itself. How can a mind, not knowing itself, know any other mind? It cannot be compared with the body's eye which sees other eyes but not itself. We see bodies with the bodily eyes, because the rays which flash from them and touch the thing seen cannot be reflected back upon the eyes, unless we are looking at a mirror. This is a very delicate and obscure subject, which needs much research before it can be clearly proved to be so or otherwise. But whatever be the truth about our power of vision, the power itself, whether it acts by rays or in some other way, is something that we cannot see with our eyes: we enquire about it with the mind, and comprehend it (if we can) with the mind. We may say then that the mind acquires knowledge of corporeal things by the bodily senses, and of things incorporeal by itself. Being itself

incorporeal, it must know itself by itself: if it does not know itself, it cannot love itself.

4. Now just as we found a duality, of mind and its love, in the fact of self-love; so there is a duality of mind and its knowledge in the fact of self-knowledge. Accordingly, the mind, its love, and its knowledge, constitute a triad. These three are one, and if perfect they are equal. If the mind's love of itself does not reach the measure of its being – if (say) the human mind, which is greater than the body, loves itself only with the love due to the human body – then there is sin: the love is not perfect. Again, if the measure of its self-love exceeds that of its being – if it should love itself with the love due to God, to whom it is incomparably inferior – then also there is great sin, and no perfect self-love. The sin is yet more perverse and iniquitous, when the body is loved with love due to God. Similarly a knowledge which falls short of its object, where full knowledge is possible, is not perfect. A knowledge which is greater than its object implies a superiority in the nature of the knower to that of the known: the knowledge of a body is greater than the body which is the object of the knowledge. For knowledge is a mode of life in the knowing mind, whereas the body is not life; and any life is greater, not in extent but in power, than any body. But when the mind knows itself, the knowledge does not exceed the self, for the self is both subject and object of the knowledge. If it knows the whole of itself, without any alien importation, the knowing is correspondent to the mind; for it is no less apparent that in this self-knowledge the knowing is not dependent on any other source. And when this knowledge takes in the whole self and nothing more, it is neither less nor greater than the self. Thus it is true to say that when each member of our triad is perfect, it follows that all three are equal.

5. At the same time we find ourselves encouraged to conceive how this triad really exists in the soul, inseparable though distinct to consciousness as so many substantive or essential realities; not as properties of a subject, like colour or shape in a body, or any other quality or quantity. For nothing of that kind can pass outside the subject to which it belongs: the colour or shape of a particular body cannot belong also to another. But the mind can love not only itself; it can also direct that love to an object outside itself. Similarly the mind knows not only itself but much else as well. Therefore love and knowledge do not belong to the mind as attributes to a subject: their existence is as substantive as that of the mind itself. They can be regarded as mutually related terms, but each exists in a substance of its own. As related terms they are not comparable to colour and the

coloured subject, where the colour possesses no substance proper to itself: the substance is the coloured body, the colour is *in* the substance. The relation is to be compared rather to that of two friends who are also men, that is, substances. 'Men' is not a relative term, 'friends' is.

6. 'Lover' and 'knower', 'knowledge' and 'love' are all substances. But while 'lover' and 'love', 'knower' and 'knowledge' are, like 'friends', relative terms, 'mind' and 'spirit', like 'men', are not. Yet it is not the case with 'lover' and 'love', 'knower' and 'knowledge', as it is with men who are friends, that they can exist apart from one another. It may appear that friends, *quâ* friends, can be separated in body only and not in soul. But it is possible for a friend to begin to hate his friend and thereby cease to be his friend, though the other may not know it and may continue to love him. On the other hand, if the love with which the mind loves itself ceases to exist, the mind will also cease to be lover; and so with the knowledge whereby the mind knows itself. A head is the head of something headed; 'head' and 'headed' are relative terms, though also substances, both being bodies, for nothing can be headed unless it is a body. But in this case severance can separate the two from one another, which is not so with 'love' and 'lover', or 'knowledge' and 'knower'.

7. If any bodies exist which cannot be cut or divided at all, they must still be composed of their own parts or they would not be bodies. Part and whole are related terms, since every part belongs to some whole, and the whole is whole by a totality of parts. But since both part and whole are bodies, they exist not only as related but as substances. May we say then that the mind is a whole, and that the love with which it loves itself and the knowledge with which it knows itself are like two parts composing the whole? Or, alternatively, that they and the mind itself are equal parts making up the one whole? The difficulty here is that no part embraces the whole to which it belongs; whereas the mind's knowledge when it knows itself as a whole, that is perfectly, extends over the whole of it; and when it loves itself perfectly it loves itself as a whole, and its love extends over the whole of it. Take another possible comparison. A single drink may be composed of wine, water, and honey: each component will extend throughout the whole, and yet they remain three: there is no part of the drink which does not contain all three – not side by side as would be oil and water, but completely mixed: all are substances, and the whole fluid is one definite substance made out of the three. Can we suppose that the triad of mind, love and knowledge exist together in the same kind of way? Apparently not.

Water, wine and honey are not themselves of one substance, though one single substance of drink results from that mixture. But it seems certain that our 'mental' triad must be of one and the same essence; since the mind loves itself and knows itself, and its 'threeness' does not involve its being loved or known by anything else. The three must then necessarily have one and the same essence. This means that if they could be intermingled so as to lose their identity, they would in no way be three or capable of mutual relation. This would be like three similar rings made out of one piece of gold: they might be linked together, but would still be mutually related on the basis of their similarity, since similarity implies similarity to something else. We should have a trinity of rings and one gold. But if they were melted down and mixed with one another in a single lump, there would be an end to the trinity. We could still speak of 'one gold' as with the three rings, but no longer of three golden objects.

8. In our triad, on the other hand, in which the mind knows and loves itself, we have a permanent trinity of mind, love, and knowledge. There is no intermingling and loss of identity; though severally each is in itself and mutually each as a whole is in the others as wholes, whether each singly in the other pair or the pairs in each singly. In other words, all are in all. The mind is in itself, being a substantive term; though it is termed knowing, known, or knowable in relation to its knowledge, and loving, loved, or lovable in relation to the love with which it loves itself. Knowledge is indeed related to the mind knowing or known, but still it is properly termed known and knowing in itself, for the knowledge by which the mind knows itself is not unknown to the knowledge itself. Similarly love, though related to the loving mind to which it belongs, still remains of itself and in itself; for love is loved, and that can only be by the love which is itself. This shows that each of the three singly is in itself. Again, they are alternately in one another: the loving mind is in the love, love is in the lover's knowledge, knowledge in the knowing mind. They are severally in the remaining pairs: the mind which knows and loves itself is in its love and knowledge; the love of the loving and self-knowing mind is in the mind and its knowledge; the knowledge of the self-knowing and loving mind is in the mind and its love, because it loves itself knowing and knows itself loving. The three pairs are in each single member; for the mind which knows and loves itself is in the love together with its knowledge, and in the knowledge together with the love; and the love and the knowledge are together in the mind which loves and knows itself. And the manner in which wholes are in wholes we have already indicated:

the mind loving and knowing the whole of itself, knowing the whole of its love, and loving the whole of its knowledge, whenever the three members are each in themselves perfect. In a wonderful way, the three are inseparable from one another, and yet each one of them is a substance, and all together are one substance or essence, though mutually related to one another.

3 Christ

The affirmation of the divinity of Christ raises questions not only about the nature of the godhead of the kind dealt with in the last section, which led to the development of the doctrine of the Trinity. It raised questions also about the person of Christ himself – how could he be both God and man? The first extract comes from an attack by Tertullian on the teachings of Praxeas written about A.D. 210. Praxeas is probably a nickname meaning 'busybody'. The distinctive feature of his teaching (not unlike what Origen appears to have objected to in Heraclides) was so strong an insistence on the unity of God that he was led to regard Father and Son as different names for God rather than indicative of different persons. This is the main problem dealt with by Tertullian in the work, but in the section given here he goes on to insist that Christ must be seen as both God and man without any diminution or loss of the essential characteristics of either nature.

The next five extracts come from the Eastern Church which was the scene of the main struggle to understand the full implications of the Church's confession on this issue. The first of them comes from a work of Eusebius of Caesarea, almost certainly written before the outbreak of the Arian controversy. It shows how the Greek Christian mind was able to see God's coming in Christ as the supreme act of divine condescension, and yet because of its conviction about the impassible nature of deity tended to think of the human nature of Jesus as something used by and external to the Word itself. A similar approach is characteristic of Athanasius (although he and Eusebius had extremely different attitudes to the teaching of Arius). Since Athanasius wished to insist against Arius that the Word was fully and unqualifiedly divine, he found it necessary to insist that though fully joined to the humanity the impassibility of the divine was not thereby impugned.

The main controversial discussion of this issue came after the time of Athanasius. The Antiochene school emphasised the reality and relative autonomy of Christ's human nature. This approach is represented by a passage from a dogmatic work of

Theodore of Mopsuestia of which only fragments (of which this is much the most substantial) remain. There follows a sermon of Proclus, preached at Constantinople in the presence of the Antiochene Nestorius on 25 March 431. It shows the religious importance which the opponents of Nestorius attached to their insistence on the intimate union of divine and human in the one Christ and the way in which an exaltation of the role of the Virgin was related to this theme. Nestorius' leading opponent was Cyril of Alexandria. In the letter of Cyril's here given he is defending his use of the formula 'one nature of the Word incarnate' (μία φύσις τοῦ λόγου σεσαρκωμένη). The phrase in fact derived from the writings of Apollinarius (passing under the name of Athanasius) who had denied the existence of a human soul in Christ. Cyril, who did affirm a human soul in Christ, seeks none the less to defend the formula as expressive of the full saving union of divine and human in the incarnation. He argues that the concluding word of the formula, 'incarnate', shows that it does not impugn the full reality of Christ's human nature, as his opponents suggest.

Leo, bishop of Rome 440–61, played a significant part in ensuring that the Council of Chalcedon did full justice to both natures. His famous *Tome*, read and accepted at the Council, was a counterbalancing influence to that of the writings of Cyril. The same characteristic emphases are represented here by one of his Christmas sermons.

10 Tertullian

Against Praxeas 27

[*CCL* 2, 1198–1200]

Why should I spend more time on matters so obvious when I ought to be dealing with issues on which they set out to obscure the obvious? On the question of a distinction between the Father and the Son they are utterly defeated; we maintain it in a form which does not destroy the union between them – a union like that between the sun and its rays or a spring and the river flowing from it, one which is inherent in the indivisible character of the two or three entities. But they try to interpret the distinction in a way which will still be compatible with their views; they make a distinction between Father and Son by which both are present in one person, by saying that the Son is the 'flesh' (or 'man', or 'Jesus') while the Father is the 'spirit' (or 'god', or 'Christ'). Thus the very people who are contending that the Father and Son are one and the same now prove to be dividing them instead of making a unity. For if there is a distinct Jesus and a distinct Christ, then there must be a distinct Son and a distinct Father, since Jesus is Son and Christ is Father. Perhaps it was from Valentinus that they learnt this kind of 'monarchy' which involves separating Jesus and Christ into two.

This line of attack has been met in advance by what we have written already, because what they are identifying as the Father is referred to as 'Word of God' or 'spirit of God' or 'power of the most high', and these cannot actually be the Father since they are referred to as his, but must come from him or belong to him. There is another way of refuting their argument drawn from the very same passage. 'Look', they say, 'it was foretold by the angel, "Therefore that which will be born shall be called holy, the Son of God" [Luke 1: 35], and it was the flesh which was born so it must be the flesh which is Son of God.' On the contrary, the reference is to the spirit of God. For it was certainly of the Holy Spirit that the virgin conceived; moreover it was what she conceived that she gave birth to. So what was there to be born was that which had been conceived and was waiting to be brought to birth – namely the spirit – and he it is whose 'name shall be called Emmanuel, which is being interpreted, God with us' [Matt. 1: 23]. Now the flesh is not God, so that the words 'shall be called holy, the Son of God' cannot refer to the flesh but to the one who was born God in it, as the psalm testifies, 'Since God was born a man in it and built it by the will of the Father' [Ps. 87: 5].* Who was the God born in it? The Word and the spirit who along with the Word was born by the will of the Father. So then the reference is to the Word in the flesh.

One then has to ask *how* the Word was made flesh – whether it was transformed into flesh or whether it put on flesh. The answer is emphatically that it put on flesh; for one must certainly† believe God to be immutable and not subject to change of form in that he is eternal. Transformation involves the destruction of what a thing was previously; everything that undergoes a transformation into something else ceases to be what it has been in the past and begins to be what it was not previously. But God cannot cease to be nor can he be anything other than himself. Now the Word is God:

* Tertullian's version of this text is not found anywhere else.
† Reading *certe enim* for *ceterum*.

45

moreover 'the Word of the Lord endures for ever' [Isa. 40: 8] – namely by continuing unchanged in its own form. So if it is impossible for him to be transformed, it follows that one must understand his being made flesh in the sense that he comes to be in the flesh and is manifested, seen and handled through the medium of flesh.

Other evidence also supports this interpretation. For if he were made flesh by a transformation and alteration of his substance, it would mean that Jesus was a single substance formed out of two substances (flesh and spirit) – a sort of mixture, like electrum formed from gold and silver, in which the gold (or spirit) ceases to be gold and the silver (or flesh) ceases to be silver, as the one is modified by the other and some third entity is produced. Jesus then would neither be God – for the Word would have ceased to be in being made flesh; nor would he be man * – for the flesh would not really be flesh since it was once the Word. Derived from both the outcome would be neither; it would be a third thing, vastly different from either. But in fact we find him described both as God and as man without qualification (as the psalm we have quoted illustrates: 'Since God was born a man in it and built it by the will of the Father'); and he is repeatedly called 'son of God' and 'son of man', no doubt because he is God and man with each substance having its own distinct characteristics, since the Word is none other than God and the flesh none other than man. The apostle also gives this teaching about his two substances, when he says: 'Who was made of the seed of David' (this must refer to man and son of man), 'who was designated son of God according to the spirit' (this must refer to God and the Word, the Son of God) [Rom. 1: 3–4]. We have here a dual condition – not fused but united – in one person, Jesus as God and man. (I am holding over till later what I have to say about Christ.) The characteristics of each substance are kept so unimpaired that the spirit performed its characteristic works in him (miracles, mighty works and signs) while the flesh similarly underwent its characteristic experiences (being hungry when tempted by the devil, being thirsty when meeting the Samaritan woman, weeping for Lazarus, being sorrowful even unto death and finally actually dying). If he were some third thing from a fusion of the two, like electrum, one would not find such distinct evidence of each substance. Either as a result of interchange between them the spirit would have done things appropriate to the flesh and the flesh things appropriate to the spirit or else as a result of fusion it would have been things appropriate neither to the flesh or to the spirit but

* Omitting *caro* (with Kroymann in *CSEL* 47, 281).

belonging to some other third category. If the Word had actually been changed into flesh, then either the Word would have died or the flesh would not have died, since either the flesh would have become immortal or the Word mortal. But since each substance operated separately in its own condition, each had its own activity and its own destiny. Learn with Nicodemus that 'what is born in the flesh is flesh and what is of the spirit is spirit' [John 3: 6]. Flesh cannot become spirit or spirit flesh. But they can clearly coexist in one. Jesus is made up of both. In that he is of flesh he is man, and in that he is of spirit he is God. It was in respect of that part of him by which he was spirit that the angel declared him to be 'son of God', keeping for the flesh the designation 'son of man'. The apostle also confirmed his having the two substances when he called him 'mediator between God and men' [1 Tim. 2: 5].

Finally, you who interpret the son of God to be the flesh, show us what the son of man can be. Is he to be the spirit? But you want the spirit to be regarded as the Father himself on the basis that 'God is spirit' [John 4: 24] – as though there could not also be 'the spirit of God', just as there is both 'the Word was God' [John 1: 1] and 'the Word of God'.*

11   Eusebius
Demonstration of the Gospel IV, 10, 15–14, 1
[*GCS*, 23, 167–73]

10. He is coexistent with the Father; with divine power he directs the providential ordering of the universe; heaven and earth and all that they contain, and the holy and incorporeal beings beyond the heavens, all fall under his care and oversight. And so the divine oracles proclaim him Word of God, wisdom of God, power of God, ruler, leader, king, and even God and Lord. He enlightens the beings of the incorporeal and spiritual order; so he is called 'sun of right-eousness' and 'true light'. He assists and cooperates with the commands of the Father; so he is called the Father's assistant and demiurge. Furthermore he alone, in virtue of his position, can give due service to God. He stands midway between the uncreated God and the created beings that come after him, and so both undertakes the oversight of the universe and acts as priest to the Father on behalf of all his subjects; he alone renders him favourable and

* *Deo sermo* in *CCL* is clearly a misprint for *Dei sermo*.

gracious to all.* So he is called eternal high-priest and the Father's Christ. ('Christs' was a title once used by the Hebrews for those whose office was a symbolic image of this primary priesthood.) Then he is set as commander over the angels; so he is entitled 'angel of great counsel' [Isa. 9: 6] and, as leader of the heavenly hosts, has the name 'captain of the Lord's might' [Josh. 5: 14]. Finally, he reaches down to earth; because of our rational nature and the presence in us of his own image, he comes to our help with the aid of the Father's love. In so far as this resembles the leading of children or even of cattle, he is called 'shepherd of the sheep' [see Isa. 63: 11 (LXX)]. In so far as he is bringing the promise of healing to souls subject to passion, he is naturally called 'saviour' or 'physician'. (That indeed is the meaning of the name 'Jesus' in Hebrew.)

But in course of time he needed a human instrument so that he could reveal himself even to men and teach them the truth about the knowledge and worship of the Father. Even this new mode of operation he was willing to accept. He entered right into our nature to appear among men, and showed the whole world a great marvel – God through the medium of man. Thus he made himself known not only, on the basis of his invisible and unseen role, as fleshless and incorporeal in nature. He now made himself visible to eyes of flesh, enabling human sight to behold superhuman miracles; and with a tongue and an articulate voice he taught corporeal ears. This was something truly divine and wonderful – nothing else like it has ever been recorded – and in it he revealed his care for the salvation and welfare of the whole world. So God the Word was called 'Son of Man' and was named 'Jesus' – because his coming among us was for the curing and healing of human souls. (The name 'Jesus' means 'saviour' in Hebrew.) So he underwent our common lot. In no way did he cease to be what he was, but preserved the godhead in the manhood. Accordingly, at the very first moment of his coming among men he effected the divine marvel of combining with the godhead a human birth. On the one hand he was born like us and, like a mortal, clothed himself in humanity; but on the other, in that he was not in fact man but God, the birth of his visible humanity was from an undefiled and unmarried maiden, not a product of sexual intercourse and corruption.

11. The whole of his life follows the same pattern. At times he shows his sharing of our passions; at other times he lets the divine

---

* Eusebius, following Origen, sees the function of the Word as that of mediator between the ultimate God and creation. For this theological tradition the Word is, as mediator, necessarily subordinate and inferior to the Father.

Word show through by performing miracles and wonders as God, by the prediction of future events, and by revealing quite openly in his deeds that divine Word who can be seen only by the few.

The way in which he finished his life, when he left the human realm, was similar to the way in which he began it. [12] The logic of his love for mankind led him even to death and the very abode of the dead. Thus he was able to recall the souls even of those long dead – for his concern was for the salvation of all men of all time. In order that (as we are taught by the holy Scriptures) 'through death he might destroy him who had the power of death' [Heb. 2: 14], he once again combined humanity and divinity in his execution of the divine plan. As man he allowed his body to be removed for customary burial, but as God he removed himself from it. For after he had cried with a loud voice and said, 'I commit my spirit to the Father' [Luke 23: 46], he left his body and made himself wholly free of it. He did not let death simply come to him; rather, death was delaying and shrinking back – more than that, it was turning round and running away – and he pursued after it and attacked it. He broke down the age-old gates of nethermost darkness and furnished the dead who lay there, bound by the cords of death, with a way of return to life. Thus in his case he who had died was raised, and many bodies of the saints who had fallen asleep rose up and entered with him into the holy, that is, the heavenly, city [Matt. 27: 53]. This is well expressed in the holy words, 'Death has been strong and has devoured, and yet God has wiped every tear from every face' [Isa. 25: 8]. So he who is the saviour of the universe and our lord, the Christ of God, is called victor. The predictions of the prophets introduce him as mocking death and uttering this song of victory as he frees the souls that were bound: 'From the hand of hell I will deliver them and from death I will ransom their souls.' 'O death, where is thy victory? O death, where is thy sting? The sting of death is sin and the power of sin is the law' [Hos. 13: 14; 1 Cor. 15: 55–6].

Such was the divine plan, extending even to the point of his death. The inquirer can find a whole number of reasons for this. The first reason, the Word teaches us, was 'that he might be lord both of the dead and of the living' [Rom. 14: 9]; the second, that he might wipe away our sins, being sacrificed for us and 'becoming a curse for us' [Gal. 3: 13]; the third, that a divine offering and a mighty sacrifice might be made on behalf of the whole world to the supreme God; the fourth, that by ways hidden from man he might destroy the power of the wandering demons. The fifth reason was that he might give to his friends and disciples the hope of a life after death with God; that the giving of this hope should be a matter not merely of words and talk, but of actual deeds; and that by making his verbal promise thus visible he might render them bold and eager to proclaim to all men, Greeks and barbarians alike, the way of true religion which he had established. Accordingly he immediately afterwards filled those friends and followers, whom he had chosen for their merits and collected as his disciples and apostles, with his own divine power. He thus strengthened them to preach to every race that knowledge of God which they had heard him declare. On all men, Greeks as well as barbarians, they enjoined one way of religion. They proclaimed the withdrawal and flight of the demons, the renunciation of polytheistic error, and the true knowledge of the one and only supreme God. They promised not only forgiveness of past sins of ignorance, provided men no longer remained in them, but also one hope of salvation for all through the supremely wise and virtuous way of life which they enjoined.

13. No one should feel perplexed at hearing of birth, body, passions and death being thus referred to the immaterial and incorporeal Word of God. If the rays of the sun suffer nothing by filling the whole world and touching even dead and unclean bodies, then surely the incorporeal power of God will suffer nothing in its essence, nor will it receive any damage or change for the worse, when it makes its incorporeal contact with a corporeal substance. How is this? Quite apart from the body in which he was incarnate, the Word of God is always and continually present in his capacity as creator throughout the basic matter of which the elements and all corporeal objects are composed, imprinting on it the rational principles of the wisdom which stems from him. To the inanimate he gives the impress of life; to the naturally formless and shapeless he gives the impress of form; in the attributes of corporeal objects he expresses the incorporeal beauties and forms inherent in himself; to things without life or motion in themselves – earth, water, air and fire – he imparts a supremely intelligent and harmonious pattern of movement. He brings all things out of chaos to order, growth and perfection. In his divine and rational power not only does he reach, pervade and touch all things, but he does so without incurring harm from anything or suffering defilement in his own nature.

The same is true of his dealings with man. In the past he appeared in a variety of ways but only to a very few people, just to the prophets and other righteous men of whom this is recorded. But in the end he was led by the surpassing kindness and love of the all-perfect Father to reveal himself to all men, to the worthless and the irreligious, to Jews and Greeks alike, as the benefactor and saviour of them all. Thus he declares explicitly: 'They that are strong have no need of the physician, but they that are sick; I did not come to call the righteous, but sinners to repentance' [Matt. 9: 12–13]. The saviour of all men called them with the words: 'Come to me all who labour and are heavy laden, and I will give you rest' [Matt. 11: 28]. He called men and healed them freely by means of the human instrument which had been brought into being, just as a musician shows his skill by means of his lyre. Like a good doctor, he gave to sick souls in human bodies the right and appropriate help – the help of his humanity. He offered himself as an example of a truly wise, virtuous and religious life. His teaching was not taken from others second-hand; it was his own, derived from the Father, and laid down in ancient times long ago in the laws given to the first men of God and to the Hebrews who were before Moses. And, since his care was no less for men's bodies than for their souls, he did physical acts for them to see with their physical eyes and uttered his teaching with a physical tongue for it to be heard with their physical ears. Everything that he did for men he did through the humanity which he had assumed; for it was thus, and thus only, that they could come to an awareness of his divinity.

All this, in accordance with the Father's will, was done by God's all-loving Word to help and aid us all. Yet he himself remained immaterial and incorporeal, just as he was before with the Father. He did not change in essence; he was not deprived of his own nature; he was not bound by the fetters of flesh; he did not lose his divinity; he did not abandon the native power of the Word. His living on earth, where his human vessel was, did not prevent his presence in the rest of the universe. Even during the time when he lived among men, he still filled all things; he was with the Father, and he was in him; even then he was still caring for the totality of things in heaven and on earth; he was in no way prevented as we are from being omnipresent. His usual divine activity was in no way hindered. He shared with his humanity the characteristics that belonged to him as Word; he did not receive in return the characteristics that belong to mortality. He bestowed on the mortal a part of his divine power; but he assumed in return no share in mortality. Bodily birth did not defile the incorporeal; the sufferings of mortality did not affect the essence of the impassible. A musician can hardly be said to suffer if his lyre happens to get damaged or its strings get broken. Or if a wise man's body is afflicted with injuries, we are unlikely to say that the wisdom within him, or the soul inside his body, is being maimed or burnt. We can far less reasonably affirm that the nature or power of the Word suffers any harm from the sufferings of the body. In the case of light we agreed that the sun's rays are not stained in any way when they come from heaven to earth and touch mud, filth and pollution of every kind. Nothing prevents us from saying that these things are enlightened by the light's rays; what we cannot say is that the sun is defiled or polluted by its contact with bodily things. Indeed, the basic nature of the sun and its rays is no different from that of bodily things. But the Word of God is immaterial and incorporeal. He is absolute life and absolute spiritual light, as well as all the other things we have earlier enumerated; therefore whatever he touches with his divine and incorporeal power, is bound to be endued with both life and spiritual light. Thus any bodily object that he touches is immediately sanctified and enlightened. Anything in the way of disease or weakness is done away, and the lack is supplied by his fullness. So even a corpse, once touched but lightly by the power of the Word, was raised to life again. Death fled from life and darkness gave place to light. 'Corruption put on incorruption and mortality put on immortality' [1 Cor. 15: 53].

14. What does this mean? That the humanity in its entirety was swallowed up by the divinity. God the Word was God once again as he was before becoming man. He made his humanity divine as a first-fruit of the hope that is ours. He reckoned it worthy to share in his own eternal life and to participate in his godhead and blessedness. Thereby he gave to us all the perfect exemplar of what it will be to share his immortality and to reign at his side.

12   Athanasius
Against the Arians III, 29–34
[Ed. W. Bright (Oxford, 1873), pp. 184–9]

29. It is, as we have frequently said, the characteristic aim of holy Scripture to present the Saviour in a two-fold manner. First, in that he is Word, effulgence and wisdom of the Father, he always was and is God and Son. Subsequently, by taking flesh for our sake from a virgin, the God-bearing Mary, he became man. Now one can find this indicated throughout inspired Scripture – as the Lord himself said: 'Search the scriptures, for it is they that bear witness to me' [John 5: 39]. But in order not to waste too much space by collecting all the relevant sayings, let us be content to be reminded of them all by the words of John, 'In the beginning was the Word, and the

Word was with God, and the Word was God; he was in the beginning with God; all things came into being through him, and without him nothing came into being' [John 1: 1–3], and then, 'And the Word became flesh, and dwelt among us, and we have seen his glory, glory as of the only-begotten from the Father' [John 1: 14]. Paul too writes: 'Who, being in the form of God, did not count equality with God a thing to be grasped, but emptied himself, taking the form of a slave, coming to be in the likeness of men; and being found in human form, he humbled himself, becoming obedient to the point of death – the death on the cross' [Phil. 2: 6–8]. Starting from these texts and going through the whole of Scripture from the same standpoint, one will discover both how in the beginning the Father said to him, 'Let there be light' and 'Let there be a firmament' and 'Let us make man' [Gen. 1: 1, 3, 6, 26], and how at the end of the ages he sent him into the world 'not to condemn the world, but that the world might be saved through him' [John 3: 17]. It is also written, 'Behold the virgin will conceive and bear a Son, and his name will be called Emmanuel, which means, God with us' [Matt. 1: 23].

30. The reader of holy Scripture will find these things stated in the Old Testament, whilst in the gospels he can see the Lord become man. For 'the Word became flesh', it says, 'and dwelt among us' [John 1: 14]. He became man, he did not come into a man. It is essential to grasp this point, in case the impious should fall into thinking, and deceive others into thinking, that it was just like the former occasions on which the Word 'came' into the various saints, and that now too he had come to reside in a man in the same way, sanctifying him and manifesting himself in him just as he had in the others. If this had been the case – if he had just appeared in a man – there would have been nothing extraordinary about him at all. No one would have been startled into saying, 'What sort of man is this?' [Matt. 8: 27] Or 'Why do you, being a man, make yourself God?' [John 10: 33] For they were accustomed to hearing the words, 'And the Word of the Lord came to' the individual prophets. But in this case the Word of God, through whom all things came into being, dared to become son of man as well, and 'humbled himself, taking the form of a slave' [Phil. 2: 7–8]. That is the reason why the cross of Christ is 'a scandal to the Jews', whereas 'to us Christ is the power of God and wisdom of God' [1 Cor. 1: 23–4]. For, as John says, 'the Word became flesh' [John 1: 14]. (It is the custom of Scripture to refer to man as 'flesh', as when it says through the prophet Joel, 'I will pour of my spirit on all flesh' [Joel 2: 28], or when Daniel says to Astyages, 'I do not worship idols made with

hands, but the living God who made heaven and earth and holds sway over all flesh' [Bel and the Dragon 5]. By 'flesh' both Daniel and Joel mean humanity.)

31. In ancient times the Word came to the individual saints and sanctified those who sincerely received him. When they were born no one said that *he* had become man; and when they suffered, no one said that *he* had suffered. But when, out of Mary, he came to reside among us 'once at the end of the ages to put away sin' [Heb. 9: 26] (for it was the Father's good pleasure to 'send his own Son, made of a woman, made under the law' [Gal. 4: 4]), then it was indeed said that he had taken flesh and become man, and that in that flesh he had suffered for us – in the words of Peter, 'Christ therefore suffered for us in the flesh' [1 Pet. 4: 1]. This was to demonstrate and to make us all believe that he who is eternally God, who sanctifies those to whom he has come, and who rules all things in accordance with the Father's will, had subsequently also become man for our sake. As the apostle says, 'the deity dwelt' in the flesh 'bodily' [Col. 2: 9]. This is equivalent to saying that, while being God, he possessed a body of his own and that, using this as an instrument, he became man for our sake.

It is on this account, namely his being in the flesh, that its properties are said to be 'his' – hunger, thirst, suffering, fatigue, and similar conditions to which the flesh is liable. On the other hand, the actions which were proper to the Word himself – such as raising the dead, restoring sight to the blind, and healing the woman with the haemorrhage, these things he did through his body. The Word bore the infirmities of the flesh as his own, because the flesh was his; and the flesh assisted the actions of the deity, since the deity was in it. For the body was God's. The prophet did well to say 'he bore' and not 'he cured our infirmities'.* Otherwise, he would have been external to the body, merely healing it as he had been doing all along, and so would have left men still subject to death. But by 'bearing our infirmities' and 'carrying our sins' [Isa. 53: 4] he shows both that he became man for our sake and that the body which bears the things in itself is his own body. In 'bearing our sins in his body on the tree' [1 Pet. 2: 24] (to use Peter's words) he received no hurt, while we men were redeemed from our own passions and filled with the righteousness of the Word.

32. When the flesh was suffering, the Word was not external to it; that is why the suffering is attributed to him. Similarly when he acted divinely doing the works of the Father, the flesh was not external to him; it was in the actual body that the Lord did these

* See the quotation of Isa. 53: 4 in Matt. 8: 17.

things. That is why, when he had become man, he said: 'If I am not doing the works of my Father, do not believe me; but if I do them, even though you do not believe me, believe the works, that you may know that the Father is in me and I in the Father' [John 10: 37–8]. Thus when he had to raise Peter's mother-in-law, who was sick with a fever, stretching out his hand was a human act, but stopping the illness a divine one. In the case of the man born blind, it was human to produce spittle from the flesh, but divine to open the man's eyes with the clay. In the case of Lazarus he spoke as man, with a voice that was human; but it was by divine act that, as God, he raised Lazarus from the dead. These things happened and were seen so to happen, because his possession of a body was fact and not illusion. It was fitting that, in putting on human flesh, the Lord put it on complete with its own passions. In consequence just as we speak of the body as his own, so too we speak of the passions of the body simply as his – though his divinity remained untouched by them. If the body had belonged to someone else, the passions also would be referred to that person. But if the flesh is the Word's (for 'the Word became flesh') then also the passions of the flesh can only be referred to him to whom the flesh also belongs. The one to whom the passions are ascribed, in particular the condemnation, scourging, thirst, crucifixion and death, together with the other weaknesses of the body, is the same as he to whom the triumph and the grace belong. It is thus consistent and appropriate to ascribe these passions to the Lord and not to someone else. For then the grace also will come from him, and our worship will not be directed to anyone else. We shall be truly religious, since the one whom we invoke is no creature, no ordinary man, but the true and natural Son of God, who also became man and yet is no less Lord and God and Saviour.

33. Who will not marvel at this? Who will not grant that this is something truly divine? If the Word's divine actions had not been performed through the body, man would not have been deified; and if the properties of the flesh had not been attributed to the Word, man would not have been liberated from them at all. They might indeed have been abated for a little, as I have said before, but sin and corruption would have remained in man. That was the state of mankind beforehand, as can easily be shown. Many men have been holy and clean from all sin – Jeremiah, for example, was sanctified from the womb and John, while still in the womb, leapt for joy at the voice of the God-bearing Mary. Yet 'death reigned from Adam to Moses, even over those who had not sinned after the manner of Adam's transgression' [Rom. 5: 14]. Thus men remained no less mortal and corruptible, in that they were liable to the

passions that belonged to their nature. But now that the Word has become man and has made the properties of flesh his own, the passions can no longer affect the body because the Word has entered it. He has destroyed them. From now on men are no longer sinful and dead in virtue of their own passions; but in virtue of the power of the Word they have been raised and are immortal and incorruptible for ever.

So when the flesh is born of the God-bearing Mary, the birth is attributed to him who bestows on all else the beginning of their existence. Thereby he has transferred our beginning to himself, and we no longer return as mere earth to earth, but are joined with the heavenly Word who carries us up with him into heaven. Similarly he has in fitting manner transferred the rest of our bodily experiences to himself; we cease to be men, and by becoming the property of the Word, we share in his eternal life. No longer, in virtue of our first birth, do we die in Adam. Our birth and all our fleshly weakness has been transferred to the Word, and from now on we are raised from earth. The curse which was on us on account of sin has been broken by him who in us 'became a curse for us' [Gal. 3: 13]. And all this has been done most fittingly. For as, in that we are of earth, we all die in Adam, so, in that we are reborn from above of water and spirit, we are all brought to life in Christ [see John 3: 3, 5; 1 Cor. 15: 22]. The flesh is no longer earthly, but from now on has been made into word by God's Word who for our sake became flesh.

34. If we wish for a clearer understanding both of the impassibility of the nature of the Word and of the weaknesses attributed to him on account of the flesh, we shall do well to listen to the blessed Peter; for he will be a trustworthy witness to the Saviour. He writes in his epistle, 'Christ therefore suffered for us in the flesh' [1 Pet. 4: 1]. So too when it is said that he was hungry, thirsty, weary and ignorant, that he slept, wept, made requests, and fled, that he was born, that he asked for the removal of the cup, and underwent all the experiences of the flesh – in each of these cases it could have been said that 'Christ therefore was hungry and thirsty for us in the flesh'; that he confessed ignorance, that he was struck, that he was weary 'for us in the flesh'; that he was exalted, that he was born, that he grew 'in the flesh'; that he was afraid and hid 'in the flesh', that he said, 'If it be possible, let this cup pass from me' [Matt. 26: 39], and that he was beaten and accepted it, 'for us in the flesh'. Of all these things it can be said that he underwent them 'for us in the flesh'. In fact, the reason why the apostle said, 'Christ therefore suffered', not in the godhead, but 'for us in the flesh', was that we should recognize that these experiences do not belong to the Word

himself in virtue of his nature, but that they belong naturally to the flesh.

So no one should be put off by the human experiences. The Word is in himself naturally impassible. But these experiences are attributed to him because of the flesh which he put on. They belong to the flesh, but the body itself belongs to the Saviour. He himself remains as he is, impassible in his own nature, not merely unharmed by the passions, but destroying them completely; while men, their passions transferred to the impassible and thereby destroyed, actually become impassible, freed from their passions from now on and for ever. This was the teaching of John: 'You know that he appeared to take away our sins; and sin is not in him' [1 John 3: 5]. All this makes it impossible for the heretic to object, 'How can the flesh rise, if it is naturally mortal? And if it rises, why does it not experience hunger, thirst and suffer again? Why does it not remain mortal? It is made of earth. How can it lose its natural condition?' The flesh can answer the contentious heretic: 'I am indeed made of earth, and am naturally mortal. But subsequently I have become the flesh of the Word. He has borne my passions, although he is impassible; I have become free of them, and because of the Lord who has freed me, I am no longer abandoned to their service. If you object to my being rid of my natural corruption, be careful you do not raise objections to God's Word having taken the form of my servitude.' For as the Lord became man by putting on the body, so we men are deified by the Word, by the fact that he has made us his own through his flesh; and henceforward we inherit eternal life.

13   Theodore of Mopsuestia
On the Incarnation VII
[Ed. H. B. Swete, *Minor Epistles of St. Paul* (Cambridge, 1880–2), 2, 293–7]

If we can discover how the indwelling is effected, then we shall know both the mode in which it is effected and also what makes for differentiation within that mode. Some people have asserted that the indwelling was a matter of essence (*ousia*), others that it was a matter of activity (*energeia*). Let us consider whether either of these is correct. First we must ask whether the indwelling is universal or not. Obviously the answer is 'No'. It is promised by God as something special for the saints or, in general terms, for those whom he wills to devote themselves to him. What would be the point of his promise,

'I will dwell among them and will walk among them and will be their God and they shall be my people' [2 Cor. 6: 16; see Lev. 26: 12], which implies some kind of special favour to them, if that is something enjoyed by all men* in the ordinary run of things? If indwelling then is not universal (and clearly it is not) even for men let alone for all existents, then we need to be able to define some special meaning of 'indwelling' according to which he is present only to those whom he is said to indwell. This makes it quite out of the question to say that indwelling is a matter of essence. For then either we would have to find God's essence only in those whom he is said to indwell and he would be outside everything else, which is absurd since he is of a boundless nature that is everywhere present and not spatially circumscribed at all; or else, if we say that in his essence God is everywhere present, then he must give a share also of his indwelling to everything – not only to all men but also to the irrational and even to the inanimate creation; this would be a necessary corollary of claiming that God's indwelling was a matter of essence. But both these are obviously out of the question. For to say that God indwells everything has been agreed to be the height of absurdity, and to circumscribe his essence is out of the question. So it would be naive in the extreme to say that the indwelling was a matter of essence.

Precisely the same reasoning applies in the case of activity. Either one has to confine it to these particular cases only – and then how could we go on talking about God's foreknowledge of everything, his governing everything, and his acting appropriately in everything? Or else if one allows that his activity is universal in its scope – and that is clearly appropriate and logical since it is by him that everything is empowered with its individual existence and with its own way of functioning – then one will have to say that his indwelling is universal.

So God's indwelling cannot be a matter of essence or of activity. What remains? What other concept can we use which will not destroy its particular character as applying to certain particular people? It is obviously appropriate to speak of indwelling being a matter of good pleasure (*eudokia*). 'Good pleasure' is the name for that very good and excellent will of God which he exercises because pleased with those who are earnestly devoted to him; the word is derived from his 'good' and excellent 'pleasure' in them. Scripture frequently speaks of God being thus disposed. So the blessed David says, 'He will not base his will on the strength of a horse nor will he find his good pleasure in the legs of a man. The Lord has good pleasure in those who fear him and in those who hope in his mercy'

---

* Reading πάντες for παρέντες.

[Ps. 147: 10–11]. This implies that he does not plan to work with or choose to cooperate with anyone other than those who fear him; they are the ones he values, they are the ones he chooses to cooperate with and to assist. This therefore is the appropriate way to define indwelling. For being of an infinite and uncircumscribed nature he is present to everyone; but in his good pleasure he is far from some and near to others. That is the meaning of these two texts: 'The Lord is near to the broken in heart and will save the humble in spirit' [Ps. 34: 18] and 'Do not cast me away from thy presence and do not take thy Spirit from me' [Ps. 51: 11]. He comes near in disposition to those who are worthy of such nearness and he goes far away from sinners. It is not a matter of being separated or coming nearer in actual nature; in both cases what happens is a question of attitude of mind.

The argument as we have developed it so far shows why we use the phrase 'good pleasure', and we have discussed the meaning of the term in full detail in order to establish this. We are now in a position to say that just as it is in his good pleasure that God can be both near and far, so too it is in his good pleasure that his indwelling operates. He does not circumscribe his essence or his activity by being present in certain people only and being separated from everyone else; he is present universally in his essence, but he is separated from the unworthy in his attitude and disposition. In this way the uncircumscribed character of his being is fully preserved; it can be seen that he is not in this respect subject to any external necessity. If on the other hand he were universally present in his good pleasure, this again would make him in a different way subject to external necessity. In that case he would not be determining his presence by choice of will; it would be a matter of his uncircumscribed nature and his will would be simply consequent on that. But as it is he is universally present in nature and separated from those he chooses in will; the unworthy are not benefited by the presence of God which they do have, while the truth is preserved intact of the uncircumscribed character of his nature.

So then in his good pleasure he is present to some and separated from others, just as if he were actually in his essence with the one group and separate from the rest. Moreover, just as the indwelling is a matter of good pleasure, so also in precisely the same way the good pleasure varies the mode of indwelling. That which effects God's indwelling and explains how the one who is universally present in his essence can indwell only some – indeed only a very small proportion – of the whole of mankind is, as I have said, good pleasure; and this good pleasure also qualifies the particular mode of indwelling in every case. Just as God is described as present to all in his essence yet not indwelling all but only those to whom he is present in his good pleasure, so similarly when he is spoken of as indwelling it is not always an identical indwelling but the particular mode of indwelling will depend on the good pleasure. Thus when he is said to indwell the apostles, or more generally the righteous, then it is an indwelling as being well pleased with the righteous, according to the mode of the pleasure he has in the virtuous. But we would never describe the indwelling in his [i.e. Christ's] case as of that kind – that would be sheer madness; in his case it is as in a son; that is the form of good pleasure by which the indwelling took place. What is the significance of this 'as in a son'? It is an indwelling in which he united the one who was being assumed wholly to himself and prepared him to share all the honour which he, the indweller, who is a son by nature, shares. Thereby he has constituted a single person (*prosopon*) by union with him and has made him a partner in all his authority. So everything he does he does in him, effecting even the ultimate testing and judgement through him and through his coming. The difference of course [i.e. between the Word and the man] is one that we can recognise by the distinguishing characteristics of each nature.

Although it is in the future that we shall be perfectly controlled in body and soul by the Spirit, yet even now we have a partial fore-taste of this in that we are so assisted by the Spirit that we are not forced to succumb to the reasonings of the soul. In the same way although it was in the end that the Lord had God the Word working in him so perfectly and completely that they were inseparably joined in every action, yet even before that he had the Word bringing to perfection in him to the highest possible degree all that he must do; in that period before the cross he was being given free room because of the necessity to achieve virtue on our behalf by his own will, though even then he was being stirred on by the Word and was being strengthened for the perfect fulfilment of what needed to be done. He had received union with him right from the start at the moment of his formation in the womb. Then at the age when men normally begin to be able to distinguish between good and bad, indeed even before that age, he demonstrated far more rapidly and quickly than other people this power of discrimination. This ability to discriminate does not arise in the same way and at the same moment for each person. Some with greater insight achieve the goal more quickly; others acquire it with the help of training over a longer period. He was exceptional in comparison with all others and it came to him at an earlier age than is normal; this is not surprising since even at the human level he was bound to have something extra by virtue of the fact that even his birth was not by the normal method of intercourse between a man and a woman but he was formed by the divine working of the Spirit. Thanks to his union with God the Word, which by foreknowledge he was deemed worthy to receive when God the Word from above united him to himself, he had an outstanding inclination to the good. For all these reasons, as soon as he was in a position to discriminate, he had a great antipathy to evil and attached himself to the good with unqualified affection. In this he received the cooperative help of God the Word proportionate to his own native will and so remained thereafter unaffected by any change to the worse. On the one hand this was the set of his own mind, but it was also a matter of this purpose of his being preserved by the cooperative help of God the Word. So he proceeded with the utmost ease to the highest peak of virtue, whether it were a matter of keeping the law before his baptism or of living the life of grace after it; in doing so he provided a type of that life for us also, becoming a path to that goal for us. Then in the end after his resurrection and assumption into heaven, he showed himself worthy of the union even on the basis of his own will, though he had received the union even before this by the good pleasure of his Maker at the time of his very creation. Thus finally he provides a perfect demonstration of the union; he has no activity separate or cut off from God the Word, but he has God the Word as the effective agent of all his actions by virtue of the Word's union with him.

14 Proclus

Sermon 1

[*ACO* I. i. 1, 103–7]

1. It is the Virgin's festival, my brethren, that summons us today to words of praise. This is a feast that has blessings to bestow on those who assemble to keep it. And surely this is right. For its subject is chastity. What we celebrate today is the pride and glory of womankind, wrought in her who was mother and virgin at once. Well-loved assembly! Behold, earth and sea are the Virgin's escorts: the sea spreads out her waves in calm beneath the ships; the earth conducts the steps of travellers on their way unhindered. Let all nature leap for joy; women are honoured. Let all mankind dance; virgins receive praise. For 'where sin increased, grace abounded yet more' [Rom. 5: 20].

She who has assembled us here is the holy Mary; the untarnished vessel of virginity; the spiritual paradise of the second Adam; the workshop of the union of the natures; the market-place of the contract of salvation; the bridechamber where the Word took the flesh in marriage; the living, human bush, which the fire of a divine childbirth did not consume [see Exod. 3: 2]; the veritable swift cloud that carried in her body him who sits on the cherubim [see Isa. 19: 1]; the purest fleece full of heavenly rain [see Judg. 6: 37–8], whereby the shepherd clothed himself with the sheep; handmaid and mother, maiden and heaven, only bridge to mankind; the awesome loom of salvation on which the robe of the union was mysteriously woven [see John 19: 23]; whose weaver was the Holy Spirit, the workman the power that overshadowed from on high [see Luke 1: 35], the wool the ancient fleece of Adam, the fabric the unsullied flesh of a virgin, the shuttle the immeasurable grace of him who wove it, and the craftsman the Word who entered through the ear.

2. Who ever saw, who ever heard of God in his infinity dwelling in a womb? Heaven cannot contain him, yet a womb did not constrict him. He was born of woman, God but not solely God, and man but not merely man. By his birth what was once the door of sin was made the gate of salvation. Through ears that disobeyed, the serpent poured in his poison; through ears that obeyed, the Word entered to form a living temple. In the first case it was Cain, the first pupil of sin, who emerged; in the second it was Christ, the redeemer of the race, who sprouted unsown into life.

The merciful God was not ashamed of the pains of a woman; for the business in hand was life. He was not sullied by dwelling in places which he had himself created without being defiled. If the mother had not remained a virgin, the child born would have been a mere man and the birth no miracle. But if she remained a virgin even after the birth, then indeed he was wondrously born who also entered unhindered when the doors were locked [see John 20: 26; Ezek. 44: 2], whose union of natures was proclaimed by the words of Thomas, 'My Lord and my God!' [John 20: 28].

3. So do not be ashamed of the pains, O man! They were the start of our salvation. Had he not been born of woman, he would not have died. Had he not died, he would not 'through death have destroyed him who has the power of death, that is, the devil' [Heb. 2: 14]. A master builder is not dishonoured if he dwells in places built by himself. Clay does not defile the potter who repairs what he himself had formed. Neither is the spotless one defiled by coming forth from a virgin's womb. From what he formed without pollution he came forth without defilement. O womb, in which was drawn

up the bond that gave us all liberty! O belly, in which was forged the sword to fight against death! O field, in which Christ, our nature's farmer, himself sprouted unsown as an ear of corn! O temple in which God became priest, not by changing his nature, but by mercifully putting on him who was 'after the order of Melchizedek' [Heb. 6: 20]! 'The Word became flesh' [John 1: 14], even if the Jews disbelieve the Lord who has said so. God has worn the form of man, even if the Greeks ridicule the wonder. The mystery is 'to the Jews a stumbling block and to the gentiles folly' [1 Cor. 1: 23], because the wonder transcends reason. Had the Word not dwelt in a womb, the flesh would never have sat on the throne. Were it a disgrace for God to have entered a womb, it would also be a disgrace for the angels to serve a man.

4. So he who is by nature impassible became in mercy most passible. Christ did not by progress become God – heaven forbid! – but in mercy he became man, as we believe. We do not preach a deified man; we confess an incarnate God. His own handmaid he acknowledged as his mother – he who in essence is without mother and in the incarnation is without father. How otherwise could Paul speak of the self-same one as both 'without mother' and 'without father' [Heb. 7: 3]? Were he merely man, he would not be without mother; and he has a mother. Were he solely God, he would not be without father; and he has a Father. Yet in fact the self-same person is both without mother, as creator, and without father, as creature.

5. You should also pay attention to the name of the archangel. He who brought the tidings to Mary was called Gabriel. What is the meaning of 'Gabriel'? God and man. Now he of whom he was bringing the tidings was God and man. So this name was an anticipation of this miracle, given to assure us of the incarnation.

Listen to the reason for his coming and glorify the power of the incarnate. Mankind was deep in debt and incapable of paying what it owed. By the hand of Adam we had all signed a bond to sin. The devil held us in slavery. He kept producing our bills, which he wrote on our passible body. There he stood, the wicked forger, threatening us with our debts and demanding satisfaction. One of two things had to happen: either the penalty of death had to be imposed on all, since indeed 'all had sinned' [Rom. 3: 23]; or else a substitute had to be provided who was fully entitled to plead on our behalf. No man could save us; the debt was his liability. No angel could buy us out; such a ransom was beyond his powers. One who was sinless had to die for those who had sinned; that was the only way left by which to break the bonds of evil.

6. What happened then? The very one who brought every

creature into existence and whose bounty never fails, he it was who for the condemned won life most sure and for death secured a fitting dissolution. He became man (he himself knows how – to explain this miracle is beyond the power of speech). By what he became he died; by what he was, he redeemed – as Paul says, 'In him we have redemption through his blood, the remission of our trespasses' [Eph. 1: 7].

What a transaction! It was for others that he procured immortality, since he himself was immortal. Another, able to do this work, there neither was nor has been nor is nor will be, beside him alone who was born of a virgin, God and man. His dignity was such as not only to outweigh the multitude of the condemned, but also to prevail against all sentences given against them. For he was the Son, maintaining his unchangeable likeness to the Father; the creator, possessed of unfailing power; the merciful, revealing his unsurpassable compassion; the high priest, who was worthy to plead on our behalf. None of these qualities could ever be found in another, whether in equal or in similar degree. Behold his love! Freely accepting condemnation, he destroyed the death that was due to those who crucified him; and the transgression of those who killed him he turned into the salvation of the transgressors.

7. A mere man could not save; for he would have needed a saviour himself since, as Paul said, 'All have sinned' [Rom. 3: 23]. By sin we were delivered to the devil, and by the devil handed over to death. Our affairs were in utmost peril; there was no means of rescue. This was the verdict of the physicians who were sent to us.

What happened then? When the prophets saw that our wounds were beyond human resource, they cried for the heavenly physician. 'Bow thy heavens and come down!' [Ps. 144: 5], says one. Another, 'Heal me, O Lord, and I shall be healed' [Jer. 17: 14]. One says, 'Stir up thy might, and come to save us!' [Ps. 80: 2]. Another, 'Will God indeed dwell with men?' [1 Kings 8: 27]. One says, 'Let thy mercies speedily overtake us, for we are brought into great poverty' [Ps. 79: 8]. And another, 'Alas my soul, for the godly man has perished from the earth, and there is none upright among men' [Mic. 7: 1–2]. Another says, 'O God, come to my help; O Lord, make haste to help me' [Ps. 70: 1]. Another, 'Yet a little while and the coming one shall come and not tarry.'* Another, 'I have gone astray like a sheep that is lost; seek thy servant whose hope is in thee' [see Ps. 119: 176]. And another, 'God, even our God, shall come manifestly and shall not keep silence' [Ps. 50: 2–3 (LXX)].

So our natural king did not allow our nature to remain for ever

* See Hab. 2: 3 (LXX) as quoted in Heb. 10: 37.

under tyranny. The merciful God did not permit us to remain
subject to the devil to the end. He came, who was always present.
He paid the ransom of his own blood. He gave to death in exchange
for mankind the body taken from the virgin that he bore. And he
redeemed the world from the curse of the law, by death destroying
death – as Paul cries, 'Christ redeemed us from the curse of the
law' [Gal. 3: 13].

8. So he who bought us was no mere man, you Jew! For human
nature was enslaved to sin. Nor was he solely God, without humanity. For he had a body, you Manichee! Had he not clothed himself
in me, he would not have saved me. Rather, when he appeared in
the virgin's womb he clothed himself in him who was condemned;
there it was that the awesome contract was concluded. He gave
spirit and took flesh. The self-same was both with the virgin and of
the virgin; by his overshadowing, he was with her; by becoming
incarnate, he was of her. If Christ and God the Word are not the
same person, there is no more trinity; there is a quaternity. Do not
rend the tunic of the incarnation which is woven from above [see
John 19: 23]. Be no pupil of Arius. He in his impiety divided the
essence; you must take care not to sunder the union, lest you be
sundered from God.

Who was it that 'shone on those who sat in darkness and in the
shadow of death' [Luke 1: 79]? A man? But how? For man dwelt
'in darkness', as Paul says: 'He was delivered us from the power
of darkness' [Col. 1: 13], and again: 'Once you were darkness'
[Eph. 5: 8]. Then who was it who 'shone'? David teaches you when
he says, 'Blessed is he who comes in the name of the Lord!' [Ps.
118: 26]. Tell us plainly, David: 'Cry with strength and spare not;
lift up your voice like a trumpet' [Isa. 58: 1]; tell us who this is.
The Lord the God of hosts! 'The Lord is God, and he has shone
upon us!' [Ps. 118: 27] For the Word became flesh;* the natures
combined and the union remained unconfused.

9. He came to save, but he also had to suffer. How were both
possible? Mere man had no power to save. One who was solely
God could not suffer. What happened then? He who was God
became man. By what he was, he saved; and by what he became,
he suffered. When therefore the Church saw the synagogue crowning
him with thorns, she bewailed the outrage in the words: 'Daughters
of Jerusalem, go forth and behold the crown with which his mother
crowned him' [see Song of Songs 3: 11]. For he both wore the crown

---

* *For the Word became flesh.* This phrase, although not printed in the
   ACO text, is strongly represented in the manuscript tradition, and
   the argument appears to make better sense if it is included.

of thorns and undid the sentence of the thorns [see Gen. 3: 18]. For the self-same was in the Father's bosom [see John 1: 18] and in the virgin's womb, in a mother's arms and on the wings of the wind [see Ps. 104: 3], adored by angels and dining with tax collectors. Seraphim would not look on him, and Pilate interrogated him. A servant struck him, and creation trembled before him. While nailed on the cross, he did not leave his throne; while shut in the tomb, he was stretching out the heavens like a curtain [see Ps. 104: 2]; while numbered with the dead, he was plundering Hades. Below he was accused as a deceiver; above he was praised as a holy one.

What a mystery! Beholding the miracles, I extol the deity; seeing the sufferings, I cannot deny the humanity. As man, Emmanuel opened the gates of human nature; as God, he left the bars of virginity unbroken. As he entered through the ear, so too did he come out from the womb; as he was conceived, so was he born. His entering in was altogether without passion, and his coming out was altogether beyond understanding – as the prophet Ezekiel said: 'The Lord brought me back by way of the outer gate of the sanctuary, which faces east; and it was shut. And the Lord said to me, "Son of man, this gate shall be shut; it shall not be opened. No one shall pass through it, but the Lord, the God of Israel, he alone shall enter and come out, and the gate shall be shut"' [see Ezek. 44: 1–2].

There you have clear testimony to the holy and God-bearing Mary. Let all contradiction now cease, and let us be enlightened by the teaching of the Scriptures, that so we may attain to the kingdom of heaven in Christ Jesus our Lord. To him be glory for ever and ever. Amen.

15 Cyril of Alexandria
Second letter to Succensus
[*ACO* 1. i. 6, 157–62]

1. Truth makes herself plain to those who love her. But she hides, I believe, and endeavours to conceal herself from the thoughts of the crafty. For they show themselves unfit to look at her with unclouded eyes. The lovers of the unsullied faith seek the Lord in simplicity of heart, as it is written [Wis. 1: 1]. But those who walk in devious paths [Prov. 2: 15] and whose heart is crooked (as it says in the Psalms [Ps. 101: 4]), amass a crafty variety of perverse notions as a means of perverting the straight paths of the Lord [Hos.

14: 9] and leading astray the souls of the simple so as to make them think thoughts which they ought not. I say this after reading your holiness' memorandum, in which I found a number of dangerous propositions advanced by persons who have come, I know not how, to love the perversity of the knowledge which is falsely so called [1 Tim. 6: 20]. They are the following:

2. *If Emmanuel is the product of two natures, but after the union one nature of the Word incarnate is envisaged, it will necessarily follow that one must speak of him as suffering in his own nature.*

When the holy fathers drew up the sacred formula of the orthodox faith,* it was the Word who is of God the Father, who is of the Father's essence, who is only-begotten and through whom all things exist, whom they spoke of as having been incarnate and made man. We cannot suppose that those holy men were ignorant of the fact that the body that was united with the Word was animated by a rational soul. Accordingly, if one asserts that the Word became incarnate, one includes a rational soul in one's confession of the flesh that was united with him. This, as I believe – or rather, as one may confidently assert – is the sense in which the wise evangelist John asserted that 'the Word became flesh' [John 1: 14]. He was not saying that the Word was united with a flesh devoid of soul, far from it; neither was he saying that the Word underwent any change or alteration. For he remained what he was; that is, by nature God. But when he took it on himself to be man as well – that is to be born like us of a woman in the realm of flesh – he still remained one Son, the only difference being that whereas formerly, that is before the time of the incarnation, he was without flesh, he had now, so to speak, put on the additional clothing of our nature. Granted that the body, even when endowed with a rational soul, is not consubstantial with the Word begotten of the Father with whom it was united, and that we do have a mental perception of the difference of nature between the two things that were united, nonetheless it is one Son and Christ and Lord whom we confess, in that the Word became flesh; and when we say 'flesh', we are saying 'man'.

Why, then, if one asserts that after the union there was one nature of the Son incarnate, should it necessarily follow that he must have suffered in his own nature? If the concept of the *oikonomia* † did not in itself include some element naturally capable of suffering, then it could have been rightly asserted that, since there was no element

* Cyril is referring to the Council of Nicaea.
† The Greek word, οἰκονομία, meaning literally 'management' or 'dispensation', is regularly used to refer to God's self-revelation as a whole and to the incarnation in particular.

naturally capable of suffering, the nature of the Word must as a matter of absolute necessity have been affected by suffering. But if in the very use of the word 'incarnate' the complete logic of the *oikonomia* in the flesh is implicit – for the way in which he was incarnate was by 'laying hold of the seed of Abraham' and 'being made like his brethren in all respects' and 'taking the form of a slave' [Heb. 2: 16–17; Phil. 2: 7] – then it is idle nonsense for them to say that it necessarily follows that he must have suffered in his own nature. For the flesh was there, and it is reasonable to suppose that it was in relation to the flesh that the suffering occurred, while the Word was impassible.

However, this does not prevent us from saying that he suffered. For just as the body belonged to him, so also all the properties of the body with the exception of sin alone [Heb. 4: 15] can be predicated of him, in that he made them his own through the incarnation.

3. *If there is one nature of the Word incarnate, there is bound to have been a confusion and mixture, involving a kind of diminution or robbery of the human nature in him.*

Once again the perverters of orthodoxy reveal their ignorance of the fact that there really is but one nature of the Word incarnate. For if there is one Son, who is such by nature and in reality, who is the Word ineffably begotten of God the Father, and if he then, by assuming a flesh that, far from being without soul, was rationally animated, came forth as a man out of a woman, that does not divide him into two *prosōpa** or sons. For he remained one, not indeed without flesh or outside a body, but in possession of a body that was his own in virtue of an inseparable union.

To say this is not to produce a confusion or mixture or anything else of the kind. Nothing like that need follow at all. Why should it? If we speak of the only-begotten Son of God, incarnate and made man, as one, this produces no mixture, as they think. The nature of the Word has not passed into the nature of the flesh, nor has that of the flesh into that of the Word. Rather, it is with each nature retaining its own distinctive character, and being perceived as such, that the ineffable and inconceivable union of the Word which we have just described discloses to us one nature of the Son – though, as we have said, one nature incarnate.

In fact, unity is not predicated only of things that are naturally

---

* The Greek word, πρόσωπον, meaning literally 'face' or 'character', conveys the idea of a person in his external characteristics and relations. Nestorius, though insisting that there was a single πρόσωπον of the Christ, did also speak of the human and divine natures each having their own πρόσωπον.

simple, but also of things that are produced by composition. An example is man, who is composed of soul and body. Things of this kind are quite different from each other; they are not consubstantial. Yet when united, soul and body produce the one nature of man, even though the difference of nature between the entities that have been brought together into unity is inherent in the very fact of composition.

It is therefore empty talk to assert that, if there is one nature of the Word incarnate, there must inevitably have been a confusion and mixture, involving the diminution and robbery of the human nature. It is neither diminished nor, as they put it, robbed. A full declaration of the fact that he became man is contained in the assertion that he became incarnate. If we had been silent on that point, there would have been some ground for their calumny. But in view of this crucial addition that he became incarnate, how can there be any diminution or robbery?

4. *If he is envisaged as being at once both perfect God and perfect man, consubstantial with the Father in respect of his deity and consubstantial with us in respect of his humanity,* what becomes of this perfection if the human nature no longer exists? And what becomes of his consubstantiality with us, if our substance or essence (that is, our nature) no longer exists?*

A sufficient explanation of this point is contained in the response that we made under the previous heading. If, after saying that the nature of the Word is one, we had kept silent and not added the word 'incarnate', thereby excluding the *oikonomia*, they could perhaps have made quite a convincing case asking what had become of the perfect humanity and of the existence of our human essence. In fact a declaration of the perfect humanity and of our essence is provided by the expression 'incarnate'. So they should stop relying on a staff of reed [see Isa. 36: 6]. If we were to reject the *oikonomia* and deny the incarnation, the objection could rightly be made that we were depriving the Son of his perfect humanity. But if, as we have said, the assertion that he was incarnate is a clear and unambiguous confession of the fact that he became man, there is nothing to prevent us from thinking of Christ as being the one and only Son at once both God and man, perfect in deity and perfect in humanity.

You, reverend sir, showed a sound understanding of the matter in your exposition of the saving passion, when you insisted that the only-begotten Son of God, inasmuch as he is conceived of as God

---

* These phrases (*perfect God...his humanity*) are drawn from an Antiochene formulary (the so-called 'formulary of Reunion') to which Cyril had assented in A.D. 433.

and is God, did not endure bodily suffering himself in his own nature, but that he did suffer in his earthly nature. Both points about the one true Son had to be maintained: that divinely he does not suffer, and that humanly he is said to have suffered. For it was his flesh that suffered.

But those people suppose that this means that we are introducing what they call the 'passion of God'. They have no sense of the *oikonomia* but make the outrageous attempt to transfer the suffering to a man on his own. The senseless aim of their disastrous piety is that the Word of God should not be acknowledged as the Saviour who gave his own blood for us, but that Jesus thought of as a man on his own and by himself should be said to have achieved this. But this way of thinking upsets the whole logic of the incarnation. It quite plainly converts the divine mystery of our religion into a form of man-worship. They do not realize that it is he who is of the Jews according to the flesh – that is, he who is of the seed of Jesse and of David – whom the blessed Paul spoke of as Christ and Lord of glory and God who is blessed for ever and over all [see Rom. 1: 3; 9: 5; 1 Cor. 2: 8]. By declaring that the body of the Word that was nailed to the tree was truly his, Paul was also assigning the cross to him.

5. I gather that there is one further point at issue. *If one asserts that the Lord suffered in flesh alone, one is excluding reason and free will from the passion. If, on the other hand, in order to make the passion a matter of free will, one asserts that he suffered with a rational soul, there can be no objection to saying that he suffered in human nature. And if that be true, are we not bound to concede that after the union two natures exist inseparably? Thus, the words 'Christ therefore suffered for us in flesh'* [1 Pet. 4: 1], *mean exactly the same as 'Christ suffered for us in our nature'.*

The target of this objection is once again those who assert that there is one nature of the Son incarnate. It is their desire to make this proposition look silly that makes them so keen to demonstrate the existence in all circumstances of two natures. But what these people fail to recognize is that it is only in the case of entities where the distinction to be drawn between them is not a matter of mental apprehension alone that there can be a complete separation of the one from the other into individual compartments on their own. Once again let us take an ordinary man as an example. In this case also we perceive two natures, one being that of the soul, the other that of the body. But although we do distinguish them in bare thought, and by careful consideration or by the use of the imagination recognize their difference, nevertheless we do not put the natures apart by themselves or let them be totally sundered from each other. We perceive that they belong to one man, so that the two natures are no longer two, but between them produce the one living being. Thus though they may speak of divine and human natures in the case of Emmanuel, nevertheless the humanity belongs to the Word; and one Son is perceived, including the humanity.

Since inspired Scripture says that he suffered 'in the flesh', it is better for us to say the same rather than 'in human nature' – even though, as long as no one uses the expression perversely, it can do no possible harm to the pattern of the divine mystery. After all, what is human nature but flesh rationally animated? And what we say is that the Lord suffered in flesh. Their saying that he suffered in human nature is therefore utterly superfluous. It tends to separate the humanity from the Word and to set it apart on its own, giving rise to the notion that the Word of God the Father, incarnate and made man, is no longer one but two.

The additional word 'inseparable' has with us an orthodox enough meaning. But that is not how they understand it. They take the word 'inseparable' in a different way, in accordance with the empty notions of Nestorius. What they say is that it is in equality of honour, in identity of will and in power, that the man is inseparable from the Word who dwelt in him. So they are producing these expressions not in simplicity of heart, but with a measure of craft and deceit.

16 Leo
Sermon 28
[*PL* 54, 221–6]

1. We are bidden, my beloved, throughout the divine Scriptures always to be rejoicing in the Lord, but we are without doubt more particularly stirred to spiritual joy on this day, when the mystery of the Lord's nativity shines so brightly upon us. We turn once again to that ineffable condescension of the divine love, whereby the creator of man deigned to be made man; our aim is to be found in his nature as we adore him in ours. God, the Son of God, the only-begotten from the eternal and unbegotten Father, continuing eternally in the form of God and possessing beyond all change and time an essence identical with the Father's, took upon him the form of a servant – yet without impairing his own majesty: he did it to promote us to his own state, not to degrade himself to ours. Each

nature continued with its own characteristics,* but so close a unity was established between them that the divine was inseparable from the humanity and the human indivisible from the divinity.

2. In celebrating our Lord and Saviour's birthday, my beloved, we must have a complete and true conception of the childbearing of the blessed Virgin. We must believe that there was no moment of time at which the power of the Word was absent from the flesh and soul that were conceived. There was no previously formed and en-souled temple of Christ's body, which the Word was to enter later and claim as a habitation. Rather it was through and in the Word himself that the new man was given his beginning. So there was one Son of God and of man, in whom the divinity was without mother and the humanity without father. By the Holy Spirit a virgin was made fruitful, and without trace of corruption gave birth at one and the same moment to the offspring and founder of her race. It was for this reason too that this same Lord, as the evangelist records, could enquire of the Jews whose son they understood Christ to be on the authority of the Scriptures, and, when they replied that it was taught that he would come from the seed of David, could ask, 'How then is it that David in the Spirit calls him "Lord"? For he says, The Lord said to my Lord, "Sit at my right hand until I put your enemies under your feet" ' [Matt. 22: 43–4]. The Jews were unable to answer the question, because they did not realize that the prophecy was speaking both of the offspring of David and of the divine nature within the one Christ.

3. The majesty of the Son of God, who is equal to the Father, clothes itself in the humility of a servant – without fear of diminution and without need of augmentation. By the power of his divinity alone he was able to achieve that operation of the divine love, which was devoted to the restoration of mankind – namely the rescue of the creature made in the image of God from the yoke of a harsh oppressor. But when the devil acted against the first man, he did not use force; he got man on to his own side with the consent of his free will. So, man's sin being voluntary and his hostility to God a matter of deliberate choice, these things had to be overcome in a manner which would not make of the requirements of justice an obstacle to the gift of grace. With the whole human race ruined in its entirety, there was in the secret depths of the divine purpose only one remedy which could help the fallen; that was for one of the sons of Adam to be born free from and innocent of the original trans-

---

* This insistence that each nature keeps its own distinctive characteristics goes back to Tertullian (see p. 46 above). It is also an important point of agreement between Leo and Cyril.

gression so that he could benefit all the rest both by his example and by his merit. But this could not happen by natural birth; no offspring of our tainted root could come except from that seed of which Scripture says: 'Who can make clean that which has been conceived of unclean seed? Art not thou the only one?' [Job 14: 4]. So David's Lord became David's son and from the fruit of the promised branch there did arise an offspring without taint. Two natures came together into one person, so that there was a single conception and a single birth of our Lord Jesus Christ, in whom was both true divinity for the working of miracles and true humanity for the endurance of suffering.

4. So then, my beloved, the catholic faith should turn her back on the errors of those heretics who rail against her. Deceived by the vanity of the wisdom of the world, they have deserted the truth of the gospel. They have made the source of true enlightenment into the occasion of their own blindness. We have examined the views of almost every form of false belief, even those which go so far as to deny the Holy Spirit, and we are confident that almost every deviation involves a failure to believe the truth of the two natures in Christ within an acknowledgement of the one person. Some have ascribed humanity only to the Lord, others divinity only. Others have said that he had true divinity but that his flesh was unreal. Others have acknowledged that he took real flesh, but have denied that he had the nature of God the Father; they have ascribed to his divinity what are really marks of his human nature, and so have invented the notion of a greater and a lesser God – although in true divinity there can be no differences of rank, since whatever is less than God is not God. Others have recognized that there is no such separation between Father and Son, but because they could not conceive the unity of the godhead except as a unity of person have affirmed that the Father is the same as the Son; on that understanding birth and growth, suffering and death, burial and resurrection are all acts of that one God, who fulfils the role of the man and of the Word at every point. Others have thought that our Lord Jesus Christ had a body which was not of the same substance as ours but composed of elements of a higher and more refined nature. Others have claimed that there was no human soul in the flesh of Christ but that the divinity of the Word itself filled the role of the soul. This rash opinion easily passes over into the view that there was a soul in Christ but it did not have a rational mind as part of it since the divinity by itself was sufficient to fulfil all the functions of reason for the man. Finally these same people have actually dared to affirm that some part of the Word was changed into flesh. Thus the various

forms of this one doctrine do away not only with the nature of the flesh and of the soul but even with the essence of the Word itself.

5. There are many other strange forms of error but we must not weary your patience by listing them all. These varied forms of impiety are linked together by the family resemblance which exists between one kind of blasphemy and another. But there are two errors in particular which we call on you to avoid with devout and special care. One of these was started some time ago by Nestorius; its attempt to gain ground was checked. The other, which is new, and which merits the same vigorous condemnation, has been propounded by Eutyches. Nestorius dared to proclaim that the blessed Virgin Mary was bearer of Christ's humanity only. This excludes the belief that in her conception and child-bearing a union was affected of flesh and the Word; the Son of God will not himself have become son of man, but will only have joined himself by an act of special favour to a created man. Catholic ears were utterly unable to accept this idea, being well enough trained in the true gospel to be absolutely sure that there is no hope of salvation for the human race unless the one who is the Virgin's son is the very one who is his mother's creator. Eutyches, the irreligious author of the more recent blasphemy, did acknowledge a union of the two natures in Christ; but he said that the outcome of that union was that only one of the two remained and that the substance of the other in no sense continued to exist – but this annihilation could only have happened by a process either of absorption or of separation. But both these notions are so directly opposed to a sound faith that one cannot accept them without losing the name of Christian. Consider what follows if the incarnation is a union of divine and human natures of such a kind that by their coming together what was double becomes single; it is divinity alone that was born of the womb of the Virgin, divinity alone that went through the deceptive appearance of submitting to bodily nourishment and growth; and, if I may omit all the other occasions of mutability that are inherent in being human, it is divinity alone that was crucified, divinity alone that died, divinity alone that was buried. Indeed for those who think thus there can be no ground for hope of resurrection, and Christ cannot be 'first-begotten from the dead' [Col. 1: 18]; for only someone capable of being put to death could have a right to resurrection.

6. Keep your hearts free, my beloved, from poisonous lies inspired by the devil. You know that the eternal divinity of the Son has not grown or increased in any way in the Father's presence; be careful then to observe that the saying 'Sit at my right hand' [Ps. 110: 1]

is directed to the same nature in Christ as that to which the saying 'Earth thou art and to earth thou shalt return' [Gen. 3: 19] was directed in the case of Adam. In that nature in which Christ is equal to the Father, the Only-begotten has never been inferior to the greatness of his begetter. The glory which he has with the Father is not a temporal thing. He is on that very right hand of the Father, of which Exodus and Isaiah speak: 'Thy right hand, O Lord, is glorified in power' [Exod. 15: 6] and 'Lord, who has believed our report? and to whom was the arm of the Lord revealed?' [Isa. 53: 1]. So then the man was taken up into the Son of God; he was received at the very outset of his physical existence into the unity of the person of Christ in such a way that he could not be conceived in separation from the divinity, could not be born in separation from the divinity, could not be reared in separation from the divinity. The same person was present in the miracles and in the endurance of insults. In his human weakness he was crucified, dead and buried; in his divine power he was raised on the third day, ascended into heaven and sat down at the right hand of God the Father. In his nature as man he received from the Father what in his nature as God he himself also bestowed.

7. Ponder these things, my beloved, with a dutiful heart; always remember the injunction of the apostle, who gives this general warning: 'See that no one deceives you by philosophy or empty deceit, according to human tradition and not according to Christ: for in him the whole fullness of deity dwells bodily, and you are filled in him' [Col. 2: 8–10]. He says 'bodily', not 'spiritually', so that we will realize that it is real fleshly substance in which there is a bodily indwelling of the fullness of deity. Thereby, indeed, the whole Church also is filled; cleaving to its head, it is the body of Christ, who lives and reigns, with the Father and the Holy Spirit, God for ever and ever. Amen.

4 Holy Spirit

Christian understanding of God took the form, as we have seen, of a trinitarian belief in one God existing as three coequal 'hypostases' or 'persons'. This is not clearly or self-evidently the teaching of Scripture. It is in relation to the Holy Spirit that scriptural teaching is least clear or self-evident. In the writings of the second and third centuries the Holy Spirit figures much less prominently than the Logos or the Son. The first passage, coming from that period, shows Origen reflecting on Scripture in the light of his general philosophical convictions about God in a way which was to seem to later generations to be wholly unacceptable.

The second passage comes from the Catechetical Lectures of Cyril of Jerusalem, delivered in the Church of the Holy Sepulchre during Lent to candidates for baptism at the coming Easter, about A.D. 350. They are concerned with man's need for the gifts of the Holy Spirit and show a strong reserve about speculations concerning his person. This may be due to the fact that they are lectures for catechumens, but is none the less characteristic of almost all Christian writing about the Spirit up to that time.

But the question of the true nature and status of the Spirit did become a prominent issue in the third quarter of the fourth century. The first clear evidence of this are the four letters of Athanasius written in 359 or 360 to Serapion, bishop of Thmuis, who had drawn his attention to certain Egyptian Christians who accepted the full divinity of the Son (unlike the Arians) but who regarded the Spirit as a creature. Of the four letters, the second and third were probably originally a single letter. The passage given is the whole of the so-called third letter and gives in summary form the gist of the argument for the divinity of the Spirit which is set out at greater length in the first letter. Athanasius argues that the divine nature of the Holy Spirit's work necessarily implies his personal divinity. This line of argument was basic also to the thought of the Cappadocians in their development of trinitarian doctrine.

The last passage comes from Augustine's work on the Trinity, from which the passage above (pp. 36–42) was also taken. If there is no distinction between the persons of the Trinity either in nature or in activity, some account is called for to explain why particular attributes are associated in both Scripture and tradition with particular persons of the Trinity. It is this problem which Augustine deals with here with his customary combination of intellectual dexterity and spiritual insight.

17 Origen
Commentary on John II, 10 (6)–12 (on John 1: 3a)
[*GCS* 10, 64–7]

10. 'All things were brought into being through him.'

The phrase 'through whom' never signifies first place, but always the second. For example, the Epistle to the Romans reads: 'Paul, a servant of Jesus Christ, called to be an apostle, set apart for the gospel of God, which he promised beforehand through his prophets in the holy Scriptures, the gospel concerning his Son, who was descended from David according to the flesh and designated Son of God with power according to the spirit of holiness by his resurrection from the dead, Jesus Christ our Lord, through whom we have received grace and apostleship to bring about obedience to the faith among all the nations for the sake of his name' [Rom. 1: 1–5]. God promised his gospel beforehand through the prophets; the prophets were acting as servants and so they have the position of those 'through whom'. When later God gave grace and apostleship to bring about obedience to the faith among all the nations to Paul and the others, he did it through Christ Jesus the Saviour; so he has the position of him 'through whom'. And in the Epistle to the Hebrews Paul again says: 'In these last days he has spoken to us by a Son whom he appointed the heir of all things, through whom also he created the ages' [Heb. 1: 2].* Thereby he teaches us that God created the ages through the Son, so that with regard to the making of the ages the only-begotten has the position of him 'through whom'. So then in this passage too, if 'all things were brought into being through' the Logos, they were not brought into being by the Logos

---

* Eusebius cites Origen as saying of the Epistle to the Hebrews that 'the thoughts are the apostle's ... but who wrote the epistle in truth God knows' (*Historia Ecclesiastica* (*Church History*) VI, 25, 13–14).

but by one higher and greater than the Logos. And who else could that be but the Father?

If then it is acknowledged as true that 'all things were brought into being through him', we must enquire whether the Holy Spirit was brought into being through him. It seems to me that any one who asserts that he was brought into being and who accepts that 'all things were brought into being through him' will have to admit that the Holy Spirit was brought into being through the Word and that the Word is senior to him. And it follows that anyone who is reluctant to describe the Holy Spirit as brought into being through Christ must – if he accepts the statements of this gospel as true – say that he is unbegotten.

There is a third possibility in addition either to allowing that the Holy Spirit was brought into being or to supposing that he is unbegotten. It would be possible for someone to claim that the Holy Spirit does not have any individual existence in distinction from the Father and the Son. But perhaps such a person would be ready to agree that, if one regards the Son as distinct from the Father, it will be a matter of the Spirit being identical with the Father, since there seems to be a clear distinction drawn between the Spirit and the Son in the text: 'Whoever speaks a word against the son of man, it will be forgiven him; but whoever blasphemes against the Holy Spirit will have no forgiveness in this age or in the age to come' [Matt. 12: 32].

But we for our part are convinced that there are three distinct existents – Father, Son and Holy Spirit – and we do not believe that any of these is unbegotten except the Father. So the view which asks our approval as the most religious and truthful one is the following: that of all things brought into being through the Word the Holy Spirit is the most honourable and he is first in rank of all the things brought into being by the Father through Christ. And perhaps this is the reason why the Spirit is not called a son of God as well. The only-begotten alone is a son by nature from the very beginning; whereas the Holy Spirit seems to require the Son as an intermediary in respect of his distinct existence – not merely enabling him to exist but enabling to exist as wise, rational, just and with all the other characteristics he must be thought of as having by participation in the attributes of Christ, of which we have spoken earlier.

It seems to me that the Holy Spirit provides those who on account of him and of their participation in him are called holy, with the matter (if I may use the expression) of which the gifts that come from God consist. This matter of God's gifts, as I have called it, is worked by God, is ministered by Christ, and is given concrete existence by the Holy Spirit. I am led to this view by what Paul writes somewhere about God's gifts: 'There are varieties of gifts, but the same Spirit; there are varieties of ministration, but the same Lord; there are varieties of working, but it is the same God who works all in all' [1 Cor. 12: 4–6].

11. The text 'all things were brought into being through him' and its corollary that the Holy Spirit is something brought into being through the Word raises this difficulty. How is it that in some Scriptures he is, as it were, honoured above Christ? In Isaiah Christ acknowledges that he has been sent not only by the Father but also by the Holy Spirit; he says, 'And now the Lord sent me and his Spirit' [Isa. 48: 16]. In the gospel he promises forgiveness of sin against him but blasphemy against the Holy Spirit is declared to be without forgiveness for the man who has committed it not only in this age but even in the age to come. But the fact that forgiveness is not available for the man who has sinned against the Spirit may not have anything at all to do with the Holy Spirit's being more honourable than Christ; it may rather be due to the fact that all rational beings participate in Christ and they can be granted pardon if they turn away from their sins, whereas those who have been deemed worthy of the Holy Spirit cannot reasonably expect any pardon if in spite of so wonderful an inspiration for good they fall back again into evil and frustrate the counsels of the Spirit within them. So too with the Isaiah passage where our Lord says that he was sent by the Father and by his Spirit, one must reply that the Spirit's sending Christ does not imply that the Spirit is superior in nature, but that the Saviour was made less than the Spirit for the purpose of realizing the divine plan of the incarnation of the Son of God. And if anyone objects to our saying that the Saviour in becoming incarnate was made less than the Holy Spirit, we must bring in the quotation from the Epistle to the Hebrews where Paul declares that Jesus was made less even than the angels because of the suffering of death: the quotation is: 'We see Jesus, who was made a little lower than the angels because of the suffering of death, crowned with glory and honour' [Heb. 2: 9]. Perhaps we can also say this. In order to be freed from the bondage of corruption, the creation – and the human race too – needed a glorious and divine power to become man in order to put to rights the affairs of the world. This task fell, as it were, to the lot of the Holy Spirit, but he was unable to sustain so great a contest and proposed the Son as the only one capable of doing so. So then the Father, as head, sends the Son but the Holy Spirit joins in this, escorting him on his way with the promise to come down to the Son of God in due time and to work with him for the salvation of

mankind. This he did when he flew down on to him after his baptism in bodily form like a dove; he rested on him and did not leave him as perhaps he does with men who are unable to bear his glory continuously. That was why John, when indicating how he knew who was the Christ, referred not only to the descent of the dove on Jesus but also, in addition to its descending, its remaining in him. For John is recorded to have said, 'He who sent me to baptize said, "He on whom you see the Spirit descending and remaining, this is he who baptizes with Holy Spirit and with fire" ' [John 1 : 33]. It does not say 'on whom you see the Spirit descending' (there may perhaps have been others on whom he descended as well), but 'descending and remaining' on him.

We have spent a long time on this point with a view to showing clearly how, if 'all things were brought into being through him', then the Holy Spirit also was brought into being through the Word; he is one of the 'all things' and is to be regarded as inferior to the one through whom he was brought into being, even though some texts may appear to point in the opposite direction.

12. If anyone accepts the Gospel according to the Hebrews* where the Saviour himself says, 'My mother, the Holy Spirit,† took me just now by one of my hairs and carried me off to the great Mount Tabor', this will raise the further problem how the Holy Spirit who was brought into being through the Word can be mother of Christ. The passage can be explained without difficulty in the following way. If anyone who does the will of the Father who is in heaven is his brother and sister and mother [see Matt. 12: 50] and the name 'brother of Christ' can be applied not only to the human race but to more divine beings as well, then there is nothing absurd in the Holy Spirit being his mother even more than all those who may be called 'mother of Christ' on the grounds of doing the will of the Father in heaven.

* The Gospel according to the Hebrews probably derives from Jewish–Christian circles in Egypt. Origen quotes the same passage, with a similar qualification, in *Homilies on Jeremiah* 15, 4. For more detailed information about the Gospel see E. Hennecke, *New Testament Apocrypha* (1963) 1, pp. 120, 158–65.

† For other examples of the Holy Spirit being understood as feminine in early Gnostic thought, see Irenaeus, *Against the Heresies* 1, 3, 1 and Hippolytus, *Refutatio omnium haeresium* 9, 13. This probably arose in Aramaic-speaking circles, where the word for 'spirit' is feminine.

18   Cyril of Jerusalem
Catechetical lecture 16, 1–4 and 22–4
[Ed. J. Rupp (Munich, 1860), pp. 204–10 and 232–6]
Translation of W. Telfer in *LCC* 4, 167–73: revised.

Lesson from the first epistle to the Corinthians: *Concerning spiritual gifts, brethren, I do not want you to be ignorant ... and there are diversities of gifts but the same spirit ...* [1 Cor. 12: 1–7].

1. Verily I need spiritual grace if I am to discourse of the Holy Spirit: I do not mean, to enable me to speak as the subject deserves, for that is not possible, but simply to run through what is said in holy Scripture without imperilling my soul. For what is written in the gospels, of Christ saying unequivocally, 'Whoever speaks a word against the Holy Spirit, will not be forgiven, either in this world, or in the world to come' [Matt. 12: 32], truly makes one very much afraid. And there is oftentimes reason to fear that a person may incur this condemnation for saying what he ought not about the Holy Spirit, either through ignorance or mistaken piety. He who proclaimed that such a one should not be forgiven is the judge of quick and dead, Jesus Christ. After that, what hope is there for an offender?

2. In those circumstances it must be for the grace of Jesus Christ himself to grant me to speak impeccably and you to hear with understanding. For understanding is needed by hearers as well as speakers, lest they form a wrong impression in their minds from what they are rightly told. Therefore let us say about the Holy Spirit exactly what Scripture says and nothing else, and do not let us pry where Scripture does not answer. The Scriptures were spoken by the Holy Spirit himself, and what he said about himself is exactly what he pleased, or we could comprehend. So, let what he spoke be said, which is to say, let us not dare to utter anything that he did not.

3. There is one only Holy Spirit the Paraclete. And just as there is one God the Father, and no second Father exists, and just as there is one only-begotten Son and Word of God, having no brother, so there is only one Holy Spirit, and there is no second spirit ranking beside him. So the Holy Spirit is supreme power, a divine and ineffable reality. For he is alive and rational, and sanctifies everything that has been brought into being by God through Christ. He enlightens the souls of righteous men. He was in the prophets, and under the new covenant he was in the apostles. Such as dare to break in two the work of the Holy Spirit are to be abhorred. There is one

God the Father, Lord of the old covenant and of the new. And there is one Lord Jesus Christ, prophesied in the old covenant and present in the new. And there is one Holy Spirit, who proclaimed the things of Christ by the prophets, and then when Christ came, came down himself to make him known.

4. Let no one therefore sunder the old covenant from the new. Let no one say that the Spirit in the one is not identical with the Spirit in the other. For whosoever does so offends none other than that Holy Spirit who is honoured together with the Father and the Son and who is fully included in the holy Trinity in the moment of holy baptism. For the only-begotten Son of God commanded the apostles explicitly, 'Go, and teach all nations, baptizing them in the name of the Father, and of the Son, and of the Holy Spirit' [Matt. 28: 19]. In the Father, the Son and the Holy Spirit is our hope. We are not preaching three Gods, so let the Marcionites hold their peace; but aided by the Holy Spirit through the one Son, we preach one God. Our faith is indivisible; our worship indissoluble. We do not divide up the holy Trinity, as some do, nor, like Sabellius, do we coalesce it into one. But we reverently acknowledge one Father who sent his Son to be our Saviour; likewise one Son who promised to send the Paraclete from the Father; and likewise the Holy Spirit, who spoke in the prophets and at Pentecost descended upon the apostles in the likeness of fiery tongues. That happened here in Jerusalem in the Upper Church of the Apostles.* (We here are privileged at every point.) To this spot Christ came down from heaven, and to this spot likewise the Holy Spirit came down from heaven. And it would certainly be most appropriate that just as I talk to you of the things of Christ and Golgotha here on Golgotha, I should talk to you about the Holy Spirit in the Upper Church. Nevertheless, he who descended in that place is sharer of the glory of him who was crucified here. And so I am discoursing here of him who descended there. For our worship is indivisible.

22. Great indeed is the Holy Spirit, and in his gifts, omnipotent and wonderful. Think how, whatever number there is of you sitting here now, there is present that number of souls. On each one, he is at work to good purpose. Present in our midst, he sees how each is disposed. He sees alike the thoughts and consciences of each. He knows what we say and what we think and what we believe. What I have said might seem enough for us, but yet it falls short of the whole. For, with your minds enlightened by the Holy Spirit, I beg you to note

* For the limited information about this church in the fourth century, see J. D. Wilkinson, *Egeria's Travels* (London, 1971), pp. 38–9.

how many Christians are in the whole of the diocese, and then how many in the whole province of Palestine. Next stretch your thoughts beyond the province to take in the whole Roman empire. Then, if you please, beyond that, into the whole wide world, the peoples of Persia, the nations of India, the Goths and Sarmatians, Gauls and Spaniards, Moors, Libyans, Ethiopians, and then all those others for whom we have no names: for there are many cases where not even the name of the nation has reached us. And then think how that in each of these nations there are bishops, presbyters, deacons, celibates, virgins and all the other lay people. Finally contemplate the great guardian and dispenser of their several graces, who, throughout the world, is giving to this one chastity, and to that one lifelong virginity, making another a generous giver, and detaching another from care for worldly goods, while on yet another he bestows the gift of driving out evil spirits. And just as daylight, by one act of the sun's radiation, enlightens the whole earth, so too the Holy Spirit gives light to all who have eyes to see. For if anyone is not granted such grace because of his blindness, let him blame not the spirit but his own faithlessness.

23. You have viewed his power in all the world. But do not stay on earth. Ascend now to the realms above. Ascend in imagination as far as the first heaven, and there behold the countless myriads of angels who inhabit it. If you can bear it, ascend in imagination still further. Lo the archangels! Lo the spirits of God! Lo the virtues! Lo the principalities! Lo the powers! Lo the thrones! Lo the dominations! Of all these the Paraclete is the ruler, teacher and sanctifier who comes from God. To speak of men, Elijah has need of him, Elisha has need of him, Isaiah has need of him; to speak of angels, then Michael and Gabriel have need of him. Nothing that has come into being ranks with him. The angelic orders, even if all their hosts were gathered together in one, cannot pretend to equality with the Holy Spirit. The all-gracious might of the Paraclete overshadows them all. While they are sent to minister, he searches the very depths of God: as the apostle tells us, 'For the Spirit searches all things, even the very depths of God. For what man knows the things of a man except the spirit of man which is in him? Even so no one knows the things of God except the Spirit of God' [1 Cor. 2: 10–11].

24. He it is who through the prophets predicted the things of Christ, he again who worked mightily in the apostles. To this very day it is he who in the sacrament seals the souls of those who are baptized. What happens is that the Father gives to the Son and the Son imparts to the Holy Spirit. That is not my saying, but Jesus himself says, 'All things have been delivered to me by my Father' [Matt. 11: 27]; while of the Holy Spirit he says, 'When he, the

Spirit of truth, shall come...he shall glorify me; for he shall receive of mine, and shall show it to you' [John 16: 13–14]. Every grace is given by the Father, through the Son, together with the Holy Spirit. There are not some graces that come from the Father, and different graces from the Son, and others again from the Holy Spirit. There is but one salvation, one power, one faith; there is one God, the Father, one Lord, his only-begotten Son, and one Holy Spirit, the Paraclete. Let us be content with this knowledge and not busy ourselves with questions about nature or hypostasis. I would have spoken of that had it been contained in Scripture. Let us not venture where Scripture does not lead, for it suffices for our salvation to know that there is Father, and Son, and Holy Spirit.

19 Athanasius

Third letter to Serapion

[*PG* 26, 624–37]

Translation of C. R. B. Shapland (London, 1951), pp. 169–78: revised.

1. Perhaps you will wonder why, when I was charged to abridge and briefly to explain the letter I had written concerning the Holy Spirit, you find me, as though I had laid aside my work on that subject, writing against those who are guilty of impiety towards the Son of God and call him a creature. But you will not blame me, I know well, when you understand the cause. Indeed when you see how reasonable it is, your Reverence will welcome it.

Our Lord himself said that the Paraclete 'will not speak from himself, but whatever he hears he will speak; for he will take from what is mine and declare it to you' [John 16: 13–14]; and, 'having breathed on them' [John 20: 22], he gave the Spirit to the disciples from himself, and in this way the Father poured him out 'upon all flesh' [Joel 2: 28], in accordance with Scripture. It is natural, therefore, that I should have spoken and written first concerning the Son, that from our knowledge of the Son we may be able to have true knowledge of the Spirit. For we shall find that the Spirit has to the Son the same proper relationship as we have recognized the Son to have to the Father. The Son says, 'All that the Father has is mine' [John 16: 15]; similarly we shall find that through the Son all those things are in the Spirit also. The Father attested the Son, saying, 'This is my beloved Son, in whom I am well pleased' [Matt. 3: 17]; similarly the Spirit belongs to the Son; for the apostle says: 'God

sent the Spirit of his Son into our hearts crying, Abba, Father' [Gal.
4: 6]. And, most remarkable of all, the Son said, 'What is mine
belongs to the Father' [see John 17: 10]; similarly the Holy Spirit,
which is said to belong to the Son, belongs to the Father – for the
Son himself says: 'When the Paraclete has come, whom I shall send
to you from the Father, even the Spirit of truth who proceeds from
the Father, he will bear witness to me' [John 15: 26], and Paul
writes: 'No one knows what is in man except man's spirit which
dwells in him. Even so no one knows what is in God except God's
Spirit which is in him. Now we have received not the spirit of the
world, but the Spirit which is from God, that we may know the gifts
which come to us from God' [1 Cor. 2: 11–12]. And throughout the
divine Scripture you will find that the Holy Spirit, who is said to
belong to the Son, is also said to belong to God. This I wrote in my
previous letter.* If therefore the Son, because of his proper relationship with the Father and because he is the proper offspring of his
essence, is not a creature, but is one in essence (*homoousios*) with the
Father: the Holy Spirit likewise, because of his proper relationship
with the Son, from whom he is given to all men and whose is all that
he has, cannot be a creature, and it is impious to call him so.

2. These considerations are sufficient to dissuade anyone, be he
never so contentious, from continuing to describe as a creature him
who is in God and who searches the depths of God and who is given
from the Father through the Son; lest from this he shall be forced to
call the Son also a creature, who is Word, Wisdom, Image, and
Radiance, seeing whom we see the Father; and lest finally he should
hear the words: 'Whoever denies the Son, neither does he have the
Father' [1 John 2: 23]. For such a man will soon be saying with the
fool: 'There is no God' [Ps. 14: 1].

None the less, so that our reply to the impious may be more fully
established, it will be well to make use of those considerations which
show that the Son is not a creature, to show that the Spirit also is not
a creature. Creatures are from nothing and their existence has a
beginning; for 'In the beginning God made the heaven and the
earth' [Gen. 1: 1], and what is in them. But the Holy Spirit is, and
is said to be, from God (so said the apostle [1 Cor. 2: 12]). Now if the
Son cannot be a creature because he is not from nothing, but from
God, then of necessity the Spirit is not a creature, since he has been
confessed to be from God. It is creatures that are from nothing.

3. Again, the Holy Spirit is called, and is, unction and seal. For
John writes: 'As for you, the unction which you received from him
abides in you, and you have no need that anyone should teach you,

---

* See, for example, *First letter to Serapion* 20; 30.

but as his unction, his Spirit, teaches you about everything' [1 John 2: 27]. In the prophet Isaiah it is written: 'The Spirit of the Lord is upon me because he has anointed me' [Isa. 61: 1]. Paul writes: 'In whom, when you had come to believe, you were sealed' [Eph. 1: 13], and again, 'Do not grieve the Holy Spirit, in whom you were sealed for the day of redemption' [Eph. 4: 30]. Creatures are anointed and sealed in him. But if creatures are anointed and sealed in him, the Spirit cannot be a creature. For that which anoints is different from those which are anointed. Moreover, this unction is a breath of the Son, so that he who has the Spirit says: 'We are a sweet savour of Christ' [2 Cor. 2: 15]. The seal gives the impress of the Son, so that he who is sealed has the form of Christ; as the apostle says: 'My little children, with whom I am again in labour until Christ be formed in you' [Gal. 4: 19]. But if the Spirit is the sweet savour and form of the Son, it is clear that the Spirit cannot be a creature; for the Son also, 'who is in the form' [Phil. 2: 6] of the Father, is not a creature.

Moreover, as he who has seen the Son sees the Father [John 14: 9], so he who has the Holy Spirit has the Son and, having him, is a temple of God. For Paul writes, 'Do you not know that you are a temple of God and that the Spirit of God dwells in you?' [1 Cor. 3: 16]. John says: 'By this we know that we abide in God and he in us, because he has given us of his Spirit' [1 John 4: 13]. But if we have confessed that the Son is not a creature, because he is in the Father and the Father in him, then the Spirit likewise cannot possibly be a creature; for the Son is in him and he is in the Son. That is why he who receives the Spirit is called a temple of God.

Furthermore, it will be well to look at it in the light of the following consideration. If the Son is the Word of God, he is one as the Father is one; for 'There is one God, from whom are all things, and one Lord Jesus Christ' [1 Cor. 8: 6]. Hence he is both spoken and written of as 'only-begotten Son' [John 1: 18]. But creatures are many and diverse: angels, archangels, cherubim, principalities, powers, and the rest, as we have said. But if the Son is not a creature because he does not belong to the many, but is one as the Father is one: then the Spirit likewise – for we must take our knowledge of the Spirit from the Son – cannot be a creature. For he does not belong to the many; he too is one. [4] This the apostle knows when he says: 'All these things are the work of the one and the same Spirit who apportions to each one individually as he wills' [1 Cor. 12: 11]; and a little farther on: 'In one Spirit we were all baptized into one body, and all were made to drink of one Spirit' [1 Cor. 12: 13].

Once more, if we must take our knowledge of the Spirit from the

Son, then with propriety we may put forward proofs which derive from him. The Son is everywhere; for he is in the Father and the Father in him [John 14: 10]. He controls and contains all things; and it is written: 'In him all things hold together, whether seen or unseen, and he is before all things' [Col. 1: 16–17]. Now creatures are in the separate places that have been assigned to them: the sun, the moon and the other lights in the firmament, angels in heaven and men upon the earth. But the Son is not in separate places that have been assigned to him; he is in the Father and is therefore everywhere; he is outside all things and is therefore not a creature. It follows from this that the Spirit too cannot be a creature; for he is not in separate places assigned to him, but fills all things and yet is outside all things. Thus it is written: 'The Spirit of the Lord has filled the world' [Wis. 1: 7]. And David sings, 'Whither shall I go from thy Spirit?' [Ps. 139: 7], inasmuch as he is not in any place, but is outside all things and in the Son, as the Son is in the Father. Therefore, as we have proved, he too is not a creature.

Over and above these things, the following considerations will confirm the condemnation of the Arian heresy, and once more make plain from the Son what we know concerning the Spirit. The Son, like the Father, is creator; for he says: 'The things which I see the Father making, these things I also make' [John 5: 19]. 'All things', indeed, 'come into being through him, and without him not one thing came into being' [John 1: 3]. But if the Son, being, like the Father, creator, is not a creature; and if, because all things were created through him, he does not belong to things created: then, clearly, neither is the Spirit a creature. For it is written concerning him in the one hundred and third psalm: 'Thou shalt take away their spirit, and they shall die and return to their dust. Thou shalt put forth thy Spirit, and they shall be created, and thou shalt renew the face of the earth' [Ps. 104: 29–30].

5. As it is thus written, it is clear that the Spirit is not a creature, but takes part in the act of creation. The Father creates all things through the Word in the Spirit; for where the Word is, there is the Spirit also, and it is out of the Spirit from the Word that the things which are created through the Word have their power to exist. Thus it is written in the thirty-second psalm: 'By the Word of the Lord the heavens were established, and by the Spirit of his mouth is all their might' [Ps. 33: 6].

The Spirit is so clearly indivisible from the Son that what we are saying leaves no room for doubt. When the Word came upon the prophet, it was in the Spirit that the prophet used to speak the things he received from the Word. Thus it is written in the Acts, when

Peter says: 'Brethren, the Scripture had to be fulfilled which the Holy Spirit spoke beforehand' [Acts 1: 16]. In Zechariah it is written, when the Word came upon him: 'But receive my words and my statutes, which I charge in my Spirit to the prophets' [Zech. 1: 6]. And when, a little farther on, he rebuked the people, he said: 'They made their heart disobedient, lest they should hear my laws and the words which the Lord Almighty has sent by his Spirit in the hands of the prophets of old' [Zech. 7: 12]. And when Christ spoke in Paul – as Paul himself said, 'Since you desire proof that Christ is speaking in me' [2 Cor. 13: 3] – it was, none the less, the Spirit that he had bestowing upon him the power of speech. For he writes: 'According to the bestowal of the Spirit of Jesus Christ upon me' [Phil. 1: 19]. Again, when Christ spoke in him, he said: 'Except that the Holy Spirit testifies to me in every city, saying that imprisonment and afflictions await me' [Acts 20: 23]. The Spirit is not outside the Word but, being in the Word, through him is in God. And so the spiritual gifts are given in the Triad. For, as he writes to the Corinthians, in their distribution there is the same Spirit and the same Lord and the same God, 'who works all things in all' [1 Cor. 12: 6]. For the Father himself through the Word in the Spirit works and gives all things.

6. Assuredly, when he prayed for the Corinthians, he prayed in the Triad, saying: 'The grace of the Lord Jesus Christ and the love of God and the communion of the Holy Spirit be with you all' [2 Cor. 13: 13]. For inasmuch as we partake of the Spirit, we have the grace of the Word and, in the Word, the love of the Father. And as the grace of the Triad is one, so also the Triad is indivisible. We can see this in regard to Saint Mary herself. The archangel Gabriel, when sent to announce the coming of the Word upon her, said, 'The Holy Spirit will come upon you', knowing that the Spirit was in the Word. Therefore he immediately added: 'And the Power of the Highest will overshadow you' [Luke 1: 35]. For Christ is 'the Power of God and the Wisdom of God' [1 Cor. 1: 24]. But if the Spirit was in the Word, then it must be clear that the Spirit through the Word was also in God. Likewise, when the Spirit comes to us, the Son will come and the Father, and they will make their abode in us. For the Triad is indivisible, and its Godhead is one; and there is one God 'over all and through all and in all' [Eph. 4: 6]. This is the faith of the Catholic Church. For the Lord grounded and rooted it in the Triad, when he said to his disciples: 'Go and make disciples of all the nations, baptizing them into the name of the Father and of the Son and of the Holy Spirit' [Matt. 28: 19]. Were the Spirit a creature, he would not have ranked him with the Father; lest, by reason of some-

thing strange and foreign being ranked therewith, the Triad should contain dissimilarity. For what was lacking to God, that he should take to himself something foreign in essence and share his glory with it? God forbid! It is not so! He himself said: 'I am full' [Isa. 1: 11]. Therefore the Lord himself ranked the Spirit with the name of the Father, to show that the Triad is not composed of diverse elements, I mean of creator and creature, but that its Godhead is one. It was because he had learned this that Paul taught the oneness of the grace given in the Triad, saying: 'One Lord, one faith, one baptism' [Eph. 4: 5]. As there is one baptism, so there is one faith. For he who believes in the Father, in the Father knows the Son; he also knows the Spirit, in his knowing of the Son.* Therefore he believes both in the Son and in the Holy Spirit. For the Godhead of the Triad is one, and knowledge of it is derived from knowledge of the one, namely the Father.

7. That is the specific mark of the Catholic faith. But as for those who speak evil of the Spirit and call him a creature, if what we have said does not make them repent, then may what we are about to say overwhelm them with shame. If there is a Triad, and if the faith is faith in a Triad, let them tell us whether there was always a Triad, or whether there was once when it was not a Triad. If the Triad is eternal, the Spirit is not a creature, for he eternally exists with and in the Word. As for creatures, there was once when they were not. If he is a creature, and creatures are from nothing, it is clear that there was once when the Triad was not a Triad but a dyad. What greater impiety can man utter? They are saying that the Triad owes its existence to alteration and progress; that it was a dyad, and waited for the coming into being of a creature which should be ranked with the Father and the Son, and with them become the Triad. God forbid that such a notion should so much as enter the minds of Christian people! As the Son, because he always exists, is not a creature; so, because the Triad always exists, there is no creature in it. Therefore the Spirit is not a creature. As the Triad always was, so it now is; and as it now is, so it always was and is; and in the Triad is Father and Son and Holy Spirit. And there is one God, the Father, 'who is over all and through all and in all' [Eph. 4: 6], who is 'blessed for ever. Amen' [Rom. 9: 5].

I have written this in brief, as you directed, and am sending it. If anything is lacking therein, as a man of understanding, be kind enough to supply it. Read it 'to those who are of the household of faith' [Gal. 6: 10], and refute those who love contention and evil speech. Perhaps, even by a late repentance, they may wash away

* Literally: 'he also knows the Spirit, not outside the Son'.

from their souls the perversity which formerly was in them. It would be well for them, as it is written, 'to turn aside and not to tarry' [Prov. 9: 18a (LXX)]; lest, by delaying, they should hear that which was spoken by the Lord: 'Whoever speaks against the Holy Spirit shall not be forgiven, either in this age or in the age to come' [Matt. 12: 32].

20 Augustine
On the Trinity XV, xvii, 27–xviii, 32
[*CCL* 50, 501–8]
Translation of J. Burnaby in *LCC* 8, 157–62: revised.

27. Concerning the Father and the Son we have now said as much as we have found possible to discern by means of the puzzling reflections in the mirror of the human mind. It remains for us to consider, with such insight as God's gift may grant us, the Holy Spirit. Scripture teaches us that he is the Spirit neither of the Father alone nor of the Son alone, but of both; and so his being suggests to us that mutual charity whereby the Father and the Son love one another. But for the exercise of our understanding, the inspired word has set before us truths not lying on the surface but to be explored in the depths and thence brought up to light; so that our search calls for the greater diligence. The Scripture has not said: 'the Holy Spirit is charity'. If it had, much of our inquiry would have been foreclosed. It has said: 'God is charity' [1 John 4: 8, 16]; and so left us to ask whether God the Father be charity, or God the Son, or God the Holy Spirit, or God the Trinity itself. Now it is not open to us to say that the reason why charity is called God is merely that it is a gift of God and that it is not a substantive reality worthy to be named God. There are, it is true, passages in Scripture where God is addressed in such terms as 'thou art my patience' [Ps. 71: 5], and there the meaning is not that our patience is the substance of God, but that it comes to us from him, as indeed we read elsewhere: 'from him is my patience' [Ps. 62: 5]. But in the case of charity any such interpretation is at once refuted by the actual language of the Scriptures. 'Thou art my patience' is like 'Thou, Lord, art my hope' [Ps. 91: 9], and 'My God is my compassion' [Ps. 59: 17], and many expressions of the kind; but we do not read: 'the Lord is my charity', or 'Thou art my charity', or 'God is my charity', but 'God is charity' – just as 'God is spirit' [John 4: 24]. Anyone who cannot see the difference must seek understanding from the Lord and not explanation from us; for we have no words to make the point more evident.

28. God, then, is charity. Our question is whether this refers to Father, or Son, or Holy Spirit, or the Trinity itself which is not three Gods, but one God. I have argued earlier in the present book that the divine Trinity must not be so conceived, from the likeness of the three members displayed in our mental trinity, as to make the Father memory of all three,* the Son understanding of all three, and the Holy Spirit charity of all three. It is not as though the Father neither understood nor loved for himself, but the Son understood for him and the Holy Spirit loved for him, while he himself did nothing but 'remember', both for himself and for them; nor as though the Son neither remembered nor loved for himself, but the Father remembered for him and the Holy Spirit loved for him, while he himself did nothing but understand both for himself and for them; nor as though the Holy Spirit neither remembered nor understood for himself, but the Father remembered for him and the Son understood for him, while he himself only loved both for himself and for them. Rather must we think that all and each possess all three powers in their proper nature; and that in them the three are not separate, as in ourselves memory is one thing, understanding another, and love or charity another: but that there is one single power whose capacity is sufficient for all, such as wisdom itself, which is so to be found in the nature of each several person that he who possesses it is that which he possesses, in that he is a changeless and incomposite substance. If this be understood and its truth manifest, so far as we may be suffered to see or to conjecture in these great matters, I see no reason why, just as Father, Son and Holy Spirit are each called wisdom, and all together are not three wisdoms but one, so Father, Son, and Holy Spirit may not each be called charity, and all together one charity. In the same way the Father is God, the Son is God, and the Holy Spirit God; and all together are one God.

29. Yet there is good reason why in this Trinity we speak of the Son alone as Word of God, of the Holy Spirit alone as Gift of God, and of God the Father alone as the one of whom the Word is begotten and from whom the Holy Spirit originally proceeds. I add the word 'originally', because we learn that the Holy Spirit proceeds also from the Son.† But this is again something given by the Father

---

* In Platonic psychology 'memory' is the fundamental source of knowledge.

† For the significance of this distinction in relation to the later controversy between the Eastern and the Western Churches on the double procession of the Holy Spirit, see J. N. D. Kelly, *Early Christian Creeds* (London, 1972³), p. 359. For a characteristically Eastern approach to the Trinity, see Gregory of Nyssa's use of the image of a chain on p. 35 above.

to the Son – not that he ever existed without it, for all that the Father gives to his only-begotten Word he gives in the act of begetting him. He is begotten in such wise that the common gift proceeds from him also, and the Holy Spirit is Spirit of both. And this distinction within the indivisible Trinity is not to be admitted in passing, but to be observed with all diligence. For hence it comes that the Word of God is by a special fitness called also the Wisdom of God, though both Father and Holy Spirit are wisdom. If then one of the three is by a special fitness to be named charity, the name falls most appropriately to the Holy Spirit. And this means that in the incomposite and supreme being of God, substance is not to be distinguished from charity; but substance is itself charity, and charity itself is substance, whether in the Father or in the Son or in the Holy Spirit, and yet by a special fitness the Holy Spirit is named charity.

30. We may compare the manner in which all the oracles of the Old Testament Scripture are sometimes denoted by the name of law. A text quoted from the prophet Isaiah, where he says, 'By other tongues and other lips I will speak to this people', is introduced by the apostle with the words, 'it is written in the law' [Isa. 28: 11; 1 Cor. 14: 21]. And our Lord himself says, 'It is written in their law, that they have hated me without a cause', though we read the words in a psalm [John 15: 25; Ps. 35: 19]. But sometimes the title is assigned specially to the law given through Moses, as in the texts, 'the law and the prophets were until John', and 'on these two commandments hang the whole law and the prophets' [Matt. 11: 13; 22: 40]. Here certainly the word 'law' is being used in a special sense to refer to that coming from Mount Sinai, whereas the word 'prophets' includes the psalms in its scope. Elsewhere however the Saviour himself says, 'Everything written about me in the law and the prophets and the psalms had to be fulfilled' [Luke 24: 44]; in this case by contrast the word 'prophets' excludes the psalms. 'Law', then, may be used in a general sense to include prophets and psalms, but also in a special sense to refer to the law given through Moses; and 'prophets' may be used as a common term including the psalms, as well as in a special sense excluding them. And there are numerous other instances to show that many words can both be extended generally, and also applied in a special sense to certain things; but we need not dwell at length on so plain a matter. I am concerned only to rebut the charge of impropriety in calling the Holy Spirit charity, if made on the ground that both God the Father and God the Son are entitled to the same name.

31. We may say, then, that just as we give the name of wisdom by a special fitness to the one Word of God, though in general both the

Holy Spirit and the Father himself are wisdom, so is the Spirit by a special fitness to be called charity, though both Father and Son are charity in general. The Word of God, God's only-begotten Son, is expressly named as the Wisdom of God in the apostle's own phrase, 'Christ the power of God and the wisdom of God' [1 Cor. 1: 24]. But we can also find authority for calling the Holy Spirit charity, by a careful examination of the apostle John's language [1 John 4: 7–19]. After saying, 'Beloved, let us love one another, for love is of God', he goes on to add, 'and everyone who loves is born of God; he who does not love has not known God, for God is love'. This makes it plain that the love which he calls God is the same love which he has said to be 'of God'. Love, then, is God of (or from) God. But since both the Son and the Spirit are from God, the Son begotten and the Spirit proceeding, we must naturally enquire to which of them we should apply this saying that God is love. Only the Father is God without being 'of God'; so that the love which is God and 'of God' must be either the Son or the Holy Spirit. Now in what follows the writer refers to the love of God – not that by which we love him, but that by which 'he loved us, and sent his Son as expiator for our sins'; and bases thereon his exhortation to us to love one another, that so God may dwell in us, since God (as he has said) is love. And there follows at once, designed to express the matter more plainly, the saying: 'hereby we know that we dwell in him, and he in us, because he has given us of his Spirit'. Thus it is the Holy Spirit, of whom he has given us, who makes us dwell in God, and God in us. But that is the effect of love. The Holy Spirit himself therefore is the God who is love. A little further on, after repeating his statement that 'God is love', John adds immediately, 'he who abides in love abides in God, and God abides in him': which corresponds to the earlier saying, 'hereby we know that we abide in him and he in us, because he has given us of his Spirit'. It is the Spirit therefore who is signified in the text 'God is love'. God the Holy Spirit who proceeds from God is the one who, when given to man, kindles him with the love of God and of neighbour, and is himself love. For man has no means of loving God, unless it comes of God: that is why he says a little later on 'let us love because he first loved us'. It is the same in the apostle Paul: 'the love of God is shed abroad in our hearts through the Holy Spirit which is given to us' [Rom. 5: 5].

32. More excellent gift of God than this there is none. It alone divides between the sons of the eternal kingdom and the sons of eternal perdition. Other favours also are given through the Spirit, but without charity they avail nothing. Unless the Holy Spirit be bestowed in such measure on a man as to make him a lover of God

and of his neighbour, he cannot pass from the left hand to the right. The name of Gift belongs specially to the Spirit, only on account of love – the love which he that lacks, though he speak with the tongues of men and angels, is sounding brass and a tinkling cymbal: though he have prophecy and know all mysteries and all knowledge, and though he have all faith so as to remove mountains, he is nothing: and though he distribute all his substance, and give his body to be burned, it profits him nothing [1 Cor. 13: 1–3]. How great a blessing must this be, without which blessings so great can bring no man to eternal life! But if a man has this love or charity (both words mean the same thing), then – even if he does not speak with tongues, have the gift of prophecy, know all mysteries and all knowledge, distribute all his goods to the poor (whether because he has none to distribute or because circumstances prevent it) or give his body to be burned (because he is never faced with such a trial of suffering) – this love will bring him to the kingdom. In fact even faith is ineffective apart from charity. For there may indeed be faith without charity, but not a faith that profits. So the apostle Paul says: 'In Christ Jesus neither circumcision nor uncircumcision is of any avail, but the faith which works through love' [Gal. 5: 6]: so distinguishing this faith from that whereby the devils also believe and tremble [James 2: 19]. Thus the love which is of God and is God is specially the Holy Spirit, through whom is spread abroad in our hearts the charity of God by which the whole Trinity will make its habitation within us. And therefore the Holy Spirit, God though he is, is most rightly called also the gift of God; and the special sense of that gift must be charity, which brings us to God, and without which no other gift of God, whatever it may be, can bring us to God.

5 Sin and Grace

The most famous controversies of the patristic period were concerned with the Trinity and the person of Christ. But it will already be evident from the extracts dealing with these themes that the concern of the Fathers was to understand the persons of the Godhead in a way which safeguarded the reality of man's redemption. The extracts in this section deal with the fact of sin in human life and God's grace in relation to it.

In the first passage Origen uses his Platonism as a key to understanding the data of Scripture. He argues for a pre-mundane fall of human souls as the only way in which God's justice can be squared with the apparent unfairness of differing human lots. This line of thought, however, did not commend itself to the Church as a whole.

The comparatively long extract from Gregory of Nyssa gives an account of the emergence of evil in the world in terms of man's free-will, without recourse to Origen's idea of the pre-existence of souls. The passage is one in which the Platonist character of Gregory's thought is particularly clear. The argument is developed in a way which not only frees God from responsibility for that evil but also sets the scene for his redemptive grace.

That redemption was effected by the death of Christ. But why was that death the means by which God worked man's salvation? The patristic age offers no clear-cut agreed answer to that question. But the next passage, once again from Augustine's work on the Trinity, brings out the main thrust of much early reflection on that issue. The heart of Augustine's answer is that the salvation effected by way of the Cross represents the victory of divine justice rather than of mere power.

The last two passages are concerned with the experience of grace in redemption and Christian living. They illustrate the characteristic difference of emphasis between the Eastern and the Western Church. Chrysostom lays great stress on the priority of God's grace, but wants to set human virtue alongside it as a factor in man's salvation. Augustine also insists in the sermon from which the final extract in this section is taken that man has an active role to play, but he probes more deeply in his determination to do justice to the scriptural insistence on the absolute priority of the divine. That determination led him in the writings that belong to the last years of his life to develop the ideas of divine election and predestination in a more extreme form than is represented here.

21 Origen
On First Principles II, 9, 1–6
[*GCS*, 22, 163–70]

On the world, on the movements of rational creatures good and bad, and on the causes thereof.

1. We must now resume the plan of our discussion and consider the beginning of creation – as far as it is possible for the mind to consider the beginning of God's creative work.* In this beginning God must, by his will, have established as large a number of intellectual beings, or whatever the above mentioned minds are to be called, as he could control. For we are bound to maintain that God's power is finite; we must not be deterred by the pretext of piety from the assertion of its limitation. For if the divine power were infinite, it would necessarily be incapable of self-knowledge; for in the nature of things the infinite is incomprehensible. So God made as many beings as he could grasp and control and keep under his providence. In the same way he prepared as much matter as he could reduce to order.*

There is also the evidence of Scripture which says that God created 'all things by number and measure' [Wis. 11 : 20]. 'Number' will be rightly referred to rational creatures or minds, the inference being that there are as many of them as the providence of God can administer, rule and control. 'Measure' on the other hand will properly apply to corporeal matter, of which we are to believe that God created as much as he knew would suffice for the ordering of the world. These are the things which we are to suppose were created by God in the beginning, that is, before everything else. This, in our opinion, is what is indicated by that beginning so mysteriously introduced by Moses: 'In the beginning God made the heaven and the earth' [Gen. 1: 1]. For these words certainly do not refer to the

– Here the translation of this paragraph follows one of the Greek fragments, with one small supplement from Rufinus' Latin version.

'firmament' or the 'dry land', but to that heaven and earth from which the names of this visible heaven and earth have been secondarily derived.*

2. Now these rational beings which, as we have said, were created in the beginning, had no existence before their creation. The fact that they had no existence and then began to exist means that they are necessarily subject to alteration and change. For whatever inherent qualities they possessed were not theirs by nature but were the result of their creator's beneficence. Even their existence is not something of their own, nor is it eternal; it is given by God. For existence is not something they have always had, and anything given can be taken away again or lost. The cause of loss will lie in the fact that the movements of these minds have not been rightly and worthily directed. For the creator granted to the minds that he made the power of free and voluntary movement, so that the good which was in them might become their own through being preserved by their own free-will. But sloth and weariness in the preservation of good supervened, coupled with disregard and neglect of better things; and so the withdrawal from good began. Now to withdraw from good is simply to find oneself arrived in evil; for it is certain that evil is the want of good.† Consequently the measure of one's fall from good is the measure of one's descent into wickedness. So as each mind neglected the good either more or less in accordance with its own movements, it was drawn into the opposite of good – and that is undoubtedly evil. It is this process which seems to have presented the creator of the universe with growing-points and occasions for variety and diversity. Corresponding to the diversity of minds or rational creatures – a diversity which they must be supposed to have produced for the reason we have just stated – he created a world that was various and diverse. We now turn to this variety and diversity.

3. By the 'world' we mean everything that is above the heavens, in the heavens, on the earth or what is called 'under the earth' [see Phil. 2: 10] – in short, whatever there is that is spatial – together with the beings that are said to dwell in these places.

In this world some beings are called 'supercelestial'; that is, they are placed in the more blessed abodes and clothed with the more heavenly and resplendent bodies. Among these many differences are

* Philo (*De Opificio Mundi* 7, 29 – 10, 36) similarly distinguishes the heaven and earth of Gen. 1: 1 from the heaven and earth of Gen. 1: 8, 10. The former belong to the incorporeal and intelligible world which is the archetype of the visible world to which the latter belong.

† For a fuller development of this view of evil in a similar context, see Gregory of Nyssa, *Catechetical Oration* 7 (p. 108 below).

revealed as, for example, when the apostle says, 'There is one glory of the sun, one glory of the moon, and another glory of the stars; for star differs from star in glory' [1 Cor. 15: 41].

Some beings are called 'earthly'. Among them, too, that is, among men, there are no small differences. Some are barbarians, others are Greeks, and among the barbarians some are comparatively wild and fierce, others comparatively gentle. Some of them have laws which are most estimable, while those of others are poorer and harsher; some indeed can hardly be said to have laws but only inhuman and savage customs. Some men are in humble positions from the moment of their birth and are brought up in subjection and slavery, placed under masters or princes or tyrants. Others are brought up in a more free and rational manner. Some have bodily health, others are invalids from their earliest years. Of these some are blind, others defective in hearing and speech, some being born thus, others losing these faculties immediately after birth or suffering a similar misfortune when fully grown. But what point is there in my unfolding the whole tale of human disaster and misery, when anyone can think of these things for himself and reflect on them one by one? In addition there are invisible powers entrusted with the management of affairs on the earth. Between them there must be considerable differences, as there are between men.

Finally the apostle Paul also speaks of the existence of beings 'under the earth'. There are doubtless similar reasons which could be discovered for their diversity. (Dumb animals, birds and water creatures do not require discussion, since they should certainly be regarded as beings of a secondary and not a primary kind.)

4. Now we are told that the whole creation has come into being through Christ and in Christ. The apostle Paul indicates this quite plainly: 'For in him all things were created, in heaven and on earth, visible and invisible, whether thrones or dominions or principalities or powers; all things were created through him and in him' [Col. 1: 16]. John makes the same declaration in the gospel: 'In the beginning was the Word, and the Word was with God, and the Word was God; he was in the beginning with God. All things came into being through him, and nothing came into being without him' [John 1: 1–3]. Further, in the psalms it is written, 'Thou hast made all things in wisdom' [Ps. 104: 24].

Now since Christ is as much 'justice' as he is 'Word' and 'wisdom' [see 1 Cor. 1: 30], it follows that the things that are made in Word and wisdom can equally be said to be made in that 'justice' which is Christ. In consequence it should be clear that there can be nothing unjust or fortuitous in what is made, but that all things will follow the principle of equity and justice. How this enormous variety and diversity of circumstances can be understood as fully just and equitable is, I am sure, beyond the power of human intelligence or speech to explain – unless as prostrate suppliants we beseech the very Word and wisdom and justice himself, who is the only-begotten Son of God, graciously to pour himself into our senses, asking him to deign to illuminate what is dark, to open what is closed, and to reveal what is hidden. This he will only do if we are found to ask, to seek and to knock so worthily that when we ask we deserve to receive, when we seek we deserve to find, and when we knock we deserve to have the door opened [see Matt. 7: 7–8]. So not relying on our own intelligence but on the help of that wisdom which made all things and of that justice which we believe to be in all that is created, we shall try – in spite of our incapacity to make any firm assertion and trusting in his mercy – to find out and discover how it is that all the variety and diversity in the world is consistent with the whole principle of justice. I speak, of course, of principle in a general sense; only an ignorant man would ask for a special explanation of each individual case, and only a fool would offer one.

5. Our assertion that this diversely ordered world has, as we have explained above, been so made by God and that this God is good, just and completely fair, meets with frequent objections, particularly from the followers of Marcion, Valentinus and Basilides, who assert that souls are naturally diverse. They ask how it can be consistent with the justice of God that in making the world he should give to some beings a habitation in the heavens, and not merely grant them a better habitation, but also confer on them some specific rank of a higher and nobler kind, by favouring some with a 'principality', conferring 'powers' on others and on others again 'dominions', to others presenting the most splendid places in the judgement halls of heaven, while others shine like gold and gleam with starry splendour, there being 'one glory of the sun, another glory of the moon, and another glory of the stars, with star differing from star in glory' [1 Cor. 15: 41]. To sum it up briefly, if God the creator is deficient neither in the will to desire the supremely good nor in the power to effect it, what reason can there be for the fact that, in creating rational beings – that is, beings of whose existence he himself is the cause – he made some of a higher and others of a low and inferior rank – in second, third and many succeeding positions?

Their final objection refers to the fact that among the inhabitants of the earth some have a happier lot at birth than others. Thus, for example, one man springs from Abraham and is born of promise. Another is the child of Isaac and Rebecca who, while still in the womb, supplants his brother and, even before his birth, is said to be loved by God [see Rom. 9: 6–13]. Speaking more generally, one man is born among the Hebrews, and finds among them instruction in the divine law; another among the Greeks, who are themselves men of wisdom and no small learning. But others are born among the Ethiopians, who are accustomed to feed on human flesh; or among the Scythians, where the practice of parricide has more or less the status of law; or among the Taurians, who kill their visitors in sacrifice. The question put to us is as follows: Granted this great diversity of circumstance and this great variety of conditions of birth, and granted the fact that the faculty of free choice can have nothing to do with the case, since no one can choose where, in what nation or in what state of life he is to be born; if this state of affairs is not the result of a natural diversity of souls, whereby a soul with a bad nature is destined for a bad nation and a good one for a good nation, what alternative is there to ascribing it all to accident and chance? But if that be admitted, one can no longer believe either that the world was made by God or that it is ruled by his providence; and in that case there is no divine judgement on each man's deeds to be looked for.

Now this is a matter whose truth can be clearly known only by him who 'searches all things, even the depths of God'.* [6] We however are mere men; but since we do not wish to encourage the insolence of the heretics by keeping silent, we shall reply as best we can to their objections with such arguments as come to mind. In our earlier chapters we have repeatedly shown, with assertions which we are able to draw from the divine Scriptures, that God the creator of all things is good, just and omnipotent. When 'in the beginning' he created those things which he wished to create, that is, rational beings, he had no cause for creating them but himself, that is, his goodness. Since he himself, in whom there was neither variety, change or incapacity, was the cause of the beings which he was about to create, all the beings which he created were created similar and equal; for he had no cause for variety or diversity. But, as we have frequently shown and as we shall discuss again at the proper point, these rational creatures were endowed with the faculty of free choice; and they were induced, each one by his own free will, either to imitate God and so to advance or to ignore him and so to fall. This, as we have already said, was the cause of the diversity between rational creatures; its origin lay not in the will or judgement of the creator, but in the choice made by the creature's own freedom. God then felt it just to order his creation in accordance with merit. So he

* I.e. the Spirit of God; see 1 Cor. 2: 10.

drew the diversity of rational beings together into the harmony of a single world, in order to furnish out of these diverse vessels or souls or minds one 'house', so to speak, in which there should be 'not only vessels of gold and silver, but also of wood and earthenware, and some for noble use, some for ignoble' [2 Tim. 2: 20].

These are the reasons, I believe, for the diversity of this world. Divine providence places each creature in a position corresponding to the variety of its own movements – that is the movements of its will. On this argument the creator will not appear unjust, since it is in accordance with antecedent causes that he has placed each creature in a position appropriate to its merit. At the same time the happiness or unhappiness or any other condition that may befall an individual at birth, will not be attributed to chance. Belief in a diversity of creators or in a natural diversity of souls will also be excluded.

22　Gregory of Nyssa
Catechetical Oration 5–8
[Ed. J. Srawley (Cambridge, 1903), pp. 19–52]

5. The existence of God's Word* and Spirit is unlikely to be contested either by the Greek whose notions are those common to mankind or by the Jew with his notions derived from Scripture. But the dispensation by which the divine Word became man will be rejected by both alike as an incredible and improper thing to affirm about God. So on this issue we will have to take a different starting-point in order to convince our opponents.

They believe that all things were created by the reason and wisdom of him who constructed the whole universe – unless they have difficulty in believing even that! But if they will not grant that reason and wisdom govern the structure of things, that would amount to setting up unreason and unskilfulness as ruling principle of the universe. And that surely is both absurd and impious; so there can be absolutely no question about their admitting that reason and wisdom govern existing things.

* Gregory's argument depends on the two meanings of the Greek word, Logos – reason and word. In translation a choice between them has to be made. Also where the personal sense of 'the divine Word' seems to be uppermost we have used a capital W and the masculine rather than the neuter pronoun – distinctions not present in the Greek.

Now it has been shown in what has been said already that the Word of God is no mere utterance nor a state of possessing some knowledge or wisdom. He is a power with an existence of his own, freely choosing all that is good and with the power to do whatever he chooses. And since the world is good this power which both possesses in advance and effects the good is its cause. Now if the existence of the world in its totality depends on the power of the Word, as our argument has shown, it follows logically that we cannot ascribe the combination of the various parts of the world to any other cause; it too must be due to the Word himself, through whom everything received its entry into being. Whether people choose to call him Word or Wisdom or Power or God or any other sublime and honorific title is a matter of indifference to us. Whatever term or name is produced to indicate this reality, the meaning of the various phrases used is identical – namely, that eternal power of God which creates what exists, contrives what does not yet exist, sustains what has been brought into being and foresees what is to come. The logic of the argument shows that this reality – the divine Word, Wisdom, Power – is the creator of human nature. He was not compelled to make man by any kind of necessity; it was the overflowing of love which led him to fashion the existence of a living creature of this particular kind. It was not right that his light should remain without anyone to see it, his glory without anyone to witness it, his goodness without anyone to enjoy it and all the other attributes of deity that we apprehend lie useless with no one to share in them or to enjoy them.

Now if man came into existence for this purpose – namely to be made a partaker of the divine goodness, he must have been created with a propensity for sharing in that goodness. In the case of physical sight the eye partakes of light by virtue of a beam of light with which the eye itself is endowed by nature; this innate power enables it to attract to itself that which is akin to its own nature.* In the same way something akin to the divine had to be included in human nature, so that by virtue of that relationship man would have a desire for that which corresponds to his own nature. In the case of creatures without reason, animals whose natural habitat is the water or the air are formed with natures corresponding to their pattern of life; the particular way their bodies are constructed in each case makes air or water, as the case may be, natural and congenial to them. So, since man was created for the purpose of enjoying the divine goodness, he had to have something in his nature akin to that of which he was

* For the idea that the eye has a light of its own by which it is enabled to attract light from outside, see Plato, *Timaeus* 45B.

designed to partake. He was therefore endowed with life and reason and wisdom and all the other good things which are characteristic of God so that each of these might provide him with a desire for something which is related to his own nature. Now since one of the good things that belongs to divine nature is eternity, it would not have been right for the constitution of our nature to have had no share in that whatever; there is therefore within man's nature an immortal element so that by virtue of this inherent capacity he might recognize the transcendent and come to long for the divine eternity.

The account of the creation sums all this up in a single phrase when it says that man was created in the image of God [Gen. 1 : 27]. For the likeness which consists in being in the image of God is a summation of all the characteristically divine attributes. And everything that Moses goes on to relate in his narrative account (for that is the form in which he presents us with his doctrine) has the same teaching in view. The garden of which he speaks and the peculiarity of the fruit which does not satisfy the belly when eaten but which gives knowledge and eternal life – all these are in full accord with what we have already seen about man: namely that in its origins our nature was good and was surrounded by goodness.

But someone looking at the situation as it is now may oppose what has been said and think he can prove it false in view of the fact that we do not see man in that condition now but in an almost exactly opposite condition. Where is the soul's likeness to God ? Where is the body's freedom from passion ? Where is eternal life ? Fleeting, subject to passion, mortal, liable to every kind of suffering in body and soul – with these and similar descriptions he will run down our nature and expect thereby to refute the account of man that we have given. We will deal with these points briefly so as not to interrupt the sequence of our argument.

The fact that human life is now in so evil a state is not sufficient proof that man was never in a state of goodness. Since man was the work of God and since it was God's goodness that brought such a creature into existence at all, one cannot reasonably suppose that man's being in an evil state derives from his maker; for goodness was the very reason for his creation. There must be some other cause of our present condition and of our having lost our more desirable state.

Our basic premise on this issue is once again not one to which our opponents will object. God made man for the purpose of sharing in his own goodness. To that end he endowed his nature with potentialities for attaining excellence in all its forms, so that his aspirations might be conveyed by those varied potentialities in the direction of their corresponding forms of excellence. He would not therefore have deprived him of the most excellent and precious form of goodness, namely the gift of liberty and free-will. For if human life were ruled by necessity of any kind, that would make it wholly unlike its archetype and the image would be falsified at that point. For how could a nature that was enslaved and subject to necessity be called an image of the sovereign nature? That which has been endowed with a likeness to the divine at every point must include in its nature self-determination and liberty; so that participation in all that is good may be the reward of virtue.

How then, you will ask, did it come about that he who was honourably endowed with excellence in all these ways exchanged these blessings for something worse? The answer to this too is clear. The existence of evil did not have its origin in the divine will. Evil would not be blameworthy if it could claim God for its creator and father. Evil comes in some way or another from within. It is the product of free choice, whenever the soul withdraws in any way from the good. Just as sight is an activity of nature and blindness a privation of this natural activity, so virtue stands in the same kind of antithesis to evil. The origin of evil can only be understood as the absence of virtue. If light is removed darkness ensues; if light is present darkness does not exist. In the same way, as long as good is present in a nature, evil as such is non-existent; but the withdrawal of the good is the beginning of the existence of its opposite. And since the distinctive character of free-will is freely to choose what pleases it, God is not the cause of your present evil state. He provided you with a free and independent nature; it is your folly that has chosen the worse instead of the better.

6. You may ask the further question: what is the cause of this total misdirection of the will? That is the issue raised by the argument so far. Once again we can find a very reasonable starting-point for the clarification of this further question. We have inherited from the fathers a kind of explanation, which is not just a legendary tale but one which gains credence from our nature itself. Our experience and observation of existing things is two-fold; it is divided between the intelligible and the sensible. Nothing can be apprehended as having real existence which does not fall within this two-fold classification. It is a vast gulf that separates them from one another. The sensible has none of the characteristics of the intelligible, nor the intelligible of the sensible; rather they have opposing characteristics. Intelligible nature is incorporeal, intangible and without form; while sensible nature, as its very name indicates, is apprehended through the senses. Within the sensible world itself, different elements are directly opposed to one another; yet a harmony in

which these opposing elements have their place has been devised by the wisdom which governs the universe; thereby the whole creation is in self-consistent harmony and the opposing nature of the different elements does not destroy the bond of union. In the same way divine wisdom provides a mixture and a blending of the sensible with the intelligible, so that all things partake equally in the good and no existing thing is deprived of a share in the better nature. The sphere appropriate to intelligible nature is a subtle and mobile essence, which with its transcendent location has in its distinctive nature a close affinity to the intelligible; yet a higher wisdom has brought about a commingling of the intelligible with the sensible creation so that, as the apostle says, 'no part of the creation may be rejected' [1 Tim. 4: 4] or be deprived of participation in the divine.

Therefore it is in the form of a mixture made up of the intelligible and the sensible that man has been produced by the divine nature, as the creation story teaches. God, it says, made man by taking the dust of the earth and by his own breath implanted life in what he had made [Gen. 2: 7]. Thereby the earthly has been raised into union with the divine; this blending of the lower nature with the transcendent means that the same grace is present to the same extent throughout the whole of creation.

The intelligible creation was in existence first. Each of the angelic powers was allocated by the authority which governs all things with a particular activity in connection with the framing of the universe. One such power was appointed to maintain and take charge of the region of the earth. He had been empowered for this specific purpose by the power which governs the universe. Then there was formed that earthly creation which is an image of the power above (namely the creature, man); in this creation was present the godlike beauty of the intelligible nature, blended in by a power that surpasses all description. The angelic power who had been allocated the governance of the earth regarded it as intolerable that out of that nature which was subject to him there should be produced an essence akin to the supreme dignity of all.

Although it is no requirement of the present discussion that we should explain in detail how one who was created for no evil purpose by him who framed the universe in goodness fell into the passion of envy, it is possible to give a brief account to those prepared to profit by it. The distinction between virtue and vice should not be regarded as if it were the distinction between two existents. To give a parallel example: non-being is logically opposed to being, but we cannot say that non-being is to be distinguished from being as a different reality; what we do have to say is that non-existence is logically opposed to existence. In the same way vice contrasts with the concept of virtue; but this does not mean it is something in its own right; it is a conception arising from the absence of the good. Again we say that blindness is logically opposed to sight; but this does not mean that blindness is a natural existent in itself; it is the privation of a former condition. In the same way we claim that vice is found where there is privation of the good, just as a shadow supervenes upon the withdrawal of the sun's ray.

Uncreated nature is incapable of movement in the sense of mutability, change or variation. But everything that depends on creation for its existence has a natural tendency to change, since the very existence of the creation began from change, when non-being was changed by divine power into being. Now that angelic power already mentioned was created and was able to choose what it liked by the movement of its own free-will. It closed its eyes to the good and the generous; and just as one who closes his eyes in sunlight sees darkness, so he, by refusing to apprehend the good, in fact apprehended the opposite of good. It is that opposite that is envy.

It is generally accepted that the first cause of anything is responsible for all the consequences flowing from it. In the case of health – fitness, work, and an enjoyable life; in the case of illness – weakness, inactivity and feeling miserable. Other things all follow in the same way from their own first causes. Freedom from passion is the first cause and basis of the life of virtue and in the same way the inclination to evil which derived from envy paved the way for all those evils that have appeared since.

So having once begotten envy in himself by turning from the good, that power had an inclination toward evil. He was like a rock which once it has been broken off from a mountain ridge is carried down headlong by its own weight. Torn away from his natural affinity with the good and weighted in the direction of evil, he was as it were forced willy nilly by that weight and impelled to the ultimate limit of iniquity. The intellectual power which he had received from the creator so that he might assist in bringing about participation in the good, he now made his assistant in discovering evil devices. Thus he cunningly deceived and outwitted man, persuading him to become his own murderer and assassin.

Empowered by God's blessing man held a lofty position. He was appointed to rule over the earth and everything on it. His form was beautiful, for he was created as an image of the archetypal beauty. In nature he was free from passion, for he was a copy of him who is without passion. He was wholly free and open, revelling in the direct vision of God. But all this was fuel to the flames of the adversary's passionate envy. He could not fulfil his purpose by violence or brute force, for the power of God's blessing was stronger than such force. So he contrived to detach man from the power which strengthened him and thus to render him an easy prey to his intrigue. To give an illustration: if the flame of a lamp catches the wick and it is impossible to blow it out, the device of mixing water with the oil will dim the flame. By a similar trick the adversary mixed evil with man's free-will and thereby affected a sort of quenching or dimming of the blessing. And as the blessing failed, its opposite inevitably came in in its place. Now the opposite of life is death, of power weakness, of blessing a curse, of openness shame, and so on with whatever is thought of as the contrary of each form of goodness. This is why humanity is now in its present evil plight. In that beginning lay the starting-point which has led to such a conclusion.

7. Now we ought not to ask whether God embarked on the creation of man with foreknowledge of the disaster that would overtake him as a result of his folly, implying that it might have been better for him not to have been made at all rather than to be in such a plight. It is people who have been misled by Manichaean teaching who put forward that argument in support of their error; their aim in doing so is to prove that the creator of man's nature is evil. Allow, they argue, that God is ignorant of nothing and man is in an evil state; then if God introduced man into life when the life that he would be living was going to be a life of trouble, the principle of God's goodness cannot be preserved. For if it is characteristic of a good nature that its activity is consistently of a good kind, then the creation of this wretched and transient life cannot be ascribed to one who is good. For such a life we have to postulate another cause, with a nature that is inclined to evil. In the eyes of those who are imbued, as it were, with the indelible dye of the deceit of heresy, all these and other similar arguments with their superficial plausibility seem to have some force. But those who are more perceptive of the truth can see clearly that they are unsound and that their deceptive character can easily be exposed.

I would also like to call on the apostle to support our charge against them on this issue. In writing to the Corinthians he distinguishes between fleshly and spiritual conditions of the soul [see 1 Cor. 2: 14–15]. I think that in what he says he is indicating that one ought not to make judgements about good and evil on the basis of sensation, but that one needs rather to detach the mind from bodily phenomena altogether and to discriminate between good and its opposite in their own intrinsic character. 'The spiritual man', he declares, 'judges all things.'

The reason why such fabulous doctrines have arisen among people who advance these views is, I believe, the following. They define good with reference to the enjoyment of bodily pleasure. And since the nature of the body (being composite and liable to dissolution) is necessarily subject to suffering and weakness, and such sufferings give rise in some way to painful sensations, they imagine that the creation of man is the work of an evil god. But if they had set the sights of their mind higher, detached their thoughts from concern with pleasure and considered the nature of reality in freedom from the influence of the passions, they would have concluded that nothing is evil except wickedness. All wickedness is characterized by the privation of good; it does not exist in its own right, nor is it observed to have any subsistence of its own. For evil has no existence of its own outside the will; it is a name given to the non-existence of good. Non-being has no subsistence; and the creator of subsistent things is not the creator of that which has no subsistence. God, therefore, has no responsibility for evil for he is the author of being and not of non-being, the creator of sight and not of blindness, the source of virtue and not of its privation. The reward of the will which he holds out to those who live virtuously is the enjoyment of all that is good. He has not subjected human nature to any kind of forcible compulsion to do what he wills; he does not drag man unwillingly, like a lifeless object, in the direction of the good. If a man of his own choice closes his eyes in broad daylight, the sun is not responsible for his inability to see.

8. Nevertheless, the man who reflects on the dissolution of the body is thoroughly resentful and finds it hard that this life of ours should be dissolved in death. This, he claims, is the ultimate evil – that our life should be extinguished by death. Let him, then, take note of God's exceeding goodness even in this melancholy prospect. It may actually prove to be an inducement to him to marvel at the graciousness of God's provision for man. Life is desirable to those who have it because they can enjoy the things that appeal to them. So a man who passes his life in pain thinks it would be far preferable for him not to exist than to exist in a state of suffering. Let us then enquire whether the author of life has any other intention than that we should live under the best possible conditions.

By a movement of free-will we brought upon ourselves an association with evil; through an act of pleasure we came to mix evil with our nature like some poison sweetened with honey. This caused us to fall from that blessed state we think of as freedom from passion and to be transformed in the direction of evil. And this is the reason why man, like a clay pot, is dissolved into earth again – so that the filth which has become a part of him may be separated out and he may be refashioned in his original form through the resurrection.

This is the doctrine that Moses expounds in the veiled form of historical narrative.* However, the teaching, though veiled, is perfectly clear. Since, he says, the first humans became involved in things forbidden and were stripped naked of their blessedness, the Lord clothed his first creatures in coats of skin [see Gen. 3: 21]. I do not think he intends the word 'skin' in its literal sense. After all, what species of animal is supposed to have been slaughtered and flayed to provide this covering for them? No – every skin when taken from an animal is a dead thing and this convinces me that 'skin' here means ability to die. This is the characteristic mark of irrational or animal nature; and this is the ability with which men were thenceforth invested by the wise provision of the healer of our evil. It is a capacity to die, but not to die permanently. For a coat is something which we put on as an external covering; it is something which the body makes use of temporarily but it does not become an integral part of its nature.

Mortality, therefore, derived from the nature of irrational creatures, was by special dispensation made the clothing of the nature created for immortality. It enveloped its outward but not its inward part; it affected the sentient part of man, but did not touch the divine image itself. The sentient part is dissolved, but it is not destroyed. For destruction means passing into non-being, whereas dissolution means diffusion once more into those elements of the world from which the thing was constituted. When this happens, the thing has not perished even though it may elude apprehension by our senses.

Now the reason for this dissolution is clear from the illustration we have given. Sensation has affinity with what is solid and earthy; but the intellectual nature is better and superior to movements apprehended by the senses. So, since our judgement of the good went astray by the arbitrament of the senses and this deviation from the good brought into existence the opposite condition, that part of us which had been rendered useless by partaking of that opposite condition is dissolved. The point of the illustration can be developed in this way. Suppose someone has made a clay pot; the pot is then maliciously filled with molten lead; the lead hardens and cannot be poured out; the owner gets hold of the pot again and, being a skilled potter, breaks up the clay surrounding the lead and then remoulds

* For a fuller discussion of how, in the tradition to which Gregory belonged, the historical narrative of Scripture embodies doctrinal teaching, see Origen, *On First Principles* IV, 2, 8 (p. 144 below).

the pot, now rid of the intruding matter, into its former shape for his own use. Now the maker of our vessel acts in the same way; evil has been mixed in with the sentient, by which I mean the bodily, part of us; so he dissolves the material which contains the evil; then when it is free from any taint of this opposing kind he will remould it by means of the resurrection and will reconstitute the vessel in its original beauty.

Now there is a bond between body and soul and they share jointly in the sinful passions; moreover there is some sort of analogy between physical and spiritual death (in the case of the body we call separation from sentient life 'death' and in the case of the soul we call separation from real life by the same name – 'death'). What we observe is, as we have just said, a single joint participation in evil on the part of soul and body; wickedness makes use of both to express itself in action. Yet death in the form of dissolution which comes from being clothed with dead skins does not affect the soul. How could that which is not composite be subject to dissolution? But the soul too is in need of some remedy by which to be freed from the stains implanted by sin.* Therefore to heal these wounds the medicine of virtue has been provided for use in this life; and if the soul remains unhealed, healing is available in the life to come.

Now bodily ailments vary; some respond comparatively easily to treatment, others less readily. In the latter case surgery, cauteries and bitter medicines are used to remove the ailment which has attacked the body. This provides a picture of the kind of healing of the sickness of the soul which the future judgement promises. For the frivolous it is a threat and a harsh means of correction; its aim is to bring us to our senses and induce us to flee from evil by fear of a painful retribution. The more serious minded, however, look upon it as a healing remedy provided by God for the restoration of his special creation to its original grace.† Those who by means of surgery or cauterization remove moles or warts that have grown unnaturally on the body do not bring the benefit of healing to their patients in a painless manner – even though they are not doing their surgery with the intention of hurting them. In the same way whatever material excrescences have become encrusted on our souls, which have become fleshly through their association with the passions, are cut off and removed at the time of the judgement by that ineffable wisdom and power of him who, as the gospel says,

* See p. 194 below for the implications of this approach for Gregory's sacramental teaching.
† See pp. 257–9 below for a fuller development of Gregory's teaching on the final restoration of the whole rational creation.

heals the evil. 'Those who are well,' it says, 'have no need of a physician, but those who are ill' [Matt. 9: 12]. The excision of a wart causes a sharp pain in the surface of the body. This is because an unnatural growth affects the underlying nature to which it is attached by a kind of sympathy. A strange union arises between what is our own and what is foreign to us, so that we feel a stinging pain when the unnatural excrescence is removed. In the same sort of way the close affinity that the soul has developed with evil means that it pines and wastes away when it comes under rebuke for sin (as prophecy says somewhere) [Ps. 39: 11]; because of its profound kinship with evil, undescribable and inexpressible pains are the inevitable outcome. Those pains are just as impossible to describe as is the nature of the blessings that we hope for; neither the one nor the other comes within the range of the power of words or the conjectures of the mind.

Therefore anyone who bears in mind the goal which in his wisdom the ruler of the universe has in view could not be so unreasonable and small-minded as to attribute the cause of evil to the creator of man, alleging either that he was ignorant of what would happen or that if he did know and still created man he played a part in the first steps in the direction of evil. He did know what would happen and he did not prevent the first steps which led to its happening. He was not ignorant that humanity would deviate from the good, seeing that in knowledge he is the complete master over all things and has as clear a vision of the future as he does of the past. So he did see man's turning away; but in the same way he also perceived man's restoration once more to the good. Which then would have been better? Not to have brought our nature into being at all since he foresaw that the one to be created would stray from the good? Or to bring him into being and then (when he had become sick) to restore him again by repentance to his original grace?

Calling God the creator of evil because of bodily sufferings, which are an inevitable consequence of our nature being in flux, or actually denying that he is the creator of man at all so as to avoid attributing the cause of our sufferings to him – that is the height of small-mindedness. It is the view of people who distinguish good and evil on the basis of sensation and do not realize that nothing is good by nature except what is unaffected by sensation, and nothing is evil except alienation from the truly good. Judging good and evil on the basis of pain and suffering is characteristic of irrational nature, because not sharing in intelligence or understanding they are in no position to grasp what is truly good. But that man is a work of God, created good and for the noblest ends, is evident not only from what we have already said but for thousands of other reasons, most of which we must leave on one side because there are such an infinite number of them.

In calling God the creator of man, we have not forgotten the careful distinction we made in that part of our introduction directed to the Greeks. We showed there that God's Word is a substantial and distinct being and is in himself both God and Word. He embraces in himself all creative power – or, better, he *is* power. His inclinations are wholly in the direction of good. And since he has power that keeps pace with his will, whatever he desires he brings to pass. His will and his work is the life of all that is. It is by him that man was brought to life and endowed in godlike fashion with every noble attribute.

Changelessness of nature belongs only to what did not come into being by way of creation. Everything that stems from the uncreated nature has its subsistence from non-being; so having begun its existence by change at the very start, it progresses all the time by way of change. If it acts according to its nature, this continual change is for the better; but if it is diverted from the straight path, movement in the opposite direction ensues. This was man's condition. His mutable nature had slipped off course and was going in the opposite direction. Having once departed from the good, every kind of evil came in as a result. Turning from life brought in death instead. Loss of light produced darkness. Absence of virtue brought in vice. In place of every form of good was listed the set of opposing evils. That was the condition into which man fell through his folly. Once he had turned from prudence, it was impossible for him to be prudent; once he had abandoned wisdom it was impossible for him to decide wisely. By whom was he to be restored once more to his original grace? Whose part was it to raise him up when he had fallen, to restore him when he was lost, to lead him back when he had gone astray? Who conceivably but the Lord of his nature? Only the one who had originally given him life was able and fitted to restore it when it was lost. This is what we learn from the revelation of the truth when it teaches us that God made man in the beginning and saved him when he had fallen.

23 Augustine
On the Trinity XIII, x, 13–xv, 19
[*CCL* 50, 399–408]

13. There are those who say: 'Could God find no other way of freeing mankind from their wretched mortal state that he willed his only-begotten Son, coeternally God with himself, to be made man by taking on himself a human soul and human flesh and having thus become mortal to undergo death?' It is not enough to refute them simply by asserting that this way in which God has in fact deigned to free us through a 'mediator between God and men, the man Christ Jesus' [1 Tim. 2: 5] is good and consistent with the majesty of God. We need also to show that, while God was not incapable of finding any other way (for his power extends equally over all things), yet there neither was nor could have been any other way more appropriate for the curing of our wretched state. What could be more essential for arousing hope in us and freeing the minds of mortals from that despair of immortality that arises from the fact of their mortality than to show us how highly God values us and how much he loves us? And what could be clearer or more outstanding proof of this than that the Son of God, while continuing to be in himself what he was – unchangeably good – should for our sake take from us what he was not and without loss to his own nature should deign to enter into partnership with ours; that he should endure to the full the evils of our condition though himself deserving no evil at all; and that then with undeserved generosity he should bestow his gifts upon us, who now believe how much God loves us and who now hope for what we used to despair of, whereas far from deserving any good, we actually deserved evil on account of our previous actions.

14. In fact what are called our merits are his gifts. So that 'faith may work through love' [Gal. 5: 6], 'the love of God is shed abroad in our hearts through the Holy Spirit which is given to us' [Rom. 5: 5]. He was given when Jesus had been glorified by the resurrection. He had promised to send him then; and he did send him then because that was the time that had been written and that had been foretold: 'He ascended on high; he led captivity captive and gave gifts to men' [Ps. 68: 18; Eph. 4: 8]. These gifts are our merits, whereby we attain the supreme good, which is immortal happiness.

'But God,' says the apostle, 'commends his love towards us in that while we were still sinners, Christ died for us. Much more being now justified by his blood we shall be saved from wrath through him'

[Rom. 5: 8–9]. He then goes on to say, 'For if while we were enemies we were reconciled to God by the death of his Son, much more, being reconciled, we shall be saved by his life' [Rom. 5: 10]. Those whom he first calls 'sinners', he then calls 'enemies' of God; those whom he first describes as 'justified by the blood' of Jesus Christ, he then describes as 'reconciled by the death of the Son' of God; those whom he first speaks of as 'saved from wrath through him', he then speaks of as 'saved by his life'. So before grace we were not just any sort of sinner, but involved in the kind of sins that made us enemies of God. Earlier on as well the apostle had used of us sinners and enemies of God two names in the same sort of way – one of them apparently very mild, the other plainly very harsh: 'For if while we were still weak, at the right time Christ died for the ungodly ...' [Rom. 5: 6]. It is the same people he names 'weak' and 'ungodly'. 'Weakness' sounds like something quite trivial, but it is sometimes of such a kind as to be called 'ungodliness'. Yet if it were not weakness, there would have been no need of a doctor – in Hebrew 'Jesus', in Greek 'sōtēr', in our language, 'saviour'. Previously the Latin language had no such word, but it was capable of producing it, and it did so when it wanted it. This earlier sentence of the apostle – 'While we were still weak, at the right time he died for the ungodly' – links closely with the two subsequent ones in one of which he speaks of 'sinners' and in the other of which he speaks of 'enemies' of God. There is a kind of one to one correspondence, 'sinners' going with 'the weak' and 'enemies of God' with 'the ungodly'.

15. But why 'justified by his blood'? What, I ask you, is the power in this blood that believers are justified by it? And why 'reconciled by the death of his Son'? Is it then that, though God the Father was angry with us, he saw his Son's death for us and so was reconciled to us? In that case, was the Son already so thoroughly reconciled to us that he would even deign to die for us, while the Father was still so thoroughly angry with us that unless his Son were to die for us he would not be reconciled? What then of that other saying of that same teacher of the gentiles: 'What then shall we say to these things? If God be for us, who can be against us? He who spared not his own Son but delivered him up for us all, how can he not with him have given us all things?' [Rom. 8: 31–2] If the Father was not already reconciled, how is it that he did not spare his own Son but delivered him up for us? Does not this saying seem to be incompatible with the other? In the former the Son dies for us and the Father is reconciled by his death. But in this one it seems that it was the Father who 'first loved us' [1 John 4: 19], he who on our behalf

did not spare his Son, he who delivered him up to death for us. The same apostle's testimony shows me that the Father loved us even before that – not just before the Son died for us, but before he founded the world: 'as he chose us in him before the foundation of the world' [Eph. 1: 4]. Nor is it the case that when the Father did not spare the Son, the Son was delivered up for us in some sense un-willingly. For of the Son too he says: 'who loved us and delivered himself up for us' [Gal. 2: 20]. So the Father, the Son and the Spirit of them both work all things together in equality and concord. Yet, 'we are justified by the blood of Christ' and 'we are reconciled to God by the death of his Son'. How this is so I will now explain as far as seems necessary to the best of my ability.

16. It was by a divine justice that the human race was delivered into the devil's power; the sin of the first man was passed on from the very beginning to everyone born as a result of intercourse between the sexes and the debt of the first parents became binding on all their posterity. This handing over is indicated first in Genesis when it is said to the serpent: 'Dust shalt thou eat' [Gen. 3: 14] and to the man: 'Dust thou art and to dust shalt thou go' [Gen. 3: 19]. The saying 'to dust shalt thou go' foretells the death of the body, since man would not have experienced that either, had he remained up-right as he was created. And the fact that the words 'Dust thou art' were spoken to a living person shows that it is the whole man that has been changed for the worse. 'Dust thou art' is equivalent to that other saying: 'My spirit shall not remain in mankind for they are flesh' [Gen. 6: 3]. In saying this God showed that man was handed over to the one to whom he had just said: 'Dust shalt thou eat.'

The apostle proclaims this more explicitly in the passage that says: 'And you, when you were dead through your trespasses and sins in which you once walked following the course of this world, following the prince of the power of the air, the spirit that is now at work in the sons of disobedience, amongst whom we all once lived in the desires of our flesh, doing the will of the flesh and of the feelings and were by nature sons of wrath like all the rest ...' [Eph. 2: 1–3]. The sons of disobedience are the unfaithful – and who is not one of them before he becomes one of the faithful? Therefore all men are by virtue of their origin under the prince of the power of the air who is at work in the sons of disobedience. When I say 'by virtue of their origin', that means the same as the apostle's saying 'by nature'. When he says that he was 'like all the rest by nature', he means nature spoiled by sin, not upright as it was created in the beginning.

But the way in which man was handed over into the power of the devil should not be thought of as if it were something God did or ordered to be done; rather it was something that he simply allowed – though justly. He abandoned the sinner, and the author of sin immediately moved in. Nor indeed did God abandon his own creature without showing himself to him as a God who creates, who is life-giving and who provides not only evil things by way of punishment but also many good things for those who are evil – for he did not 'in his wrath shut up his compassion' [Ps. 77: 9]. Nor did he let man go out of the law of his power when he let him fall within the power of the devil, for the devil himself is not unrelated to God's power any more than he is to God's goodness. For how could the evil angels continue in life at all except through him 'who gives life to all things' [1 Tim. 6: 13]? If then the commission of sin subjects man to the devil by the just wrath of God, most certainly the remission of sins rescues man from the devil by the kindly reconciliation of God.

17. But the devil had to be overcome not by the power of God but by his justice. For what is more powerful than the omnipotent? What creature's power can be compared with the power of the creator? Through the fault of his own turning away the devil became a lover of power and a deserter and opponent of justice; and men imitate him more fully the more they ignore or even detest justice and set their hearts on power, consumed either by delight in its acquisition or by desire for its possession. So in rescuing man from the power of the devil God chose that the devil should be conquered not by power but by justice, so that men too in imitation of Christ should seek to conquer the devil by justice and not by power. It was not that power had to be avoided as if it were something evil, but that the priority of justice over power needed to be preserved. After all what sort of power is possible to mortals? Let mortals keep hold on justice; power will be given to the immortal. Compared with that power whatever characterizes those who are called powerful on earth turns out to be a ludicrous weakness. Where evil men seem to be most powerful, there 'a pit is dug for the sinner' [Ps. 94: 13]. But the song of the just man declares: 'Blessed is the man whom thou dost instruct, O Lord, and whom thou dost teach out of thy law to give him respite from evil days until a pit is dug for the sinner. For God will not reject his people and will not abandon his inheritance until justice be turned into judgement; and those who have justice are all of an upright heart' [Ps. 94: 12–15]. At the present time the power of the people of God is a very different matter. But 'God will not reject his people and will not abandon his inheritance' however much bitterness and humiliation it may suffer in its lowliness and weakness, 'until justice', which is now the possession of the godly in their weakness, 'be turned into judgement', in other words receives the power of

judging, which is something kept for the just at the end when in its due order power will follow the justice that precedes it. Power added to justice or justice joined to power produces judicial power.

Now justice is connected with good will, as in the words of the angels at the birth of Christ: 'Glory to God in the highest and on earth peace to men of good will' [Luke 2: 14]. Power however must follow justice, not precede it. It belongs to things 'following'* – that is, to things favourable. The word 'following' derives from 'to follow'. We have already argued that two things make a man happy – a good will and the power to do what one wills. Something which we noted in our earlier discussion ought therefore not to occur – namely that perversity of choice whereby of these two conditions for happiness a man chooses only the power to do what he wills and neglects to will what he ought. First he should have the good will; and only later the strong power. A good will needs to be purged of those vices which if they prevail over a man prevail upon him to will badly. And then what will have happened to his good will? So one should desire the gift of power now, but power against those vices whose conquest is not the goal of men's will for power, which is willed rather for the conquest of men. That is simply to make an un- real conquest while really being the conquered; it is to be conquerors not in reality but in imagination. Let a man will to be prudent, will to be brave, will to be moderate, will to be just and then so that he may be able to be these things in reality, let him most certainly desire power, let him seek to be powerful in himself and (strange though it sounds) let him be powerful against himself for himself. There will be other things, such as immortality and perfect felicity, which he wills with a good will but has not the power to achieve; let him not cease to long for them but wait for them with patience.

18. What then is that justice whereby the devil was conquered? What was it but the justice of Jesus Christ? And how was he con- quered? Because, although he found nothing worthy of death in him, he killed him. So it is unquestionably just that the debtors whom he was holding should be allowed to go free on the strength of their believing in the one whom he killed despite his having no debt. That is what is meant when we are said to be 'justified by the blood of Christ'. Thus was his innocent blood shed for the remission of our sins. In the psalms he speaks of himself as 'free among the dead' [Ps. 88: 5]; for he alone was dead and free from the debt of death. So too in another psalm he says: 'What I did not rob, I then repaid'

* The Latin word 'secundus' means both 'second' – i.e. following in time or order – and 'favourable' (as, in English, a 'following' wind).

[Ps. 69: 4]. By robbery he means to refer to sin, because sin is illicit appropriation [see Phil. 2: 6]. So with words actually spoken in the flesh he declares as is recorded in the gospel: 'Behold the prince of this world comes and finds nothing in me' – that is no sin – 'but that all may know that I do my father's will, rise, let us go hence' [see John 14: 30–1]. And from there he proceeds to the passion to repay on behalf of us debtors what he himself did not owe.

The conquest of the devil would surely not have been achieved in so perfectly just a manner, had Christ chosen to deal with him by power instead of justice. But in fact he put power second and obligation first. That is why he had to be both man and God. If he had not been man, he could not have died. If he had not been God, no one would have believed that he did not will to exercise his power but would rather have believed that he was not able to do what he willed; we should have thought not that he had preferred justice to power but that he had lacked power. But, as things are, he suffered humanly for us because he was man; had he not willed to do so, he could have avoided this suffering because he was also God. Justice is the more attractive for being done in humility. Had he not willed the humility he need not have endured the suffering, so great was the power inherent in his divinity. But by the dying of one so powerful we powerless mortals have been given the commendation of justice and the promise of power. The first he did by dying, the second by rising again. What could be more just than going 'even to the death of the cross' [Phil. 2: 8] for the sake of justice? And what could be more powerful than to rise from the dead and ascend into heaven with that very flesh in which he had been killed? So he conquered the devil first by justice and then by power – by justice because he had no sin and was most unjustly killed by him; by power because 'being dead he came to life again never to die any more' [Rom. 6: 9]. He could have conquered the devil by power, though then he could not have been killed by him; but in fact it was a work of greater power to conquer even death itself by rising again than to avoid it by remaining alive. But that is something distinct from the source of our being justified by the blood of Christ when we are rescued from the power of the devil through the remission of sins; that is related to Christ's conquest of the devil by justice and not by power. It was in virtue of the weakness that he accepted in taking human flesh, not in virtue of his immortal power that Christ was crucified – that weakness of which the apostle said: 'The weakness of God is stronger than men' [1 Cor. 1: 25].

19. So it is not difficult to see that the devil had been conquered once he who was killed by him had risen again. It is a matter of

greater and more profound understanding to see that the devil had been conquered at the very moment when he thought he was the conqueror – namely when Christ was killed. Then it was that his blood – the blood of him who had no sin at all – was shed for the remission of our sins. Its purpose was that those whom the devil was justifiably holding bound in a condition of death since they were guilty of sin should be justifiably released by him on whom the devil had unjustifiably inflicted the penalty of death when he was guilty of no sin. By this justice he was conquered; by this chain the strong man was bound, so that his vessels could be plundered and those which had been in his house and had been like him and his angels 'vessels of wrath' might be changed into 'vessels of mercy' [see Matt. 12: 29; Rom. 9: 22–3].

The apostle Paul records words that the Lord Jesus Christ himself spoke to him when he was first called. Amongst other things that he heard, he says that he was addressed as follows: 'For this purpose I have appeared to you, to appoint you a minister and a witness of those things that I am showing you and to which I shall guide you, delivering you from the people and from the gentiles to whom I send you to open the eyes of the blind, that they may be turned away from darkness and from the power of Satan to God, that they may receive forgiveness of sins, a place among the saints and faith in me' [Acts 26: 16–18]. And that same apostle in exhorting believers to give thanks to God the Father says: 'who delivered us from the power of darkness and transferred us to the kingdom of the son of his love, in whom we have redemption for the remission of sins' [Col. 1: 13–14]. In that redemption Christ's blood was given as payment on our behalf. But in accepting it the devil was not enriched but bound. Thereby we were freed from his clutches. Of those whom Christ, himself free from all obligation or debt, had redeemed by the shedding of his own blood, freely and without obligation, not one could be held by the devil in the nets of sin; not one could he drag with him to the destruction of the second and eternal death. Those who attain to the grace of Christ, being foreknown, foreordained and chosen before the foundation of the world, have to die only to the extent that Christ himself died for them – a death of the flesh only, not of the spirit.

24 John Chrysostom
Homilies on Ephesians 1, 1–2 (on Eph. 1: 4–5)
[Ed. F. Field (Oxford, 1852), pp. 107–11]

Even as he chose us in him before the foundation of the world, that we should be holy and blameless before him.

His meaning is something like this. The one through whom God has blessed us is also the one through whom he chose us. He is also the one who will give us our heavenly rewards. He is the judge who will say, 'Come, you blessed of my Father, inherit the Kingdom prepared for you from the foundation of the world' [Matt. 25: 34], and also 'Where I am I desire that these also may be' [John 17: 24].

In almost all his epistles Paul is keen to show that our faith is no newfangled thing but was designed to be as it is from the very beginning; it was not a matter of divine afterthought but was planned and foreordained as it now is. It is the fruit of long providential care.

What then is the meaning of 'chose us in him'? That Christ established this way of faith in himself before ever we came into existence, or rather before the foundation of the world. (The word 'foundation' is well chosen because it indicates something being laid down from a great height. And the height of God is great and ineffable, not in terms of spatial distance but in the remoteness of his nature, for there is a great gulf between creation and creator. Let the heretics take note and blush!)

And why did he choose us? 'That we should be holy and blameless before him.' So that you may not suppose, when you hear that he chose us, that faith alone is sufficient, he goes on to refer to manner of life. This, he says, is the reason and the purpose of his choice – that we should be holy and blameless. Once too he chose the Jews. How so?* 'He chose this nation,' it says, 'out of all the nations' [Deut. 14: 2]. When men choose, they choose the best; that is even more true of God. Indeed the fact of their being chosen is evidence both of God's loving-kindness and of their virtue. For in choosing them he must certainly have been choosing those who were approved. In our case he has himself made us holy, but we have to stay holy. Being holy is a matter of sharing in faith; being blameless is a matter of living an irreproachable life. But it is not what is holy and irreproachable without any further qualification that he is looking for but people who will appear so 'before him'. Some are holy and blameless but only in men's eyes; they are like whited sepulchres, like those

---

* Reading πῶς; (with *PG*) rather than ποῖον.

who wear sheep's clothing. These are not the people he is looking for, but those described by the prophet: 'and according to the cleanness of my hands' [Ps. 18: 24]. What cleanness? That which is so 'in his sight'. He is looking for that holiness which God's eye sees.

After speaking of the good works of men, he goes back to the grace of God. For all this does not come about by toil and good works, but by love: yet not by love alone, nor by our virtue alone. For if it were by love alone, then everyone would be saved; and if it were by our virtue alone, then the incarnation and all that it accomplished would be superfluous. So it is not by love alone, nor by our virtue alone, but comes from both. 'He chose us,' says the text; and the chooser knows what he is choosing. 'He predestined us in love.' For virtue without love would never have saved anybody. Where would Paul have got to, how would he have achieved what he did, if God had not first of all called him and in his love drawn him to himself? In any case the fact that he bestows such great benefits on us is the outcome of his love and not of our virtue. Our becoming virtuous, our believing and our coming to him – these are all the work of him who called us, though admittedly they are our works also. But to bestow such great honours on those who come to him, translating them immediately from enmity to adopted sonship, is most emphatically the outcome of a love that knows no bounds.

He predestined us, he says, *in love to be adopted as sons to him through Jesus Christ.*

You see how nothing happens apart from Christ and nothing happens apart from the Father. The Father predestined us; Christ brought us over. In saying this he is adding something more to his praise of all that has been done – as he says elsewhere: 'Not only so, but we also rejoice through our Lord Jesus Christ' [Rom. 5: 11]. God's gifts are great but they are made much greater by the fact that they are given through Christ. It was not one of his servants that he sent to his servants, but the only-begotten Son himself.

According to the good pleasure of his will.

In other words, because he willed it so strongly. His desire, we might call this. 'Good pleasure' always indicates antecedent will. There is a further will as well. For example it is God's primary will that sinners should not perish; it is his secondary will that those who do become evil should perish. For their punishment is not a matter of inevitable necessity but of God's will. One can take an example from Paul's case too. First: 'I will that all men were even as I am myself' [1 Cor. 7: 7]. Secondly: 'I will that the younger women marry and bear children' [1 Tim. 5: 14]. So here when he speaks of 'good pleasure', he means the primary will, the strong will, the will accompanied by inner desire, or what in our own case – for I am not afraid of using quite ordinary terms to make the point clear to the simplest person – we call our firm intention; as when we say: 'It is our firm intention.' What Paul is saying is this. God earnestly longs for, earnestly desires our salvation. Why does he love us like this? What is the source of such affection? It comes solely from his goodness. For grace itself is a product of goodness. The reason, says Paul, why he predestined us to be adopted as sons was his will and strong intent that the glory of his grace should be displayed. 'According to the good pleasure of his will', he says, 'to the praise of the glory of his grace, with which he has been gracious to us in the beloved.'

25 Augustine
Sermon 156, ix, 9 – xiii, 14 (on Rom. 8: 13–15)
[*PL* 38, 854–7]

9. *But if by the Spirit you put to death the deeds of the flesh you shall live.*

This is our task in this life – by the Spirit to put to death the deeds of the flesh, each day to strike them down, reduce them, bridle them, destroy them. The man who is progressing in the faith is no longer attracted by a host of things which once did attract him. When something used to attract him and he did not give way to it, it was being put to death; if it no longer attracts him, it has been put to death. Trample on the dead and turn to the living; trample on the fallen, do battle with those still fighting. One attraction is dead, but another is still alive; when you do not give way to that one, you are putting it to death: when it has ceased altogether to attract you, you have put it to death. That is our task, that is our warfare. As we do battle in this contest, we have God to watch us; as we toil in this contest, we entreat God to help us. For if he did not himself help us, we would be unable – I do not say to win – but even to fight at all.

10. When the apostle says 'but if by the Spirit you put to death the deeds of the flesh you shall live', he is referring to those desires of the flesh, not to give way to which is matter for great praise, and to be without which is a sign of perfection. If, he is saying, by the Spirit you put to death these deadly deeds of the flesh, which struggle to bring death, you will live. But here we must beware that no one ventures to rely on his own spirit for putting to death the deeds of the flesh. It is not only God who is spirit; your soul is spirit and your mind is spirit. (Compare 'with my mind I serve the law of God but

with my flesh the law of sin' with 'the spirit lusts against the flesh and the flesh against the spirit' [Rom. 7: 25; Gal. 5: 17].) So do not rely on your own spirit for putting to death the deeds of the flesh or your pride will destroy you; you will be resisted in your pride and grace will be withheld from you in your lack of humility, for 'God resists the proud, but gives grace to the humble' [James 4: 6].

To ensure that no such pride arises in your case, take note of what comes next. Having said, 'If by the Spirit you put to death the deeds of the flesh, you shall live', he wants to prevent the human spirit from raising itself up and boasting of its own fitness and strength for this task; so he goes on to say: *For all who are directed by the Spirit of God, they are the sons of God.* How could you propose to raise yourself up on hearing the words: 'If by the Spirit you put to death the deeds of the flesh you shall live'? You were on the point of saying: 'My will can do that, my free-will can do that.' What will? What free-will? Unless he rules, you fall; unless he lifts you up, you are down. How can this be done by your spirit when the words of the apostle are, 'For all who are directed by the Spirit of God, they are the sons of God'? You want to direct yourself, you want to be directed by yourself in putting to death the deeds of the flesh. What is the use of not being an Epicurean and being a Stoic instead? Whether you are an Epicurean or whether you are a Stoic, you will not be among the sons of God. 'For all who are directed by the Spirit of God, they are the sons of God' – not those who live according to their own flesh, nor those who live according to their own spirit; not those who are guided by the pleasures of the flesh, nor those who are directed by their own spirit, but 'all who are directed by the Spirit of God, they are the sons of God'.

11. Someone will say to me: 'So we are directed and do not direct; we are acted on and do not act.' My reply is: You both direct and are directed; you act and are acted on; and you direct your life well when you are directed by that which is good. For the Spirit of God who acts on you is helping you in your acting. The very word 'helper' shows that you too are yourself an agent. Realize what you are praying for and realize what you are confessing when you say: 'Be my helper; do not forsake me' [Ps. 27: 9]. You call God 'helper', but no one can be helped, if he is not doing anything for himself. 'All who are directed by the Spirit of God, they are the sons of God' – directed not by the letter but by the Spirit, not by the law with its injunctions, threats and promises but by the Spirit with his encouragement, enlightenment and help. The apostle also says: 'We know that God works all things together for good for those who love

him' [Rom. 8: 28]. * If you were not a worker, God would not be a co-worker.

12. At this point be especially on your guard that your spirit does not say: 'If God's cooperation and God's help are withdrawn, my spirit can do it – admittedly with effort and with some difficulty, but all the same it can complete it.' That is like someone saying: 'We'll get there by rowing but it will be hard work. If only we had some wind! Then we could get there more easily.' God's help is not like that; Christ's help is not like that; the Holy Spirit's help is not like that. If it is lacking, you cannot do anything good. You can indeed act without his help by your own free-will, but only badly. Your will, which is called a free-will, is capable of that; it has become the cursed slave of evil doing. When I tell you: 'Without God's help, you can do nothing', I mean 'nothing good'. For doing evil you have without God's help a free will – though it is not really free. 'Whatever overcomes a man, to that he is enslaved'; 'everyone who commits sin is a slave of sin'; 'if the Son makes you free, you will be truly free' [2 Pet. 2: 19; John 8: 34; 8: 36].

13. Believe this with all your heart; you can act with a good will – and this is how. If you are alive, you can certainly act. He cannot be your helper unless you act; he cannot be your co-worker unless you work. But you must realize that if you do good it is because the guiding Spirit is your helper, and that if he is absent you can do nothing good at all. This is something very different from what has been said by some of those who have at last been compelled into admitting grace. (In fact we thank God that they have come round to saying even this much; by getting this far they will be able to get further and might even reach the full truth in the end.) What they say is that the grace of God helps us by enabling us to do things more easily. 'God gave his grace to men', they say, 'so that they can fulfil more easily by grace what they are commanded to do by free will.' It is easier sailing and harder rowing, yet even rowing gets you there; it is easier on a horse and harder on foot, but even your feet will get you there. This is not how it is. What did the true master say – he who flatters no one and deceives no one, the truthful teacher and saviour, to whom the exceedingly hard schoolmaster †

---

* Reading 'cooperatur' in place of 'cooperantur' of the text. The emendation seems to be required by the following sentence. The text appears in both forms in the writings of Augustine. For 'cooperatur' see *The City of God* I, 10; XVIII, 51; *On the Trinity* XIII, xvi, 20. That God is the subject of the verb is also implicit in Augustine's allusion to the text in *On the Trinity* XIII, xi, 15; see p. 115 above.

† I.e. the law. See Gal. 3: 24.

has led us? When he was speaking about good works (or in other words the fruit of the vine branches) he did not say: 'Without me you can do such and such but by me you can do it more easily'; he did not say 'Without me you can bear your fruit, but by me you can bear it more plentifully.' That is not what he said. Read what he said: it is the holy gospel; the proud necks of all men are placed under its yoke. It is not Augustine who says it; it is the Lord who says it. What does the Lord say? 'Without me you can do nothing' [John 15: 5].

So when you now hear the words, 'All who are directed by the Spirit of God, they are the sons of God', you must not give up. In building his temple God does not use you like stones which have no power of self-movement. They are simply picked up and put in place by the builder; but it is not like that with living stones – and you are being built like living stones into a temple of God [see 1 Pet. 2: 5; Eph. 2: 22]. You are led, but you yourselves run too; you are led but you follow; and because you must follow, it is true that without him you can do nothing. 'It is not a matter of the one who wills or the one who runs, but of God who shows mercy' [Rom. 9: 16].

14. Perhaps you were about to say: 'The law is enough for us.' What the law produced was fear. Notice how the apostle continues. First he says: 'All who are directed by the Spirit of God, they are the sons of God'; and those who are directed by the Spirit of God are directed by love, for 'the love of God has been shed abroad in our hearts by the Holy Spirit which has been given to us' [Rom. 5: 5]. So he goes on: *For you did not receive the spirit of slavery again with fear.* Why 'again'? That was how the exceedingly hard schoolmaster used to frighten us. Why 'again'? It was the spirit of slavery you received in the past at Mount Sinai. Someone will object: there is one spirit of slavery and a distinct spirit of freedom. If they were distinct the apostle would not say 'again'. It is the same Spirit, but when it is on tables of stone it is with fear and when it is on tables of the heart it is with love. Those of you who were here the day before yesterday heard how voices, fire and smoke from the mountain terrified the people even though they stood afar off [see Exod. 19: 16–18], but how when that same finger of God, the Holy Spirit, came on the fiftieth day after the shadow of the Passover,* he came with tongues of fire and actually settled on each of them [Acts 2: 1–3]. This time it was not with fear but with love, so that we might be sons and not slaves. The man who still does good for fear of punishment does not love God; he is not yet a son – but it is good

* I.e. the Jewish Passover which for the Christian is a shadow of the true festival.

that he should at least fear punishment. Fear is a slave; love is free: we can even say that fear is love's slave. To prevent the devil getting possession of your heart, let the slave come in there first and keep a place for its master who will come later. You must act; and you must act from fear of punishment, if you cannot yet act from love of righteousness. In time the master will come and the slave will go away, for 'perfect love casts out fear' [1 John 4: 18].

'You did not receive the spirit of slavery again with fear.' This is the New Testament, not the Old. 'Old things have passed away, behold all things are become new. And all this is from God' [2 Cor. 5: 17–18].

6 Tradition and Scripture

The extracts so far given have all been concerned with the substance of Christian doctrine. But the proper sources for determining Christian truth and the right use of them was also a matter for debate. The heading 'Tradition and Scripture' should not be allowed to suggest that these were thought of as rival sources in the way that has been characteristic of much later Christian history. In debate with the Gnostics of the second century insistence was placed both on the apostolic nature of the accepted writings of the New Testament and on the public nature of the Church tradition handed down from apostolic times. This is the main burden of the first passage of Irenaeus' work against the Gnostics.

Next we have Tertullian arguing for the importance of unwritten tradition in determining the Christian attitude on issues not dealt with in Scripture. But even more fundamental was the problem of how to interpret what was accepted as scriptural. The passage from Origen gives a clear account of the allegorical method of interpretation, which is so characteristic of his own work and of the Alexandrian tradition in general. In the next passage we see that approach applied by Dionysius, bishop of Alexandria shortly after Origen's time, in discussion with people who drew millenarian conclusions from the book of Revelation. The passage also displays an unusually acute literary critical sense in its discussion of the authorship of the writings that make up the Johannine corpus.

The passage from Theodore of Mopsuestia illustrates the approach of the Antiochene school which is normally contrasted with that of Alexandria. The Antiochene approach was far from being literalistic in character, but it was strongly opposed to any form of spiritual interpretation which involved denying the truth of the text at a historical level.

Finally we have from Augustine a discussion of how the interpreter is to deal with ambiguities in Scripture. Through the discussion of detailed examples, it provides an interesting account of the interrelation of biblical interpretation and Christian doctrine.

26 Irenaeus

Against the Heresies III, Preface – 4.2
[*SC* 34, 94–118]
Translation of E. R. Hardy in *LCC* 1, 369–75: revised.

The Lord of all gave to his apostles the power of the gospel, and by them we also have learned the truth, that is, the teaching of the Son of God – as the Lord said to them, 'He who hears you hears me, and he who despises you despises me, and him who sent me' [Luke 10: 16].

1.1. For we learned the plan of our salvation from no others than from those through whom the gospel came to us. They first preached it abroad, and then later by the will of God handed it down to us in Scriptures, to be the foundation and pillar of our faith. For it is not right to say that they preached before they had come to perfect knowledge, as some dare to say, boasting that they are the correctors of the apostles. For after our Lord had risen from the dead, and they were clothed with the power from on high when the Holy Spirit came upon them, they were filled with all things and had perfect knowledge. They went out to the ends of the earth, preaching the good things that come to us from God, and proclaiming peace from heaven to men, all and each of them equally being in possession of the gospel of God.

So Matthew among the Hebrews issued a written version of the gospel in their own tongue, while Peter and Paul were preaching the gospel at Rome and founding the Church. After their decease Mark, the disciple and interpreter of Peter, also handed down to us in writing what Peter had preached. Luke also, the follower of Paul, recorded in a book the gospel as it was preached by him. Finally John, the disciple of the Lord, who had also lain on his breast, himself published the gospel, while he was residing at Ephesus in Asia.

1.2. All of these handed down to us that there is one God, maker of heaven and earth, proclaimed by the law and the prophets, and one Christ the Son of God. If anyone does not agree with them he despises the companions of the Lord, he despises the Lord himself, he even despises the Father, and he is self-condemned, resisting and refusing his own salvation, as all the heretics do.

2.1. But when they are refuted from the Scriptures they turn around and attack the Scriptures themselves, saying that they are not correct, or authoritative, that they are mutually inconsistent and that the truth cannot be found from them by those who are not acquainted with the tradition. For this, they say, was not handed down in writing, but orally, which is why Paul said, 'We speak wisdom among the perfect, but not the wisdom of this world' [1 Cor. 2: 6]. Each of them utters a wisdom which he has made up, or rather a fiction; so that, according to them, the truth was at one time to be found quite properly in Valentinus, then at another time in Marcion, at another time in Cerinthus, then later in Basilides, or in anyone who opposes the Church and has no saving message to utter. Each one of them is wholly perverse, and is not ashamed to preach himself, corrupting the rule of faith.

2.2. But when we appeal again to that tradition which has come down from the apostles and is guarded by the successions of elders in the churches, they oppose the tradition, saying that they are wiser not only than the elders, but even than the apostles, and have found the genuine truth. For the apostles, they say, mixed matters of the law with the words of the Saviour, and not only the apostles, but even the Lord himself, spoke sometimes from the Demiurge, sometimes from the middle power, sometimes from the highest,* while they know the hidden mystery without doubt or corruption, and in its purity. This is nothing less than shameless blasphemy against their Maker. What it comes to is that they will not agree with either Scriptures or tradition.

2.3. It is such people, my dear friend, that we have to fight with, who like slippery snakes are always trying to escape us. Therefore we must resist them on all sides, hoping that we may so rebut and confound them that we may be able to bring some of them to turn to the truth. For although it is not easy for a soul which has been seized by error to turn back, still it is not absolutely impossible to put error to flight by putting the truth beside it.

3.1. The tradition of the apostles, made clear in all the world, can be seen in every church by those who wish to behold the truth. We can enumerate those who were established by the apostles as bishops in the churches, and their successors down to our time,

---

* Irenaeus is referring to the Valentinian belief, which he mentions in his account of the system of Ptolemaeus, that the words of Scripture originate in, and are revelatory of, various levels of being in the Gnostic system. The tripartite composition of Scripture corresponds to the tripartite composition of Jesus himself. 'They divide the prophecies, maintaining that one part was spoken by the mother, another by the seed, and the third finally by the Demiurge. Similarly they hold that Jesus spoke partly under the influence of the Saviour, partly of the mother, and partly of the Demiurge' (*Against the Heresies* 1.7.3; see also 1.6.1). In his *Letter to Flora*, which survives, Ptolemaeus applies this hermeneutical principle to the law of Moses. See G. Quispel's edition of the *Letter to Flora* (*SC* 24), pp. 23–4, 84–5.

none of whom taught or thought of anything like their mad ideas. Even if the apostles had known of hidden mysteries, which they taught to the perfect secretly and apart from others, they would have handed them down especially to those to whom they were entrusting the churches themselves. For they certainly wished those whom they were leaving as their successors, handing over to them their own teaching position, to be perfect and irreproachable, since their sound conduct would be a great benefit, and failure on their part the greatest calamity.

3.2. To enumerate the successions of all the churches would take up too much space in a volume of this kind. But in order to put to shame all of those who in any way, either through self-conceit, or through vain-glory, or through blind and evil opinion, gather as they should not, I need only cite the case of that very great, most ancient and universally known church founded and established at Rome by those two most glorious apostles Peter and Paul and draw attention to the tradition which that church has received from the apostles and to the faith it preaches which has come down to our time through the succession of bishops. For in view of the outstanding pre-eminence of this church, there cannot be any disagreement between it and every other church (that is, the faithful in every place) – every church, that is, in which men in every place have at all times preserved the apostolic tradition.*

3.3. When the blessed apostles had founded and built up the Church they handed over the ministry of the episcopate to Linus. Paul mentions this Linus in his Epistles to Timothy. Anencletus succeeded him. After him Clement received the lot of the episcopate in the third place from the apostles. He had seen the apostles and associated with them, and still had their preaching sounding in his ears and their tradition before his eyes – and not he alone, for there were many still left in his time who had been taught by the apostles. In this Clement's time no small discord arose among the brethren in Corinth, and the church in Rome sent a most appropriate letter to the Corinthians, leading them to peace, renewing their faith, and declaring the tradition which they had recently received from the apostles, which declared one almighty God, maker of heaven and

---

* Following the interpretation of the passage first proposed by H. G. J. Thiersch in *Theologische Studien und Kritiken* (1842), p. 527, n. 11, and supported by A. von Harnack in 'Das Zeugniss des Irenäus über das Ansehen der römischen Kirche' (*Sitzungberichte der königlich prussischen Akademie der Wissenschaften* [1893], pp. 939–55, esp. pp. 953ff.). For a more recent full discussion of the exegetical problems of the passage, see P. Nautin, 'Irénée, Adv. Haer. III, 3, 2: église de Rome ou église universelle?' (*Revue d'histoire ecclésiastique* 151 (1967), 37–78).

earth and fashioner of man, who brought about the deluge, and called Abraham; who brought out the people from the land of Egypt; who spoke with Moses; who ordained the law and sent the prophets; and who has prepared fire for the devil and his angels. Those who care to can learn from this writing that he was proclaimed by the churches as the Father of our Lord Jesus Christ, and so understand the apostolic tradition of the Church, since this epistle is older than those present false teachers who make up lies about another God above the demiurge and maker of all these things that are. Evarestus succeeded to this Clement, and Alexander to Evarestus; then Xystus was installed as the sixth from the apostles, and after him Telesphorus, who met a glorious martyrdom; then Hyginus, then Pius, and after him Anicetus. Soter followed Anicetus, and Eleutherus now in the twelfth place from the apostles holds the lot of the episcopate. In this very order and succession the apostolic tradition in the Church and the preaching of the truth has come down even to us. This is a full demonstration that it is one and the same life-giving faith which has been preserved in the Church from the apostles to the present, and is handed on in truth.

3.4. Similarly there was Polycarp, who not only was taught by apostles and associated with many who had seen the Lord, but also was installed by apostles in Asia as bishop in the church in Smyrna. I saw him myself in my early youth, for he survived for a long time and was of a ripe old age when he departed this life by a glorious and magnificent martyrdom. He too always taught what he learnt from the apostles. This is what the Church continues to hand on. This alone is true. The churches in Asia all bear witness to this, as do those who have succeeded Polycarp down to the present time; he is certainly a much more trustworthy and dependable witness to the truth than Valentinus and Marcion and the other false thinkers. When he visited Rome under Anicetus, he converted many followers of the above-mentioned heretics to the Church of God, proclaiming that he had received from the apostles the one and only truth, the same which is handed on by the Church. There are those who have heard him tell how when John the disciple of the Lord went to bathe at Ephesus, and saw Cerinthus inside, he rushed out of the baths without washing, but crying out, 'Let us escape, lest the baths should fall while Cerinthus the enemy of the truth is in them.' Polycarp himself, when Marcion once met him and said, 'Acknowledge me!', answered, 'I acknowledge you – I acknowledge the first-born of Satan.' The apostles and their disciples took such great care not even to engage in conversations with the corrupters of the truth, as Paul also said, 'A heretical man after a first and second warning avoid, knowing that such a man has fallen away and is a sinner, being self-condemned' [Titus 3: 10–11]. There is also a most appropriate letter of Polycarp addressed to the Philippians, from which those who care to, and are concerned for their own salvation, can learn the character of his faith and his preaching of the truth. The church in Ephesus also, which was founded by Paul, and where John survived until the time of Trajan, is a true witness of the traditions of the apostles.

4.1. Since there are so many clear testimonies, we should not seek from others for the truth which can easily be received from the Church. It was there, in the Church, that the apostles, like a rich man making a deposit, fully bestowed everything that belongs to the truth. She is the entrance to life; all the others are thieves and robbers. Therefore we ought to avoid them, but to love with the greatest zeal the things of the Church, and so to lay hold of the tradition of the truth. What if there should be a dispute about some matter of moderate importance? Should we not turn to the oldest churches, where the apostles themselves were known, and find out from them the clear and certain answer to the problem now being raised? Even if the apostles had not left their Scriptures to us, ought we not to follow the rule of the tradition which they handed down to those to whom they committed the churches?

4.2. Many barbarian peoples who believe in Christ follow this rule, having their salvation written in their hearts by the Spirit without paper and ink. Diligently following the old tradition, they believe in one God, who made heaven and earth and all that is in them through Christ Jesus the Son of God, who on account of his abundant love for his creation submitted to be born of a virgin, himself by himself uniting man to God, and having suffered under Pontius Pilate, and risen, and having been received up into splendour, is to come in glory as the Saviour of those who are saved, and the judge of those who are judged, and will send into eternal fire those who alter the truth, and despise his Father and his coming. Those who believe in this faith without written documents are barbarians in our speech, but in their convictions, habits and behaviour they are, because of their faith, most wise, and are pleasing to God, living in all righteousness and purity and wisdom. If anyone should preach to them the inventions of the heretics, speaking in their own language, they would at once stop their ears and run far, far away, not enduring even to listen to such blasphemous speech. Thus the old apostolic tradition ensures that their minds do not even entertain the least particle of the impressive claptrap of the heretics.

27 Tertullian
The Crown 1–4
[*CCL* 2, 1039–45]

1. I record a recent occurrence. The bounty of our most excellent Emperors was being dispensed in a military camp.* The soldiers were approaching with laurel crowns on their heads. One man present was first and foremost a soldier of God; the other Christians had thought they could serve two masters, but he was more faithful than they. He was the only one with head bared; his crown remained in his hand unused. By this act he stood out publicly as a Christian. People begin to point him out; those further away jeer; those closer by snarl at him. A general hubbub soon builds up. He is denounced to the tribune – he had already come out of his place in the ranks. The tribune immediately asks: 'Why are you dressed differently?' He says that he is not allowed to dress like the others. He is told to give his reasons. 'I am a Christian', he replies. 'Proud warrior'† – of God! A vote is taken; the case is recorded; he is sent for sentence to the prefects. There and then he removes his heavy cloak (he is beginning to be lightened of his burden); he takes his cumbersome boots off his feet (he is beginning to stand on holy ground [see Exod. 3: 5]); he hands over his sword (his Lord did not need one to defend himself [see John 18: 10–11]); the laurel wreath falls from his hand. Instead he is clad in the crimson of the blood he expects to shed; he is shod with the preparation of the gospel; he is girded with the word of God sharper than any sword – thus he puts on the whole armour of which the apostle speaks [see Eph. 6: 13–16; Heb. 4: 12]. Then as one who is to receive a far better crown, the dazzling laurel crown of the martyr, he waits in prison for the bounty which Christ will give him. Views are expressed about him (I hesitate to call them the views of Christians, as they were no different from those of non-Christians): he was headstrong, rash, eager to die, he had made things difficult for Christians by getting himself interrogated on a matter of dress – whereas the truth of the matter is that he was the only brave man among all his Christian fellow-soldiers,

---

* The occasion of the incident is most probably the donative provided for the army by the emperors Caracalla and Geta shortly after their accession in A.D. 211, though T. D. Barnes, *Tertullian: A Historical and Literary Study* (Oxford, 1971), p. 37, argues for an earlier occasion in the reign of Severus in A.D. 208.

† *Miles gloriosus*: the title of a play by Plautus.

in fact the only true Christian at all. Obviously the next step for people who have rejected the prophecies of the Holy Spirit is to plan how to refuse martyrdom too.* They complain that the peace which has served them so well for so long is being endangered. Some no doubt, following the Scriptures, are clearing out, packing their bags and preparing to flee from city to city [see Matt. 10: 23]. That is the only bit of the gospel they are keen to remember. I know their pastors too – lions in peace and deer in battle. But we will deal elsewhere with the public confession of Christ and the issues it involves. For the moment I want to take up a different objection – namely 'Where are we forbidden to be crowned?' Here is the nub of this particular case. Some ask the question out of genuine ignorance; them I seek to instruct. Others do it with the definite intention of exculpating the offence; them I seek to refute – and particularly those crowned Christians themselves who seem to find consolation in the raising of the question on the ground that if the matter is open to question the offence must be regarded either as non-existent or at least open to doubt. That it is neither non-existent nor open to doubt is what I shall now show.

2. No believer, I assert, is ever to be found with a crown on his head except on an occasion of testing like this. This is a universally observed practice with everyone from catechumens to confessors and martyrs or (as the case may be) deniers of the faith. Now consider where this custom gets its authority; that is the issue before us. The mere fact of discussing why something is observed is evidence of general agreement that it is observed. So one can see straightaway that the offence is neither non-existent nor open to doubt on the simple ground that it is committed against our observed custom; the very title 'observed custom' is its own defence and is supported by the authority of established usage. Clearly in enquiring about the reason for an observed custom, the observation of the custom is unaffected; the aim is not to overthrow the custom but to strengthen it, so that you can observe it more fully when your mind is satisfied about the reason behind it. Think what would be involved in someone raising the question of the observation of a particular custom just as he himself has abandoned it or asking what had been the basis of the custom just when he himself has given it up. He may like it to appear that he is raising the question in order to show that he has done nothing wrong in abandoning the practice – but if so it must follow that he has done wrong previously in his earlier

* Tertullian, by this time a Montanist, is referring to the Catholic rejection of the claim that Montanist prophecies were the work of the Holy Spirit.

following of it. If he has done no wrong in accepting the crown today, he must have done wrong in refusing it on some previous occasion. This treatise is not directed therefore to those whom the question does not concern; it is directed to those who really want to learn, whose interest is less in the debating of a question than in the discussion of a principle. Not all inquiries are of this latter kind, and I applaud the faith which believes a custom should be observed even before it has learnt the reason behind it.

It is easy to start off by demanding where it is written that we should not be crowned. But for that matter where is it written that we should be crowned? If you insist on scriptural support for your opponent's position, you commit yourself in advance to the need for scriptural support for your own position too. If you are going to say that it is permissible to be crowned because Scripture does not forbid it, you are fully open to the retort that it is impermissible to be crowned because Scripture does not command it. What is the faith to teach? Shall it allow either, because neither is forbidden? Or shall it reject both, because neither is commanded? 'What is not forbidden is expressly permitted', you will say. I reply, 'On the contrary, what is not expressly permitted is forbidden.'

3. How long shall we go on with this see-saw when we have an ancient custom which has settled the issue in advance? If there is no Scripture which settles the matter decisively, it has certainly gained strength from established usage, which in its turn undoubtedly originated from tradition. For how can anything become a matter of regular practice, unless it has first been handed down by tradition? 'But', you say, 'even where the plea is one of tradition, one must call also for written authority.' Let us then investigate the question whether tradition ought to be accepted only if it is written. Obviously we will have to say that unwritten tradition ought not to be accepted, unless we can cite as precedents examples of other observed customs, which we justify without the aid of anything written but under the heading of tradition alone and therefore on the grounds of established usage. I begin with baptism. In that rite, a little before we actually enter the water, we swear that we renounce the devil, his pomp and his angels; this we do in the presence of the congregation and under the hand of the presiding minister.* Then

* The precise implications of this phrase, which we have translated literally, is uncertain. It could mean no more than 'under the authority of the presiding minister' but it is much more likely that 'hand' is to be understood literally. This may have involved no more than a stretching out of the hand over all the candidates together (see A. H. Couratin in *The Pelican Guide to Modern Theology* 2 [ed. J. Daniélou, A. H. Couratin and J. Kent], 168–9). It probably refers

we are immersed three times and make a rather fuller response than the Lord laid down in the gospel [see Matt. 28: 19]. When we have been taken up from the water, we are given a mixture of milk and honey as a foretaste of what is to come; also starting from that day we abstain from the regular daily bath for a whole week. I turn to the sacrament of the Eucharist. This was entrusted by the Lord to all, and at a meal time; yet we receive it at meetings before dawn and only from the hand of those who preside. Again we make offerings* for the dead as birthday celebrations on their anniversaries. We think it wrong to fast or to kneel in worship on the Lord's day. We enjoy this privilege also between Easter and Whitsun. We feel uneasy if any of the wine or bread (even that which has become our own) is dropped on the ground. At every new movement or action, on entering or leaving the house, getting dressed, putting on shoes, having a bath, beginning a meal, lighting the lamps, going to bed, sitting down – in fact in all the activities of ordinary life – we make the sign of the cross on our foreheads.

4. If you demand a scriptural injunction as the basis for these and other similar practices, you will not find any. The arguments for them will be tradition, usage and faith – tradition as supplying their origin, usage their confirmation and faith their observance. That tradition, usage and faith are supported by reason is something that you will either come to see for yourself or that you will learn from someone else who has come to see it. Meanwhile you will believe that some reason does exist to which compliance is required.

I will give one more example as it will be a good idea to draw instruction from the ancients also. With the Jews the veiling of women is so firmly established that it is a way of recognizing them as Jews. Where do we find the rule for this? I leave the apostle out of it for the moment. Rebecca veiled herself when she saw her betrothed in the distance [see Gen. 24: 64–5]. An individual case of modesty like that could not have established a law. If it had, it would have done so only for that kind of situation; then only virgins would be covered, specifically virgins on the way to their weddings and even then not before they had recognized their betrothed.

to the action of the minister at the time of the renunciation (see B. Capelle, 'L'introduction du Catéchuménat à Rome', *Recherches de théologie ancienne et médiévale*, 5 [1933], 147, n. 25). Without independent knowledge of the rite in question, we cannot tell whether it was part of an exorcism (as in Hippolytus, *Apostolic Tradition* 20, 8) or even possibly of an anointing as in the early Syrian tradition.

* Eucharistic offerings are meant. Tertullian provides our earliest evidence for the offering of the Eucharist for the dead (see also Tertullian, *De Monogamia* 10, 4).

Again, the case of Susanna whose veil was removed at her trial, might seem to offer a reason for veiling [see Susanna 32]. But her veiling was a matter of deliberate choice. She was there as the accused party. She was embarrassed at the infamy attributed to her and very properly hid her beauty – or perhaps she was afraid she might prove too attractive once again. But I do not imagine that she was veiled when she walked in her husband's garden and proved so attractive. Suppose she was always veiled. I still do not find in that fact a law about dress – nor in any other similar incident. If then I fail to find a law anywhere, it follows that it was tradition that provided established usage with this custom, and it was only at some later date that it was to receive apostolic authority with an explanation of the reason behind it [see 1 Cor. 11: 4–15].

These examples then lead to the conclusion that even unwritten tradition can be defended on the ground of its being observed; established usage confirms it and this provides all the evidence that is needed for the approval of a tradition on the basis of its long continued observance. Even in civil matters established usage can take the place of law where no specific law exists. It makes no difference whether it rests on something written or on reason, since it is in fact reason that secures our approval of law. So if law rests on reason, everything that rests on reason (whatever its source) will be law. Surely every Christian is at liberty to decide and to determine what is conducive to good conduct and helpful for salvation, provided it is agreeable to God. Does not the Lord say, 'Why do you not judge of yourselves what is right?' [see Luke 12: 57]. And the apostle speaks not only of judging but of forming an opinion on all sorts of issues that come up for consideration, when he says: 'If there is anything you do not know, God will reveal it to you' [see Phil. 3: 15]. It was his custom to supply advice, where he had no command of the Lord, and to give instructions of his own – as, of course, a man who had the spirit of God who leads into all truth [see 1 Cor. 7: 25, 40; John 16: 13]. Therefore his advice and instructions have now acquired the status of divine commands because grounded on the authority of divine reason. It is for this reason that you must ask. Maintain your respect for tradition, whoever you may judge to have started the tradition; be concerned not about its author but about its authority, and especially the authority of well-established usage. Revere such usage, that you may not want for an interpreter to explain the reason behind it. And if God gives you one, what you will learn from him is not whether you ought to observe established custom but why.

28 Origen
On First Principles IV, 2, 1–9
[*GCS* 22, 305–23]

1. We have spoken briefly about the inspiration of the divine Scriptures. We must now tackle the question of how they should be read and understood, since many mistakes have been caused by the failure of the multitude to discover the right way to approach the sacred writings.

First, there are the hard-hearted and ignorant members of the circumcision who have refused to believe in our Saviour because they are accustomed to stick to the letter of the prophecies about him. They do not see him as having literally 'proclaimed release to the captives' [Isa. 61: 1], as having built what they consider a real city of God [see Isa. 45: 13], as having 'cut off the chariots from Ephraim and the horse from Jerusalem' [Zech. 9: 10], or as having 'eaten butter and honey and chosen good before he knew or preferred evil' [Isa. 7: 15]. Further, they think that it is the four-footed animal that is meant by the 'wolf' of which it is prophesied that it 'shall feed with the lamb, and the leopard shall rest with the kid, and the calf and bull and lion shall feed together, led by a little child, and the cow and the bear shall pasture together, their little ones growing up with each other, and the lion shall eat chaff like the ox' [Isa. 11: 6–7]. Because they did not see any of these things happening literally during the sojourn of him whom we believe to be Christ, they did not accept our Lord Jesus but crucified him for having improperly called himself Christ.

Secondly, there are heretics. They read passages like: 'Fire is kindled out of my anger' [Deut. 32: 22; Jer. 15: 14]; 'I am a jealous God, visiting the sins of the fathers upon the children to the third and fourth generation' [Deut. 5: 9]; 'I repent that I anointed Saul king' [1 Sam. 15: 11]; and 'I am a God who makes peace and creates evil' [Isa. 45: 7]. Other such texts are: 'There is no evil in a city which the Lord has not done' [Amos 3: 6]; and again, 'Evil has come down from the Lord on the gates of Jerusalem' [Mic. 1: 12]; and 'An evil spirit from the Lord tormented Saul' [1 Sam. 16: 14]. When they read these and innumerable similar passages, they do not venture to disbelieve that the Scriptures are divine, but they believe that they belong to the creator worshipped by the Jews. Since, on this view, the creator is not perfect or good, they suppose that the Saviour came to proclaim a more perfect god who, they say, is not the creator; about this god too they hold a variety of opinions. Once they have denied the creator, who is the only un-originate God, they give themselves to inventions; they make up mythical theories to account for the origin of things seen and of various unseen things as well – all of them the product of their own imagination.

Finally there are the more simple believers from within the number of those who are proud to belong to the Church. These hold that there is none greater than the creator; and in that they do well. But they also hold notions about him which would never be held about the most savage and unjust of men.

2. Now the reason for all these false, impious and ignorant assertions about God is simply that Scripture is not understood spiritually, but in accordance with the bare letter. To those there-fore who believe that the sacred books are no human composition but have been written and handed down through the inspiration of the Holy Spirit by the will of the Father of the universe mediated through Jesus Christ, we must explain what, in the opinion of those who hold to the rule of the heavenly Church of Jesus Christ handed down by the apostles, are the right methods of interpreta-tion.

That there are various mysterious revelations indicated by the divine Scriptures is believed by all who adhere to the Word, even the simplest. But what they signify, men of good sense and humility admit that they do not know. If someone is in difficulty about the intercourse of Lot with his daughters or the two wives of Abraham or the two sisters married to Jacob or the two slave-girls who bore children by him, they have nothing to say except that these are mysteries that we do not understand. Again, when the passage about the construction of the tabernacle is read, they believe that the things described there are types and this leads them to look for things that they can fit to each item in the tabernacle. In their belief that the tabernacle is a type of something they are not mistaken. Where they do sometimes fall into error is in providing a correct fit between the matter of which the tabernacle is a type and the particular details of Scripture. Everything that is reckoned to be narrative about marriages or the begetting of children or wars, everything in fact that the multitude will accept as pieces of history – all these things, they say, are types. But types of what? Here the interpretation of the individual points is not so clear. Sometimes this is due to lack of training and sometimes to hasty judgement. But sometimes a person's training is good and his judgement steady; then the cause is man's extreme difficulty in discovering these things.

3. Again, what are we to say about the prophecies which, as we all know, are full of riddles and dark sayings [see Prov. 1: 6]? Even in the case of the gospels, if their meaning is to be understood correctly, we need, since it is the meaning (or mind) of Christ that is in question, the grace once given to him who said, 'We have the mind of Christ, that we may understand the gifts bestowed on us by God; and we impart this in words not taught by human wisdom but taught by the Spirit' [1 Cor. 2: 16, 12–13]. Again, what reader of the revelations made to John is not amazed at the ineffable mysteries hidden there, whose presence is evident even to one who does not understand what is written? And no expert in literary interpretation would suppose that the letters of the apostles are clear or easy to understand; for in them there are innumerable passages that provide, so to speak, narrow openings leading to a vast number of the deepest thoughts.

In these circumstances, in which such vast numbers of people go astray, it is not without risk for a reader to claim that he can with ease understand things for which 'the key of knowledge' is required – the key which our Saviour said was with 'the lawyers'. And if anyone does not want to admit that the truth was with them before the coming of Christ, then he must explain how it is that Christ spoke of 'the key of knowledge' as being with them, that is, with men who, according to these objectors, were without books containing the ineffable and all-complete mysteries of knowledge. For what the text says is, 'Woe to you lawyers! for you have taken away the key of knowledge; you did not enter it yourselves, and you hindered those that were entering' [Luke 11: 52].

4. The right way to read the Scriptures and to grasp their meaning is, in our view, the following. It is drawn from the Bible itself. In Proverbs we find this sort of injunction given by Solomon concerning the divine teachings of Scripture: 'You are to register them thrice in counsel and knowledge, that you may answer words of truth to those who attack you' [see Prov. 22: 20–1 (LXX)]. Accordingly, one must register the thoughts of the holy Scriptures in one's soul in a triple manner. The simple man will be edified by what we may call the flesh of Scripture, by which we mean its obvious interpretation; he who has made some progress will be edified by its soul; whilst the perfect man who is like those of whom the apostle speaks – 'We speak wisdom among the perfect, although it is not a wisdom of this age or of the rulers of this age, who are passing away; but we impart a secret and hidden wisdom of God, which God decreed before the ages for our glory' [1 Cor. 2: 6–7] – such a man will be edified by 'the spiritual law' [Rom. 7: 14] which 'contains a shadow

of the good things to come' [Heb. 10: 1]. For just as man consists of body, soul and spirit, so too does the Scripture which God has provided for the salvation of men.

It is for this reason that we interpret as follows the passage in the Shepherd (a book despised by some) * where Hermas is told to 'write two books' and then to 'proclaim to the elders of the Church'. The text is: 'You shall write two books, and shall give one to Clement and one to Grapte. Grapte shall admonish the widows and orphans, Clement shall send to the cities outside, and you shall proclaim to the elders of the church.' † Now Grapte, who 'admonishes the widows and orphans', is the bare letter; it admonishes the infant souls that are not yet even able to claim God as their father and are therefore called 'orphans'. It also admonishes those who no longer associate with the unlawful bridegroom but are in widow-hood because they are not yet worthy of '*the* bridegroom'. Clement has passed beyond the letter. He is said to send the sayings 'to the cities outside', that is to say, to such souls as are outside all bodily and lower thoughts. Finally, there is the disciple of the Spirit himself; it is not through letters at all but in living words that he is instructed to 'proclaim to the elders' of the whole Church of God, that is, to those who have grown grey in wisdom.

5. However, there are some passages of Scripture which, as we shall show, have no bodily sense at all. There are therefore places where one need look only for the 'soul' and the 'spirit' of the passage. This is perhaps the reason why the waterpots which are described, as we read in the gospel according to John, as 'standing there for the purification of the Jews', 'contains two or three measures each' [John 2: 6]. The passage alludes to those the apostle calls 'Jews in secret' [Rom. 2: 29], that is people who are purified by the words of the Scriptures, and suggests that in some places those Scriptures contain 'two measures', that is, what I may call the 'soul meaning' and the 'spiritual meaning', and in other places 'three', since some passages also contain a bodily sense capable of edifying its reader. 'Six waterpots' is appropriate to those who

---

* Origen regularly treats the *Shepherd of Hermas* as an inspired book, while acknowledging that it does not have universal acceptance in the Church. For an example of Origen's readiness to quote a work even further removed from general acceptance in the Church, see his use of the Gospel according to the Hebrews in his commentary on St John, 2: 12 (p. 80 above).

† A free citation of *Hermas* 8, 3 (= *Vis.* II. 4.3). Origen plays on the fact that the name Grapte means 'written'.

are being purified in the world, since the world was made in six days – a perfect number.*

6. That profit can be had from the first meaning, which is helpful at its own level, is evident from the multitudes of sincere and simple believers. The kind of interpretation which rises to the level of 'soul' is exemplified by a passage from Paul's first letter to the Corinthians. 'It is written', he says, ' "You shall not muzzle a threshing ox." ' He then explains this precept by continuing, 'Is it for oxen that God is concerned? Does he not speak entirely for our sake? It was written for our sake, because the ploughman should plough in hope and the thresher should thresh in hope of a share in the crop' [1 Cor. 9: 9–10]. Most of the interpretations current which are suitable for the multitude and edify those incapable of higher truths are of this character.

Interpretation is spiritual when one is able to show of what heavenly things the Jews after the flesh were serving a copy and shadow [see Heb. 8: 5], and of what good things to come the law has a shadow [see Heb. 10: 1]. In general, one should always follow the apostolic injunction by looking for the 'secret and hidden wisdom which God decreed before the ages for the glory' of the righteous, 'which none of the rulers of this age understood' [1 Cor. 2: 7–8]. Elsewhere the same apostle, after citing various incidents recounted in Exodus and Numbers, says, 'These things happened to them as types, but they were written down on our account, upon whom the end of the ages has come' [1 Cor. 10: 11]. He gives us hints about what these events were types of, when he says, 'For they drank from the spiritual rock which followed them, and the rock was Christ' [1 Cor. 10: 4].

In another epistle, while giving a brief account of the tabernacle, he quotes the words, 'Make everything in accordance with the type that was shown you on the mountain' [Heb. 8: 5]. Again, in the letter to the Galatians, he reproaches those who suppose that they are reading the law while in fact not understanding it; he condemns them for not understanding it inasmuch as they suppose that the Scriptures contain no allegories. 'Tell me', he says, 'you who desire to be under law, do you not hear the law? For it is written that Abraham had two sons, one by the slave and the other by the free woman. But the son of the slave was born according to the flesh, the son of the free woman through promise. Now these things are

* See Philo, *De Opificio Mundi* 3, where it is explained that six is a perfect number because it is both the product and the sum of its factors (i.e. $6 = 1 \times 2 \times 3$ and $1 + 2 + 3$). It is also the product of the first male number, 3, and the first female number, 2.

an allegory; for these two women are two covenants ...' [Gal. 4: 21–4]. We must be careful to notice exactly what he says. He says, 'You who desire to be under the law' (not 'You who *are* under the law'), 'do you not hear the law?' 'Hearing' he judges to consist in knowing and understanding.

In the letter to the Colossians he briefly sums up the purpose of the whole code of law: 'Therefore let no one pass judgement on you in questions of food and drink or with regard to a festival or a new moon or a sabbath. These things are a shadow of the things to come' [Col. 2: 16–17]. Again, in Hebrews, when discussing those who belong to the circumcision, he writes that 'they serve a copy and shadow of the heavenly things' [Heb. 8: 5].

Now those who admit the inspiration of the apostle will probably, after this evidence, have no doubts about the five books ascribed to Moses. They will want to know whether the other narratives also 'happened as types' [see 1 Cor. 10: 11]. But notice the quotation from the third book of Kings in the letter to the Romans: 'I have kept for myself seven thousand men who have not bowed the knee to Baal'. Paul takes these to stand for the Israelites 'according to election' [Rom. 11: 4–5]; for it is not only the Gentiles who have profited from the coming of Christ, but also some members of the holy nation.

7. In view of all this we must give a sketch of what, in our view, are the characteristics of a right understanding of the Scriptures. The first thing to indicate is their aim. The principal aim with which the Spirit, by the providence of God through the Word who was 'in the beginning with God' [John 1: 2], enlightened the servants of the truth, that is, the prophets and apostles, concerns those ineffable mysteries that have to do with the affairs of men (by 'men' I refer to souls employing bodies); it is that anyone capable of learning should, by 'searching out' and devoting himself to 'the depths' [see 1 Cor. 2: 10] of the meaning of the words of Scripture, become a partaker of the complete teachings of the divine counsel.

Souls can only reach perfection through the rich and wise truth about God. The most important part of this is of course teachings about God and his only-begotten Son; about the nature of the latter and the mode in which he is God's Son; about the causes of his descent to human flesh and complete assumption of humanity; about the nature of his activity, towards whom it is directed and in what circumstances it is exercised.

Other topics necessarily included in the scriptural records of divine teaching relate to rational beings, to those akin to the Word as well as to others, that is, to the more divine as well as to those that have fallen from blessedness; and to the reasons for the fall of the latter. Other questions are the differences between souls and the origin of these differences; the nature of the world and the reason for its existence; why there is such great and widespread evil on earth, and whether it is to be found not only on earth but elsewhere too. All these are questions about which we need to be taught.

8. It was with these and similar ends in view that the Spirit enlightened the souls of the holy servants of the truth. But Scripture also has a second aim, related to those unable to endure the toil of searching out such great matters. This is to conceal the teaching on the themes I have just mentioned in words that present a narrative account of the visible creation, the formation of men, and the successive descendants from those first humans to the point when mankind had multiplied; and in other stories it recounts the deeds of the just and the sins that those same men, in that they were human, sometimes committed, as well as the acts of wickedness, licence and greed performed by the lawless and the impious.

But the most remarkable thing is the way in which narratives about wars and about who conquered whom are used to reveal some of these ineffable mysteries to those capable of examining these stories. Even more wonderful is the way in which a written code of law prophetically discloses the laws of truth. All these things are recorded in orderly series, with a skill that truly befits the wisdom of God. The intention was that even the covering of the spiritual truths, that is, the bodily sense of the Scriptures, should be made quite useful and capable in all sorts of ways of improving the multitude in accordance with their capacities.

9. Now if the written law were in its entirety immediately and clearly useful, or if the narratives were similarly smooth and elegant throughout, we should not have come to believe that there was anything to be understood in the Scriptures beyond their obvious meaning. Consequently the Word of God has arranged the insertion of a number of stumbling-blocks, obstacles and impossibilities in the middle of the law and the narrative. For the sheer attractiveness of the language might otherwise have led us either to abandon their teachings entirely, through supposing that there was nothing worthy of God to be learned from the Scriptures, or else, through not moving beyond the letter, never to discover anything of a more divine character.

There is something else that we must realize. The main aim of Scripture is to reveal the coherent structure that exists at the spiritual level in terms both of events and injunctions. Wherever the Word found that events on the historical plane corresponded with these mystical truths, he used them, concealing the deeper meaning from the multitude. But at those places in the account where the performance of particular actions as already recorded did not correspond with the pattern of things at the intellectual level Scripture wove into the narrative, for the sake of the more mystical truths, things that never occurred – sometimes things that could never have occurred, sometimes things that could have but did not. In some cases it is a matter of only a few words being inserted which in the literal sense are not true, in others more.

A similar method can also be found in the law. There one can often find matter which is useful in itself, being relevant to the period when the law was given. Other sayings appear to have no use. And in some places there are utterly impossible injunctions, inserted in order to get the more skilful and inquiring readers to apply themselves to the work of examining what is written and so become thoroughly assured of the necessity of searching for a meaning worthy of God in such instances.

It was not only in relation to the events before the coming of Christ that the Spirit arranged things in this way. Because he is the same Spirit and comes from the one God, he has acted in the same way with the gospels and the writings of the apostles. Even they contain a narrative that is not at all points straightforward; for woven into it are events which in the literal sense did not occur. Nor is the content of the law and commandments to be found in them entirely reasonable.

29 Dionysius of Alexandria
On the Promises as preserved by Eusebius, *Church History VII, 24–5*
[*GCS* 9, 684–700]

24. *Dionysius also composed two books entitled* On the Promises. *This work was occasioned by the teaching of an Egyptian bishop, Nepos. Nepos taught that the promises made to the saints in the divine Scriptures should be given a thoroughly Jewish interpretation and held that there would be a millennium on this earth given over to bodily enjoyment. He thought that he could find support for this notion of his in the Revelation of John and wrote a book on the subject entitled* Refutation of the Allegorists. *It is this work which Dionysius attacks in his books* On the Promises; *in the first book he sets out his own view of the doctrine and in the second he discusses the Revelation of John. He mentions Nepos at the start in the following terms:*

They produce a work by Nepos, on which they place excessive reliance as proving beyond dispute that Christ's kingdom will be on this earth. Now in many other respects I approve and love Nepos – for his faith, for his devotion to work, for his diligent study of the Scriptures and for all his hymn-writing, which is a source of encouragement to many Christians to this day; and I hold him in all the greater respect as one who has already gone to his rest. But truth is the most dear and precious thing of all;* one must give unqualified praise and assent to whatever is rightly said, but examine and correct anything that may seem to be unsoundly written. Were it a case of someone present and propounding his ideas orally, then unwritten discussion, with its use of question and answer, would be sufficient to persuade and convince one's opponents. But it is a different matter when we have to deal with a published work (and, in the eyes of some, a very persuasive one at that) and with teachers who attach no value to the law and the prophets, have abandoned following the gospels and have come to despise the epistles of the apostles and yet hold out great expectation about the teaching o this book as though it were some great and hidden mystery. These are men who prevent our simpler brethren from having any sublime or noble conception either of the glorious and truly divine appearing of our Lord, or of our own resurrection from the dead, our being gathered together to him and our being made like him and who persuade them that it is petty, mortal things, such as we now enjoy, that we should hope for in the kingdom of God. In such circumstances we have no choice but to argue with Nepos our brother as if he were present.

Later on he says:

In the district of Arsinoë† this doctrine had, as you know, been prevalent for a long time, and had caused schisms and defections of entire congregations. When I was there, I called together the elders and teachers of the brethren in the villages (with such of the brethren as wished it also present) and urged them to undertake a public examination of the issue. They produced this book for me like some piece of impregnable defensive armour; so I sat with them for three days running, from dawn till dusk, and tried to correct what was written in it. I was filled with admiration for the brethren – for the steadiness of character, the love of truth, the readiness to follow an argument and the intelligence which they displayed as we dealt systematically and sensibly with the various questions, difficulties

* See Plato, *Republic* 10, 1 (595C); Aristotle, *Nicomachaean Ethics* 1, 4 (1096A).

† About 50 miles south of modern Cairo.

and points of agreement. We refrained from clinging obstinately and persistently to our old beliefs when they could be seen to be in error. At the same time we did not shrink from putting the counter-arguments; we tried our best to master the issues before us and to settle them. If convinced by argument we were not ashamed to change our minds and express our assent to the opposing view. Thus conscientiously, sincerely and with our hearts laid open to God we accepted whatever was demonstrably established by the teachings of the holy Scriptures. In the end the leader and spokes-man of this teaching, whose name was Coracion, solemnly confessed to us in the hearing of all the brethren present that he would no longer hold to this position, and that he would neither discuss, mention nor teach it since he had been fully convinced by the argu-ments against it. Some of the other brethren expressed their pleasure at the conference and at the general spirit of conciliation and agreement.

25. *Later on, he has this to say about the Revelation of John:*

In the past some have rejected the book and done away with it altogether. They criticize it chapter by chapter and allege that it is unintelligible and illogical and its title false.* They say that it is neither John's nor a revelation since it is so heavily veiled with a curtain of unintelligibility; indeed they claim that its author was not only not one of the apostles but was not even one of the faithful or a member of the Church; it was written, they say, by Cerinthus (who organized the Cerinthian sect that bears his name) and he used John's name in order to give respectability to his own forgery. They argue that this was the doctrine he taught – namely that Christ's kingdom would be an earthly one; he dreamed that it would consist of those things which he himself (a thoroughly sensual man devoted to bodily pleasure) hankered after, the satisfaction of the belly and the lower lusts; that is, it would consist of eating and drinking and marrying and (what seemed to him a more reputable way of getting the same thing) feasts, sacrifices and the slaughter of victims. But I personally would not be so bold as to reject the book, since there are many brethren who hold it in high regard; I regard

---

* Epiphanius (*Haereses* 51) describes a heretical group, whom he calls the 'Alogi', who rejected both St John's Gospel and the Apocalypse. Gaius, a presbyter at Rome at the beginning of the third century, whose attack on Cerinthus in terms very similar to those used here is reproduced by Eusebius in *Church History* III, 28, 2, may have been associated with the same group. But the evidence is insufficient to warrant any firm conclusions. Dionysius uses here the technical language of the grammarians (see F. H. Colson, in *JTS* xxv [1924], 365ff.).

my own ability as too limited to make a proper evaluation of it and assume that everything in it has some hidden and higher meaning. Where I fail to understand it, I still presume that there is some deeper meaning in the words; I do not judge them by the measure of my own reasoning powers but, giving full scope to faith, I conclude that they are too lofty for me to grasp. I do not reject what I have not completely comprehended; my awe is the greater because of my failure to comprehend.

He then examines the whole book of Revelation and demonstrates that it cannot be understood in the literal sense. He goes on:

When he has completed practically the whole prophecy, the prophet pronounces a blessing on those who keep it, and indeed on himself: 'Blessed', he says, 'is he who keeps the words of the prophecy of this book and I, John, who saw and heard these things' [Rev. 22: 7–8]. So I certainly will not deny that he was called John and that the book is by someone called John. I further agree that it is the work of a holy and inspired man. But I cannot readily agree that he was the apostle, the son of Zebedee, the brother of James, the author of the 'Gospel according to John' and the catholic epistle. I base my judgement that it is not the same John on the character of the two authors, the nature of the language and on what may be called the structure of the book. Nowhere indeed does the evangelist include his name or announce his identity, either in the gospel or in the epistle.

Later on he makes the same point again:

John never appears either in the first person or in the third person. The author of the Revelation, however, introduces himself right at the beginning: 'The Revelation of Jesus Christ, which he gave him to show to his servants speedily; and he made it known by sending his angel to his servant John, who bore witness to the word of God and to his testimony, even to all that he saw' [Rev. 1: 1–2]. Then he also writes an epistle: 'John to the seven churches that are in Asia; grace to you and peace' [Rev. 1: 4]. But the evangelist did not write his name even at the beginning of the catholic epistle but without any superfluous words began with the mystery of the divine revelation itself: 'That which was from the beginning, that which we have heard, that which we have seen with our eyes' [1 John 1: 1]. (This was the revelation for which the Lord called Peter blessed, saying: 'Blessed art thou, Simon Bar-Jonah, for flesh and blood has not revealed it unto thee, but my heavenly father' [Matt. 16: 17].) Not even in the very short second and third epistles attributed to John is John mentioned by name: they are written anonymously from 'the Elder' [2 John 1; 3 John 1]. By contrast the author of

Revelation did not think it sufficient just to give his name once at the outset of his work. He brings it in yet again: 'I, John, your brother and companion in the tribulation and the kingdom and in the patient endurance of Jesus, was on the island called Patmos on account of the word of God and the testimony of Jesus' [Rev. 1: 9]. And again near the end he says: 'Blessed is he who keeps the words of the prophecy of this book and I, John, who saw and heard these things' [Rev. 22: 7–8].

So one must believe that the man who wrote these things was John, since he himself says so. But what John is not clear. For he does not speak of himself as 'the Lord's beloved disciple' (which we find frequently in the gospel) or as 'the one who leaned on Jesus' breast' or as 'the brother of James' or as 'eye-witness or hearer of the Lord'.* Surely he would have used one of these designations in view of his intention to identify himself clearly. But he did not use any of them; instead he called himself 'our brother and companion', 'a witness of Jesus' and 'one blessed in seeing and hearing the revelations' [Rev. 1: 9; 22: 7–8]. Many people, I think, have taken the same name as John the apostle; because of their love towards him, their admiration and esteem for him and their desire to be loved by the Lord as he was, they were keen to bear the same name too. (In the same way children of Christian parents are often given the name of Paul or Peter.) There is indeed another John mentioned in the Acts of the Apostles, 'surnamed Mark', whom Paul and Barnabas 'took with them' [Acts 12: 25]; and the text has a further reference to him where it says, 'they also had John for their assistant' [Acts 13: 5]. I would not claim that he was the author; the text says he did not even get to Asia with them, but 'when Paul and his company set sail from Paphos and came to Perga in Pamphylia, John left them and returned to Jerusalem' [Acts 13: 13]. I think it was somebody else in Asia, since there is a record of two tombs at Ephesus each belonging to a John.

Moreover the ideas, the language and the arrangement of the two books immediately suggest different authors. The gospel and the epistle go together. They start in similar ways. One begins, 'In the beginning was the word', the other, 'That which was from the beginning' [John 1: 1; 1 John 1: 1]; the one has, 'The word became flesh and dwelt among us and we beheld his glory, glory as of the only-begotten from the Father', and the other says the same thing in a slightly different form: 'That which we have heard, that which

* John 13: 23; 19: 26; 20: 2; 21: 20; 13: 25; 21: 20; the last two phrases do not occur in the gospel or the epistles but see Matt. 4: 21, Mark 1: 19; John 21: 2 and 1 John 1: 1.

we have seen with our eyes, that which we beheld, and our hands handled, concerning the word of life; and the life was manifested' [John 1: 14; 1 John 1: 1–2]. He begins in this way, since he is dealing, as he makes clear later on, with those who allege that the Lord did not come in the flesh. So he is careful to go on: 'And it is that which we have seen, to which we bear witness and which we declare to you, the eternal life which was with the Father and which was manifested to us; that which we have seen and heard we declare to you' [1 John 1: 2–3]. He is consistent with himself, sticking closely to his expressed intentions. He makes use of the same headings and terms throughout. I will mention some of them briefly; the attentive reader will find many examples in both books of 'life' and 'light' driving away darkness, and frequent occurrences of 'truth', 'grace', 'joy', 'the Lord's flesh and blood', 'judgement', 'forgiveness of sins', 'God's love towards us', 'the commandment that we should love one another' and our duty 'to keep all the commandments'; similarly there is 'the conviction of the world, of the Devil and of antichrist', 'the promise of the Holy Spirit', and 'adoption as sons of God'; 'faith' is repeatedly required of us; 'the Father and the Son' keep recurring.* To sum up there can be no doubt that anyone who studies the characteristics of the gospel and the epistle as a whole will see at once that they have precisely the same feel to them. But the Revelation is totally different and alien in these respects; it has no connection or affinity with them on any of these points; it has, one can almost say, hardly a syllable in common with them. The epistle (let alone the gospel) makes no mention or hint of the Revelation, nor the Revelation of the epistle. Yet Paul in his epistles does refer to his revelations, even though he never wrote them down on their own [see 2 Cor. 12: 1–4].

A difference between the gospel and the epistle on the one hand and Revelation on the other can also be detected on the basis of style. The former are not only faultless in their use of the Greek language but show great elegance in their use of words, their method of reasoning and the manner of their presentation. There is no trace in them of barbarous words, of faulty construction or of idiosyncrasies of any kind. The author, it would seem, had received from the Lord the gift of the word in both its forms – that of knowledge and that of expression. The other writer certainly saw revelations and received knowledge and prophecy; that I do not deny. But I observe the incorrect Greek of his style and language, which involve bar-

* Most of the terms cited here are to be found frequently in the gospel and the first epistle. 'Adoption', however, is exclusively Pauline, even though sonship is a fundamental Johannine theme.

barous peculiarities and sometimes even faulty constructions. There is no need to go into detail about these now. I would not like anyone to think I had said this in order to make fun of him; my only aim is to establish the dissimilarity of the writings.

30   Theodore of Mopsuestia
Commentary on Galatians 4: 24
[Ed. H. B. Swete, *Minor Epistles of St Paul* (Cambridge, 1880-2), I, 73–9]

These things are said allegorically.

There are some people who make it their business to pervert the meaning of the divine Scriptures and to thwart whatever is to be found there. They invent foolish tales of their own and give to their nonsense the name of 'allegory'. By using the apostle's word, they imagine that they have found a way to undermine the meaning of everything in Scripture – they keep on using the apostle's expression 'allegorical'. They do not realize what a difference there is between their use of the term and the apostle's use of it here. For the apostle does not destroy history; he does not get rid of what has already happened. He sets things out as they happened in the past and uses the history of what happened in support of his own purpose – as when he says, 'it corresponds to the Jerusalem that now is' and 'as then the one who was born according to the flesh persecuted the one who was born according to the spirit'. This shows that he acknowledged the history to be primary. Otherwise he would not have described the things that happened in relation to Hagar as corresponding to 'the Jerusalem that now is' – something, that is to say, which he acknowledges to be a present reality. And he would not have said 'as' except with reference to something he believed to exist; for the use of the word 'as' clearly implies a comparison, and one cannot draw a comparison where the terms of the comparison do not really exist. And by the addition of the word 'then' he declares himself uncertain of the length of time involved; but the whole question of time would be irrelevant, if it never happened.

That is how the apostle speaks. But they act in a totally opposite way; their wish is to deny any difference between the whole of the history recorded in divine Scripture and dreams that occur at night. Adam, they say, is not Adam – this being a place where they are especially prone to interpret divine Scripture in a spiritual way (spiritual interpretation is what they like to have their nonsense called) – paradise is not paradise and the serpent is not a serpent. What I would like to say in reply to them is that once they start removing bits of history they will be left without any history at all. In that case, they must tell us how they will be in a position to say who was the first man to be created or how man became disobedient or how the sentence of death was introduced. If it is from the Scriptures that they have learnt their answers to these questions, it follows that their talk of 'allegory' is obvious nonsense, because it is clearly irrelevant at all these points. If on the other hand they are right and what is written is not a record of things that happened but is a pointer to some other profound truth in need of interpretation – some spiritual truth it may be, to use the phrase they like, which they have grasped through being such spiritual people themselves – then they must tell us by what means they have acquired these notions. How can they assert these notions, as if they were things they had learnt from the teaching of divine Scripture?

I pass over in silence for the moment the fact that if this were the case, one would be unable to see any reason for the events concerning Christ. The apostle says that he revoked the disobedience of Adam and did away with the sentence of death. What are these things that are said to have happened in the past and where did they happen, if (as they say) the historical account of them does not mean that but means something else? What is to be made of the apostolic saying, 'I am afraid that as the serpent seduced Eve' [2 Cor. 11:3], if there was no serpent, no Eve, and no seduction by him at all? Many other passages too show clearly that the apostle always treated the history of the ancients as something real.

So in this passage he is at pains to prove his point on the basis of things that had happened and which were acknowledged by the Jews. That was his intention all along. And the substance of that intention was to show the superiority of the things of Christ to those of the law and the far greater dignity of the righteousness we have compared to that of the law. So he says there are two testaments, one given through Moses and the other through Christ. What he calls the testament in Christ is the resurrection Christ promised to us all when he was the first to rise from the dead. We have dealt with this point more explicitly in our commentary on the Epistle to the Hebrews.* The things that were given by Moses had the intention of enabling those who received the law to live under it

* The surviving fragments of this commentary have been edited by K. Staab, *Pauluskommentare aus der griechischen Kirche* (Münster, 1933), pp. 200–12.

and to receive the righteousness that comes from it. (That was why they came out of Egypt and were established in a distant place where they could be free from all intermingling with other nations and could keep the law given to them with appropriate care.) In a similar way the things concerning Christ have the intention and goal of doing away with death, of bringing about the resurrection of all men who have lived at any time, of enabling them to live the life of an immortal and, greatest of all, of making it impossible for them to sin any more by virtue of that grace of the Spirit which is in them and by which we will be kept safe from every kind of sin. This is true and complete justification. He appropriately gave them both the same name 'testament'; for the things taught by the law were the very things put into practice by grace, namely love of God and neighbour. These are the commands that the law told us to keep, clearly teaching that we ought not to sin in any way. Grace brings it to practical fulfilment by means of the resurrection and of that immortality which will then be ours through the Spirit by whom we will then be controlled and so enabled not to sin at all.

So there is justification both in the law and also with Christ. With the law it is achieved by anyone who is able with much effort and sweat to achieve it. It is very hard, or to speak more accurately, impossible – if one chooses to judge the matter with full legal exactitude. For it is impossible for any living man to be wholly free of sin. That can be acquired only by grace; for we shall be enabled not to sin any more at that future time when all effort having been laid aside we will receive the justification that comes from Christ.

He mentions Hagar and Sarah. One of them had a child in the ordinary course of nature while the other was unable to bear a child but had Isaac by grace; and of the two the child born by way of grace turned out to be much the more highly esteemed. He compares them in order to show that now too the justification by Christ is far better than the other, because it is acquired by grace. He relates the one who had a child in the course of nature to the justification which is according to the law and makes the one who had a child against all hope correspond to that justification which is according to grace. This is because a life according to law is appropriate to the present, whereas for those who have once risen again and been made free of corruption, circumcision and the offering of sacrifices, not to mention the observation of special days, are all irrelevant.

There are things that happen in the course of nature – for example the entry into this life by birth – where life according to the law does seem still to have a place. But there is also a birth of grace, by which everyone rises again and is born into a future life in which the justification of Christ is fully implemented. So to represent the justification according to the law he has taken the one who bore a child in the order of nature, since the law has a role in controlling those who are born in this life, born according to the order of nature. To represent the justification according to Christ, he has taken the one who bore a child by grace, since this is fulfilled in those who are seen to have risen again at some time and who by grace look forward to that second birth beyond all hope.

This then is why he said: 'These things are said allegorically'. By allegory he means the comparison which can be made between things which have happened in the past and things which are the case now.

31 Augustine
On Christian Doctrine III, i, 1 – v, 9
[*CCL* 32, 77–83]

1. The godfearing man earnestly seeks out the will of God in the holy Scriptures. If he is to have no love of controversy, he needs to be tamed by piety. He must also be well equipped with linguistic knowledge, so that he does not get stuck on unknown words and phrases; he must be similarly equipped with knowledge on a number of basic subjects, so that he does not fail to grasp the point or significance of illustrative material. He also needs the help of reliable texts, which are produced by skilled and careful correction. With these preparations he is ready to turn to the discussion and solution of the ambiguities of Scripture. To avoid his being deceived by ambiguous expressions, we will provide such instruction as we can. It may be that people of exceptional ability or greater insight will scorn the advice we intend to give as too childish. Nevertheless, as I was about to say, we will provide such instruction as we can for the man who is disposed to benefit from our instruction.

The first thing for him to recognize is that an ambiguity in Scripture may be inherent either in the straightforward meaning of the words or in their applied meaning (a distinction we dealt with in Book II).

2. If the straightforward meaning of the words gives an uncertain sense, the first thing to consider is whether we have punctuated the passage wrongly or mispronounced it in some way. If after careful consideration one is led to the conclusion that it is still not possible

to be sure how the passage should be punctuated or how it should be pronounced, then one should consult the rule of faith which is derived from clearer passages of Scripture and from the authority of the Church. (There is no need to add to what we said on that subject in Book I.) If both or, if it is a matter of more than two, all the possible renderings give a sense which is in harmony with faith, one is left with the need to consult the context of the passage so that on a basis of the passages which surround the one in question we can judge which of the various possible senses we ought to adopt and which is capable of being woven into the sense of the context.

3. Take some examples. 'In the beginning was the Word, and the Word was God, and God was. The Word – that was in the beginning with God' [John 1: 1–2]. That is a heretical punctuation of the passage; it refuses to acknowledge the Word to be God. This is to be refuted by the rule of faith, which lays down in advance for us the equality of the Trinity so that we say: 'And God was the Word. That was in the beginning with God.'

4. But in the writings of the apostle there is a case where neither way of punctuating a doubtful passage conflicts with faith and the issue has therefore to be decided by the context of the passage alone. 'Which I shall choose, I cannot tell. I feel the strong pull of the two. I have a desire to depart and be with Christ, for that is far better. But to remain in the flesh is necessary on your account [Phil. 1: 23–4].' It is not clear whether it is, 'Of the two I have a desire ...' or 'I feel the strong pull of the two. I have a desire to depart and be with Christ.' But since it goes on 'for that is far better' it is evident that he is speaking of himself as having a desire for the thing that is far better; thus while he feels the strong pull of the two, he has a desire for one of them and in the case of the other experiences a necessity – namely a desire to be with Christ but a necessity to remain in the flesh. This ambiguity therefore is settled by the one word which stands immediately following – the word 'for'. (The translators who have deleted the particle have been misled by the notion that he not only felt the strong pull of the two but also had a desire for the two.) So the passage should be punctuated as follows: 'Which I shall choose I cannot tell. I feel the strong pull of the two. I have a desire to depart and be with Christ.' Then, as if he were being asked why he has a preferential desire for this alternative, he says: 'for that is far better'. Why then does he feel the strong pull of the two? Because there is a necessity to remain, which he goes on to say in this way: 'To remain in the flesh is necessary on your account'.

5. But where the ambiguity cannot be settled either by the ruling of faith or by the context of the passage itself, there is no objection

to punctuating the passage in any of the possible ways. In the epistle to the Corinthians, for example, there is the passage: 'Since we have these promises, beloved, let us cleanse ourselves from every defilement in flesh and in spirit, making holiness perfect in the fear of God. Be open to us. We have wronged no-one' [2 Cor. 7: 1–2]. It is not clear whether it should read, 'let us cleanse ourselves from every defilement in flesh and in spirit' (in the sense of 'to be holy in body and spirit' [1 Cor. 7: 34]) or 'let us cleanse ourselves from every defilement in flesh' – new sentence – 'And in spirit making holiness perfect in the fear of God, be open to us.' Doubtful cases of punctuating sentences of this kind are open to the reader to decide for himself.

6. What we have said about passages where the punctuation is in doubt applies equally to cases where it is the pronunciation that is in doubt. These cases too, unless it is just a case of the reader being excessively careless, are to be checked by the rule of faith and by coherence with the preceding or following passage; and if neither of these tests leads to a settlement of the issue, the doubt will remain but no blame will attach to the reader however he pronounces the passage.

Unless the faith by which we believe that God will not bring any charge against his elect and that Christ will not condemn his elect restrained us, it would be possible to read the passage 'Who shall bring any charge against God's elect?' in such a way that it appears to be a question to which the words that follow are a reply: 'God who justifies'; and similarly, 'Who is to condemn?' would appear to be a question to which 'Christ Jesus who died' is the reply [Rom. 8: 33–4]. But it would be utterly outrageous to believe that; so the passage must be read in such a way that it has an open question (*percontatio*) followed by a specific question (*interrogatio*). The ancients describe the difference between these two by saying that the former can have many different answers, whereas the latter can only be answered yes or no. The passage will then read like this: First comes the open question, 'Who shall bring any charge against God's elect?'; what follows must be pronounced with an interrogative note: 'God who justifies?' – implying the answer No. Then another open question: 'Who is to condemn?', and again in the interrogative, 'Christ Jesus who died, who rose again, who is at the right hand of God, who indeed intercedes for us?', with the implied answer No throughout.

But in the passage which says, 'What shall we say, then? That the Gentiles who did not pursue righteousness have attained it', it is different [Rom. 9: 30]. Unless 'that the Gentiles who did not pursue righteousness have attained it' is an answer following on the open question 'What shall we say, then?', the sequence of the passage does not hold together.

An example of a passage which can be read either way is the one where Nathanael says: 'Out of Nazareth something good can come?' [John 1: 46]. It could be an affirmation with the interrogation applying only to 'out of Nazareth' or the whole thing could be a question with a note of uncertainty. I do not see how this can be decided. Neither meaning is a hindrance to faith.

7. Then there are also ambiguities where there is doubt about the sound to be given to particular syllables; those of course are also a matter of pronunciation. There is a text: 'My *os* is not hidden from thee, which thou didst make in secret' [Ps. 139: 15]. It is not obvious to the reader whether he should pronounce *os* with a short vowel or a long one. If he makes it short it will be understood as the singular of *ossa* (a bone); whereas if he makes it long it will be understood as the singular of *ora* (a mouth). Such cases are decided by looking at the earlier language. The Greek has *ostoun* (bone) and not *stoma* (mouth). Thus the popular style of speech is frequently more serviceable than a correct literary style in making clear the meaning of something. Indeed I would rather the slang form were used, 'My *ossum* is not hidden from thee', than the sense be made less clear for the sake of better Latin.

Sometimes the correct pronunciation of a syllable is determined by another word nearby which is of identical meaning. There is a passage of the apostle's; '*Praedico* you, as I warned (*praedixi*) you before that they who do such things shall not inherit the Kingdom of God' [Gal. 5: 21]. If he had said simply '*Praedico* you' and had not gone on to say 'as I warned (*praedixi*) you before', it would have been impossible, without reference back to a manuscript of the earlier language, to know whether the middle syllable of *praedico* should be long or short. But as it is it is clear that it must be long as he does not say 'as I preached (*praedicavi*) to you' but 'as I warned (*praedixi*) you'.

8. Ambiguities which are not a matter of punctuation or pronunciation need to be dealt with similarly. There is a passage in the epistle to the Thessalonians: 'Consequently we have cheered, brethren, over you' [1 Thess. 3: 7]. It is not clear whether 'brethren' is in the vocative or the accusative case. Neither is contrary to faith, but in Greek the two cases are not the same and an inspection of the Greek enables one to affirm that it is definitely a vocative: 'O brethren'. If the translator had chosen to say, 'Consequently we have been of good cheer, brethren, over you', he would have kept

less closely to the wording but there would have been less doubt about the meaning. Or the word 'ours' could have been added; then no one would have been in any doubt that it was a vocative on hearing: 'Consequently we have cheered, brethren ours, over you'. But such additions are a dangerous liberty to take. There is an instance in the Epistle to the Corinthians where the apostle says: 'I die daily, by my pride in you, brethren, which I have in Christ Jesus' [1 Cor. 15: 31]. One translator says, 'I die daily, I swear it by my pride in you', since the Greek leaves no doubt than an oath is being uttered.

So it is very rare and very difficult to find an ambiguity in the straightforward meaning of the words, as far as the books of divine Scripture are concerned, which cannot be settled either by the context of the passage which reveals the author's intention, or by a comparison of the different translations or by reference to the original language.

9. Ambiguities in the applied meanings of words, which we must discuss next, call for no small care and attention. To begin with, one must avoid taking a figurative expression literally. The saying of the apostle, 'the letter kills, but the spirit gives life' [2 Cor. 3: 6], is relevant here. For when something that was spoken figuratively is taken as if it had been spoken literally, it is being grasped at the level of flesh. And nothing can be more appropriately described as the death of the soul than when that very part of it in which it excels the beasts, namely the intelligence, is subordinated to the flesh by following the letter. For the follower of the letter treats words with an applied meaning as if they had their straightforward meaning and fails to move on from what the word means in its straightforward sense to a further meaning. For example, if he hears the word 'sabbath', he understands simply one day in seven, which comes round with regular repetition; and when he hears the word 'sacrifice', he does not get beyond the thought of what regularly happens to animal victims and the fruits of the earth. This really is a terrible slavery of the soul – this taking of symbols for reality, this inability to raise the eyes of the mind beyond the physical creation and take in the eternal light.

7 Church

The lines on which the Latin doctrines of the Church and sacraments developed were largely determined by controversy, much of it centered in North Africa. In the first two passages of this section we find two African bishops, Cyprian in the middle of the third century and Augustine early in the fifth, grappling with the questions of the identity and limits of the Catholic Church.

The election of Cornelius as bishop of Rome in A.D. 251 was disputed, and the impeccably orthodox but rigorist Novatian was consecrated as a rival bishop. For Cyprian the issue was clear-cut. The orthodoxy of Novatian's teaching was irrelevant. He had broken with the one and only Church and therefore had no part in her. In consequence, Novatianist baptism was worthless, and persons baptized as Novatianists who wished to join the Catholic Church must be rebaptized.

The Roman Church took the opposite view, holding that those who had received schismatical, as opposed to heretical, baptism did not need to be rebaptized if they became reconciled to the Catholic Church. When the Donatist schism broke out in North Africa in the third century, the Donatist party held to Cyprian's view of the matter, while the Catholic party adopted the Roman practice. Augustine's work *On Baptism* is directed against the Donatists. He could not hope to convince his opponents unless he could enlist the authority of Cyprian on his side. It is for that reason that his argument circles round the same texts of Scripture as Cyprian had used. Whereas for Cyprian the boundary between those who are 'outside' and those who are 'inside' coincides simply with the bounds of the visible Church, Augustine distinguishes the visible Church from the 'elect' whose number and limits are known only to the predestinating foreknowledge of God.

The note of controversy is quite absent from the Greek discussion of the Church. The passage from Cyril of Jerusalem comes, like the passage on the Holy Spirit (see pp. 81–4), from his lectures to candidates for baptism. The extract from Cyril of Alexandria is notable for the way in which Cyril's teaching on the Church is integrated with his trinitarian, Christological, soteriological and sacramental teaching.

32 Cyprian
Letter 69, 1–5
(*CSEL* 3, 749–54]

Cyprian to his son, Magnus, greeting:

1. My dear son, you show your customary scrupulous care in consulting so inferior a person as myself about the question whether, along with other heretics, those who come over from Novatian after receiving his profane washing ought to be baptized and sanctified within the catholic Church with the Church's one true and lawful baptism. On the basis of the evidence of such faith as I have and of the holiness and truth of the divine Scriptures, I reply that no heretic or schismatic whatsoever has any power or rights at all. There is therefore no reason or possibility of Novatian's being exempted from being classified among the adversaries and antichrists, since he like the others stands outside the Church and acts against the peace and love of Christ. When our Lord Jesus Christ declared in his gospel that those who were not with him were his enemies he did not specify any particular form of heresy; his statement was universal that *all* who were not with him and who did not gather his flock with him but scattered it were his adversaries: 'He who is not with me is against me; he who does not gather with me scatters' [Luke 11: 23]. So also the blessed apostle John did not specify any particular form of heresy or schism; all without exception who had gone out from the Church and who were acting against the Church he called antichrists: 'You have heard that antichrist is coming, but now many antichrists have come into being. Therefore we know that it is the last hour. They went out from us but they were not of us. If they had been of us, they would have continued with us' [1 John 2: 18–19]. It is therefore plain that in every case where someone has clearly withdrawn from the love and the unity of the Church that person is an adversary of the Lord and antichrist. Indeed the Lord makes this point in his gospel: 'If he refuses to take notice even of the Church, let him be to you as a gentile and a tax-collector' [Matt. 18: 17]. If those who refuse to take notice of the Church are to be regarded as gentiles and tax-collectors, there is obviously a far greater obligation to classify as gentiles and tax-collectors those who show themselves to be rebels and enemies by

devising false altars, illegal priesthoods, sacrilegious sacrifices and counterfeit titles. It must be so, when the Lord himself has adjudged those who have committed the lesser sin of merely refusing to take notice of the Church to be gentiles and tax-collectors.

2. That the Church is one is declared by the Holy Spirit in the Song of Songs, speaking in the person of Christ: 'My dove, my perfect one, is one; she is the only one of her mother, the chosen one of her who bore her' [Song of Songs 6: 9]. He also says of her: 'A locked garden is my sister, my bride; a sealed fountain, a well of living water' [Song of Songs 4: 12]. If then the bride of Christ, which is the Church, is a locked garden, something locked cannot possibly be open to the stranger or the profane; if it is a sealed fountain, the man who is outside and without access to the fountain cannot either drink from it or be sealed there; and if there is only one well of living water, namely that which is inside, the man outside cannot receive the life or sanctification from that water which only those inside are allowed to drink or to use in any way. Peter also shows that the Church is one and that only those who are in the Church can be baptized: 'In the days of Noah a few, that is eight, persons were saved by water; in a similar way baptism now saves you' [1 Pet. 3: 20–1]. This passage shows that the one ark of Noah is a type of the one Church. If it had been possible for anyone who was not in the ark of Noah to be saved in that baptism by which the world was expiated and purified, then it would also be possible now for a person to receive life through baptism when he is not in the Church, to which alone baptism has been granted. Paul makes this same point even clearer and more explicit in the Epistle to the Ephesians: 'Christ loved the Church and gave himself up for her, that he might sanctify and cleanse her by the washing of water' [Eph. 5: 25–6]. If then there is only one Church which is loved by Christ and it alone is cleansed by his washing, how can those who are not in the Church be either loved by Christ or cleansed and purified by his washing?

3. Therefore since the Church alone has the living water and the power of baptizing and cleansing men, anyone who asserts that a man can be baptized and sanctified with Novatian, will have first to demonstrate that Novatian is in the Church or presides over the Church. Now the Church is one, and what is one cannot be both inside and outside. If it is with Novatian, it was not with Cornelius. If it was with Cornelius, who was made Bishop Fabian's successor by lawful ordination and to whom the Lord gave not only the honour of priesthood but also the glory of martyrdom, then Novatian is not in the Church; nor can he be reckoned to be a bishop, seeing

that his office originated with himself and that in defiance o
evangelical and apostolic tradition he was not in succession to anyone else. One who was not ordained in the Church cannot conceivably have or maintain any authority over the Church.

4. The testimony of divine Scripture shows that the Church
cannot be outside, that it cannot be split or divided against itself,
but that it possesses the unity of a single indivisible house. Of the
passover lamb (which signifies Christ) it is written: 'In one house
shall it be eaten; you shall not take any of the flesh outside the
house' [Exod. 12: 46]. We see the same thing in the command
given to Rahab who is a type of the Church: 'You shall gather your
father and your mother and your brothers and all your father's
household to you in your house; and any who goes outside the door
of your house, his blood will be on his own head' [Josh. 2: 18–19].
In this figurative event it is shown that those who are to live and to
escape the destruction of the world must be gathered into one house,
namely the Church; and if anyone goes outside from that gathering,
in other words if anyone even though he has received grace in the
Church later goes away and leaves the Church, his blood will be
on his own head: in other words he will have only himself to blame
for his destruction. Paul makes this clear by enjoining that a heretic
is to be shunned as perverse, a sinner and self-condemned. He is
speaking of the man whose blood is to be on his own head, the man
who has not been expelled by the bishop but who has deserted the
Church of his own free choice, the man who for his heretical presumption stands self-condemned.

5. The Lord shows us that this unity has a divine basis by his
saying: 'I and the Father are one' [John 10: 30]. It is to this unity
that he relates his Church in the saying: 'There will be one flock
and one shepherd' [John 10: 16]. If there is one flock, how can
someone be counted as belonging to the flock when he is not one
of the flock? Or how can he be regarded as a shepherd of the flock,
when the true shepherd is still there presiding in the Church of
God on the basis of an ordination in succession and he on the other
hand is in succession to no one but originates with himself? Thereby
he makes himself a stranger and profane, an enemy of the peace of
the Lord and of the unity of God, not dwelling in the house of God,
that is the Church, where only those who are in harmony and of
one mind can dwell. In the Psalms the Holy Spirit says: 'God who
makes those who are of one mind dwell together in a house' [Ps.
68: 6].

There is a final demonstration that it is firm and unbreakable
mutual love that maintains this Christian unity of mind, in the

dominical sacrifices themselves. The Lord called bread his body (bread which is made up of a union of many grains), thus showing that we, his people, whom it signified, have been made a unity. Similarly he called wine his blood (wine which is made by gathering together what has been pressed out from a multitude of grapes), thus indicating that we, his flock, are bound together by the mingling of vast numbers united into one. If Novatian really is united to this bread of the Lord, and if he is also mingled in the cup of Christ, then there is a possibility that he will have the grace of the one baptism of the Church as well – but it must first be clearly established that he maintains the unity of the Church.

33 Augustine
On Baptism V, xxvii, 38 – xxviii, 39
[*CSEL* 51, 293–7]

38. The description of the Church in the Song of Songs – 'A locked garden is my sister, my bride; a sealed fountain, a well of living water, an orchard with choice fruits' [Song of Songs 4: 12–13] – must be interpreted as referring to the holy and the righteous; these words cannot refer to the greedy or to the fraudulent, to robbers or usurers, to drunkards or to the envious. These men admittedly share the same baptism with the righteous, but they do not share the same love with them. All this, as I have often said before, is to be found fully set out in the letters of Cyprian himself; it is from these that we have learned it and from these that we teach it. I should like to be told how these people, whom Cyprian describes as having renounced the world in word alone and not in deed and yet being within, have got into the locked garden and the sealed fountain. If they too are there, they too must be the bride of Christ. But is this what the one without spot or wrinkle is really like? Is the beautiful dove besmirched in some of her members [see Eph. 5: 27; Song of Songs 2: 14]? Or are they the thorns in the midst of which she is like a lily, as the same song declares [Song of Songs 2: 2]? She is a closed garden and a sealed fountain precisely in so far as she is a lily – namely in the persons of those righteous people who are Jews secretly by circumcision of the heart [see Rom. 2: 29] (for 'all the beauty of the king's daughter is within' [Ps. 45: 12]), who moreover constitute the fixed number of the saints predestined before the foundation of the world. The multitude of the thorns, whether their separation be concealed or open, lies outside, beyond this number.

'I have proclaimed and spoken', he says, 'they are multiplied beyond number' [Ps. 40: 5]. It is this number of the righteous, those called according to his will [Rom. 8: 28] (and referred to in the text: 'The Lord knows those who are his' [2 Tim. 2: 19]) who are the locked garden, the sealed fountain, the well of living water, the orchard of choice fruits.

Of this number some live spiritual lives and follow the supreme path of love; if anyone is overtaken in a fault, they instruct him in a spirit of gentleness and look to themselves lest they also be tempted; and if they themselves happen to be overtaken in a fault, that disposition of love receives a set-back but is not extinguished; it rises up, burns strongly once again and resumes its original course. They have learnt to say: 'My soul became drowsy through weariness; strengthen me in your words' [Ps. 119: 28]. And if there is anything where their knowledge is amiss, God will reveal it to those who remain in the burning ardour of love and do not break the bond of peace.

Then there are some who are still living their lives at the carnal or natural level. They vigorously pursue their own advancement. So that in time they may become ready for the food suited to spiritual men, they are nourished on the milk of the holy mysteries. Things which are obviously corrupt practices even in the eyes of people at large they avoid by reason of their fear of God. They take great care and trouble to diminish by degrees their love of earthly and temporal things. They give careful study to the rule of faith and hold firmly to it. If they do deviate from it, they are soon put right by the authority of what is catholic; but because of their carnal understanding they are liable to find all sorts of extraordinary ideas in its words.

Then there are yet others in that number who are still living evil lives, and as yet still belong to heretical bodies or even to gentile superstitions. But in their case too, 'God knows those who are his'. For in that ineffable foreknowledge of God, there are many who seem to be outside who are really inside, and many who seem to be inside who are really outside.

All these people – those, if I may so put it, who are inwardly and secretly within – go to make up the locked garden, the sealed fountain, the well of living water, the orchard of choice fruits. And of the gifts which heaven bestows on them some are theirs exclusively (such as unceasing love in this age and in the age to come life eternal) while others are shared with evil and wicked men (including, among all the other gifts, the holy mysteries).

39. The next point which we must consider – the ark built and

captained by Noah – will now be even easier and more straight-forward to deal with. Peter says: 'In Noah's ark a few, that is eight persons, were saved by water. Baptism now saves you in a similar way, not as a removal of dirt from the body but as the appeal of a good conscience' [1 Pet. 3: 20–1]. So then those who have been baptized but whose renunciation of the world is a matter of words only and not of deeds may appear outwardly to men to be within the fold of catholic unity, but how can they belong to the mystery of the ark of which Peter speaks when they lack 'the appeal of a good conscience'? How can those who make a false use of holy baptism and continue to the very end of their lives in profligate and dissolute ways be 'saved by water', even though they may seem to be within? How, too, can those whom Cyprian himself records as having been simply admitted into the Church with the baptism that they had received among the heretics not be 'saved by water'? It is the same unity of the ark that saves them and there no one is saved except by water. For Cyprian himself says: 'The Lord in his mercy is able to grant forgiveness to those who were simply received into the Church and then died in the Church and not to hold them back from the gifts that belong to his Church.'* If they are not 'by water', how can they be 'in the ark'? If they are not 'in the ark', how can they be 'in the Church'? So if they are in the Church, they must be in the ark and if they are in the ark, they must be by water.

It must therefore be the case that some of those who are baptized outside are by the foreknowledge of God classed as really having been baptized inside; for it is here that the water has begun to be of saving help to them. (After all one cannot speak of their being saved in the ark without their being saved by water.) And on the other hand some of those who looked as if they had been baptized inside are by that same foreknowledge of God classed as really having been baptized outside. Those who misuse baptism die by water and that can only happen to someone who is outside the ark.

It is then perfectly clear that when we speak of people being 'inside' or 'outside' the Church, we need to think of it as a matter of the heart and not of the body. Everyone who is 'inside' in heart is saved in the unity of the ark by the same water, by which everyone who is 'outside' in heart (whether or not he is 'outside' in body) perishes as an enemy of that unity. It is not some different water but the same water which saves those who are in the ark and destroys

---

* Cyprian, *Letter* 73, 23. Augustine establishes as a rule what Cyprian admitted as an exception.

those who are outside it; in the same way it is not some other baptism but the same baptism by which the good catholic is saved and the bad catholic or the heretic perishes.

34 Cyril of Jerusalem
Catechetical lecture 18, 22–7
[Ed. J. Rupp (Munich, 1860), pp. 324–30]
Translation of W. Telfer in *LCC* 4, 185–8: revised

22. The faith we profess contains in due order the words 'and in one baptism of repentance for the remission of sins, and in one holy catholic Church, and in the resurrection of the flesh, and in eternal life'. I dealt with baptism and repentance in my opening lectures. And I have dealt with 'and in the resurrection of the flesh' in what I have just been saying about the resurrection of the dead. Now we must deal with the rest; first with 'and in one holy catholic Church'. It is a subject about which there is a great deal to say, but I shall speak of it quite briefly.

23. The Church, then, is called catholic because it is spread through the whole world, from one end of the earth to the other, and because it teaches fully (*katholikōs*) and without any omission every doctrine which ought to be brought to men's knowledge, concerning things visible and invisible, in heaven and on earth. It is called catholic also because it brings into religious obedience every sort of men, rulers and ruled, learned and simple, and because it brings a universal (*katholikōs*) remedy and cure to every kind of sin whether perpetrated by soul or body, and possesses within it every form of virtue that is named, whether it expresses itself in deeds or words or in spiritual graces of every description.

24. The Church is well named *Ekklesia* because it calls everyone out (*ekkaleisthai*) and assembles them together, according as, in the book Leviticus, the Lord says, 'And assemble thou (*ekklesiason*) all the congregation to the doors of the tabernacle of witness' [Lev. 8: 3]. We should note that this is the first time that this word for 'assemble' (*ekklesiason*) occurs in Scripture, at the point where the Lord places Aaron in the office of high priest. In Deuteronomy, also, God says to Moses, 'Assemble to me the people, and I will make them hear my words, that they may learn to fear me' [Deut. 4: 10]. The word *Ekklesia* is recalled again in the passage about the tables of the Law, 'And on them was written according to all the words which the Lord spake with you in the mount out of the midst of the

fire on the day of the assembly (*ekklesia*)' [Deut. 9: 10]; which is the same thing as saying, in plainer words, 'on the day when God called you and gathered you together'. And the psalmist says, 'I will give thee thanks in the great assembly: I will praise thee among much people' [Ps. 35: 18].

25. So, then, in the old dispensation, the psalmist sang, 'Bless ye God in the assembly, even the Lord, from the fountains of Israel' [Ps. 68: 26]. But since then the Jews have fallen out of favour because of their conspiring against the Lord, and the Saviour has built up from among the gentiles a second assembly or Church, our holy Christian Church, and spoke of it to Peter, saying 'And upon this rock I will build my Church, and the gates of hell shall not prevail against it' [Matt. 16: 18].

David prophesied clearly concerning the two churches, of the first, that it is cast off, 'I have hated the church of the evil doers' [Ps. 26: 5]; and in the same psalm of the second church that is abuilding, 'Lord, I have loved the beauty of thine house' [Ps. 26: 8]; and straightaway after, 'In the churches, will I bless thee, O Lord' [Ps. 26: 12]. For since the single church that was in Judaea was cast off, henceforth the churches of Christ abound in all the world. These are they of which it is said in the Psalms, 'Sing unto the Lord a new song, and his praise in the church of the saints' [Ps. 149: 1]. In agreement with these passages is that where the prophet said to the Jews, 'I have no pleasure in you, saith the Lord of hosts', and immediately afterwards, 'For from the rising of the sun even unto the going down of the same, my name shall be great among the gentiles' [Mal. 1: 10–11]. It is of this holy Catholic Church that Paul writes to Timothy, 'that you may know how you ought to behave in the house of God, which is the church of the living God, the pillar and ground of the truth' [1 Tim. 3: 15].

26. Now the word *Ekklesia* has different applications, as when it is used in Scripture of the crowd that filled the theatre at Ephesus, saying, 'And when he had thus spoken, he dismissed the assembly' [Acts 19: 41], or when one applies it, quite properly and correctly, to heretical gatherings since there is a 'church of the evil doers', I mean the conventicles of the Marcionites, Manichees and others. And because of this variety of use, there has been given to you the article of faith 'and in one holy Catholic Church', so that you should flee their wretched gatherings, and ever keep within the holy Catholic Church in which you are regenerate. Should you ever be staying in some strange town, do not just ask, 'Where is the Lord's house (*kyriakon*)?', seeing that all those sects of the ungodly would have their dens called Lord's houses. And do not be content to ask,

'Where is the church (*ekklesia*)?', but say 'Where is the Catholic Church?' For that is the unequivocal name of this holy Church and mother of us all. She is the bride of our Lord Jesus Christ, the only-begotten Son of God (as it is written, 'As Christ also loved the Church, and gave himself for it ...' and so on) [Eph. 5: 25–7]. She also presents the form and image of 'Jerusalem which is above' which 'is free and the mother of us all', that once was barren, but now has many children [Gal. 4: 26–7].

27. For after the rejection of the first church, then (as Paul says) in the second and Catholic Church, 'God has set first apostles, second prophets, third teachers, after that miracles, then gifts of healings, helps, governments, diversities of tongues' [1 Cor. 12: 28]; yes, and every sort of virtue, such as wisdom and understanding, moderation and righteousness, generosity and kindness, and patience that will not break down under persecution. 'By the armour of righteousness on the right hand and on the left, by honour and dishonour' [2 Cor. 6: 7–8], this Church in days of old, when persecutions and afflictions abounded, wove chaplets for the holy martyrs of the many tints and flowers of patience. And now, when God has favoured us with times of peace, this Church receives from emperors and men of high estate, as from every condition and race of men, the honour that is her due. And while the sovereigns of the nations in this or that part of the earth have borders set to their dominion, the holy Catholic Church alone bears sway in all the world, and knows no bounds: as it is written 'for God hath made her border peace' [Ps. 147: 14]. I should need to lecture for many more hours if I were to say everything about the Church that I would like to say.

35 Cyril of Alexandria
Commentary on John XI, 11 (on John 17: 20–1)
[Ed. P. E. Pusey, 2 (Oxford, 1872), 733–7]

I do not wish to dwell on these things more than the present context warrants. But I cannot refrain from reiterating this much. Christ is taking the substantial unity which he has with the Father and the Father with him as an image or model of that indestructible love, harmony and unity which is recognized where there is real and deep concord. He thus expresses his will that in the strength of the holy and consubstantial Trinity, we too should be as it were commingled with one another; so that the whole body of the Church may be seen as one – as moving in Christ, through the union of two peoples, towards the constitution of a perfect single whole. This is what Paul says: 'For he is our peace, who has made the two one, and in his own body of flesh and blood has broken down the dividing wall of hostility, by abolishing in his flesh the law of commandments and ordinances, that he might create in himself one new man in place of the two, so making peace, and might reconcile both to God in one body through the cross, thereby bringing the hostility to an end' [Eph. 2: 14–16]. And this purpose is actually accomplished when those who put their trust in Christ are of one soul with one another and receive as it were a single heart; and that comes from the total affinity which true religion gives, from the obedience which is implicit in faith and from the mind that is set on the good life.

I think that what we have said so far is not only appropriate but also requisite. However the meaning of the passage, and in particular the words of the Saviour, 'As thou, Father, art in me, and I in thee, so also may they be in us' [John 17: 21], compel us to enter the realm of more profound doctrines; we need therefore to weigh our words with particular care. We have already emphasized at an earlier stage that the oneness of mind and soul which constitutes the unity of believers ought to be an imitative expression of the pattern of divine unity, the substantial identity and perfect interweaving of the holy Trinity. Now we are concerned to show further that this unity, by which we are bound to one another and all of us to God, is also a natural unity; and as far as our unity with one other is concerned, we shall not exclude unity even at the bodily level – even though we are distinct in virtue of our bodily separation, and each of us can as it were retreat within the frontier of his own individual existence. For no one would suggest that Peter was Paul or Paul was Peter because he recognized them both to be one with the kind of unity which Christ supplies.

Well then, in the case of the Father and the Son – and of course the Holy Spirit – the unity we acknowledge is a natural unity; in the holy Trinity it is a single godhead in which we believe and which we worship. So let us again think carefully about the way in which we too are one in body and spirit in relation to one another and also to God. The Only-begotten has shined on us from the very substance of God the Father; having in his own nature the fullness of the one who begat him, he became flesh, as Scripture says [John 1: 14], and mixed himself as it were with our nature by virtue of an inexpressible conjunction and union with this earthly body. So he who is God by nature was called – indeed actually became – a heavenly man (not a god-bearing man as he is called by some who do not correctly understand the profundity of this mystery).* So he was God and man in one. He made a sort of union in himself of two things which are utterly distinct and remote from one another in nature, and thereby made man to share and participate in divine nature.

The participation in the Holy Spirit and his abiding presence which began through and in Christ has also been transmitted to us. When he appeared at our level, that is as man, he was the first to be anointed and sanctified, even though in his nature, as he comes from the Father, he is God. With his own Spirit he sanctified his own temple and the whole creation that was brought into being through him, for which the act of sanctification was appropriate. Thus the divine plan was effected in Christ as a beginning of the road whereby we too might receive a share both in the Holy Spirit and in union with God. For we all are sanctified in him in the way that we have just described.

We too then are to be combined and commingled into a unity with God and with one another, in spite of our observable separation as individuals distinct in soul and body. To this end the Only-begotten has found a means devised by the Father's own will and wisdom. With one body, namely his own, he blesses those who believe in him as they partake of the holy mysteries and makes them members of the same body with himself and with one another. Who could detach or exclude from a natural unity with one another those who are bound into unity with Christ by the one holy body? For if we all partake of one loaf, then we are all made one body [see 1 Cor. 10: 17]; for Christ cannot be divided. And so the Church is also called body of Christ and we individually are limbs, as Paul teaches [see 1 Cor. 12: 27]. For we are all united to the one Christ through the holy body, since we receive him who is one and indivisible in our own bodies. Our obligation then as limbs of his is to him rather than to ourselves. The Saviour's role is that of head and the Church is the remainder of the body, made up of the various limbs. This is shown by the words of Paul: 'We are no longer to be children, tossed to and fro and carried about with every wind of doctrine, by the cunning of men, by their craftiness in deceitful wiles. Rather, speaking the truth in love we are to grow up in every way into him who is the head, into Christ, from whom the whole body, joined and knit together by every joint with which it is supplied, when each part is working properly, makes bodily growth and upbuilds itself in love' [Eph. 4: 14–16]. Paul again testifies that we who come to share in Christ's holy flesh also enjoy a union of a

* Cyril is referring to teachers of the Antiochene school.

bodily kind with him when he speaks of the mystery of religion 'which was not made known to the sons of men in other generations as it has now been revealed to his holy apostles and prophets by the Spirit; that is, how the gentiles are fellow heirs, members of the same body, and partakers of the promise in Christ Jesus' [Eph. 3: 5–6]. So if we are all one body with one another in Christ, not simply with one another but clearly also with him who is in us by virtue of his own flesh, then surely we are all of us already one both in one another and in Christ. For Christ is the bond of unity, being at once both God and man.

As to our unity in the Spirit, we can follow the same line of reasoning and say that as we all receive one and the same Spirit, namely the Holy Spirit, we are all in a manner conjoined to one another and to God. As individuals we are many but Christ makes the Spirit of his Father, which is his own Spirit, dwell in each one of us. That Spirit is one and indivisible, and it brings into unity our spirits which are cut off from unity with one another at the level of being by their individual identities, and through his own agency reveals us all as one in him. Thus as the power of the holy flesh makes one body of those in whom it is present, in just the same way the 'indwelling' in us all of the one indivisible Spirit makes of us a spiritual unity. So the divine Paul addresses us again: 'Be forbearing to one another in love, and eager to maintain the unity of the Spirit in the bond of peace. There is one body and one Spirit, just as you were called to the one hope that belongs to your call, one Lord, one faith, one baptism, one God and Father of all, who is above all and through all and in all' [Eph. 4: 2–6]. If the one Spirit makes his dwelling in us, then the God and Father of all will be in us, drawing those who have a share in the Spirit into unity – a unity with one another and with him. The fact that we are made one with the Holy Spirit though sharing in him is also clear from the following consideration. If once we turn our back on the life of the natural man and let the laws of the Spirit control our lives, then the rest must follow; we have as it were said 'no' to our own life and adopted the other-wordly mould of the Spirit who is so intimately linked with us; we are as it were being changed into another nature, no longer mere men but also sons of God with the title of heavenly men, in that we have been made partakers of the divine nature.

So we are all one in Father, Son and Holy Spirit, one in identity of attitude (to recall what we said at the beginning), one in conformity to the ways of piety, in participation in the holy flesh of Christ and in participation in the one Holy Spirit, as we have said.

8 Sacraments

We now turn to the sacraments: Baptism and the Eucharist. The meaning of the sacraments was intimately bound up with the understanding of the Church in the thought of the Fathers. Thus, in the previous section, baptism was a central issue in the first two pieces and the Eucharist was an important theme in the last. Here our concern is more specifically with what the Fathers thought was going on in the rites themselves.

The first passage, from Tertullian, comes from the earliest treatise on baptism known to us. Already, at the beginning of the third century, one notices points of confusion and ambiguity that were to cause trouble in the further development of Western thinking on Christian initiation. Was the gift of the Holy Spirit to be associated with the actual baptism, with the anointing that immediately followed it, or with the imposition of the bishop's hand which followed that? Did one of these views necessarily exclude another? At one point Tertullian seems to say one thing, at another something else.

Baptism was normally administered during the Easter vigil, and was immediately followed by the Easter Eucharist, at which the newly baptized received communion for the first time. The five sermons addressed to the newly baptized by Cyril of Jerusalem in the middle of the fourth century (or possibly by his successor John some years later) give a vivid impression both of these ceremonies themselves and of the Church's reflection on their meaning. The second of the addresses on baptism is given here. One notices the strongly scriptural imagery in the light of which Cyril interprets the ceremonies of Christian initiation.

The notion of the Eucharist as an offering or sacrifice receives its earliest extended exposition in the passage of Irenaeus which we print. This aspect of the Eucharist is of particular importance to Irenaeus because of his polemic against the Gnostics; in the Eucharist the Church offers to the Father of Jesus Christ the fruits of his own creation. He is also a witness to the strongly-held belief that the 'eucharistized' bread and wine are the body and blood of Christ.

The next two passages are the fourth and fifth of Cyril (or John) of Jerusalem's addresses to the newly baptized. In the first he expounds the eucharistic presence in terms of the transformation of bread and wine into the body and blood of Christ. The second is a commentary on the eucharistic liturgy as a whole. He enunciates the doctrine, which was to become traditional in the Eastern Church, that it is the invocation of the Holy Spirit that effects the transformation of the eucharistic elements. He also presents a further development of the doctrine of the eucharistic sacrifice: it is an offering of Christ himself.

Gregory of Nyssa, writing for a less popular audience, offers an explanation of the mechanism whereby the Eucharist divinizes those who receive it. Finally, John Chrysostom and Augustine explore the social connotation of participation in the Eucharist: the body of Christ is not only what lies on the altar, it is also the body of the faithful. This approach is particularly characteristic of Augustine.

36 Tertullian
On Baptism 1–9
[*CCL* 1, 277–84] *

1. The subject of this treatise is the mystery of that water by which the sins of our original blindness are washed away and we are set free for eternal life. It will serve a useful purpose in building up not only those who are at present under instruction, but also those whose faith is similarly vulnerable through inexperience because they have been content to believe without examining the reasons for the traditions they have received. In point of fact a viper from the Cainite heresy † who recently spent some time here succeeded in carrying off a fair number with her poisonous teaching – and one of its primary features was an assault on baptism. That was natural enough, since vipers and asps and even basilisks generally frequent arid and waterless places. But we are little fishes, called after our great fish Jesus Christ.‡ We are born in water and can only survive by staying in

---

* The texts of E. Evans (London, 1964), and of R. F. Refoulé, *SC* 35, have also been consulted.

† A form of Gnosticism.

‡ Tertullian is alluding to the early Christian acrostic 'Ιησοῦς Χριστὸς Θεοῦ Υἱὸς Σωτήρ. (Jesus Christ, Son of God, Saviour.)

water. So this monstrosity of a woman, who had no right to teach even if it had been sound doctrine, knew very well how to kill little fishes – by taking them out of water.

2. The power of error, as it seeks to overthrow faith or to prevent its acceptance altogether, lies in the way it uses those very things that go to make up faith in order to attack it. There is nothing which so hardens men's hearts as the contrast between the simplicity apparent in the performance of God's works and the grandeur promised as their eventual outcome. In this particular case a man is sent down into the water without any* pomp or ceremony and not least without financial charge, he is washed there while a few words are spoken, and comes up again little, if any, cleaner than he was before; it is all done with such simplicity that it is regarded as incredible that this should be the means of attaining eternal life. I am fully convinced that the solemn ceremonies and secret rites of idolatry build up credence and prestige for themselves by means of their pretentious magnificence – and by the fees that are charged. What wretched unbelief to deny to God his distinctive attributes – simplicity and power! Is it then not a marvel that death is washed away by bathing? It is indeed a marvel; but is that a reason for not believing it?† On the contrary, it is a positive reason for believing it. What quality better befits the works of God than to be beyond all marvelling? We marvel as well: but we believe. Unbelief marvels because it does not believe. It marvels at simple things as futile and at sublime things as impossible. Allow that it is as you suppose. To each objection God's pronouncement has provided a full answer in advance: 'God has chosen the foolish things of the world to confound its wise things' [1 Cor. 1: 27] and 'Things that are difficult with men are easy with God' [see Luke 18: 27]. For if God is both wise and powerful, as even those who disregard him do not deny, he has appropriately established the materials he uses for his working in the opposites of wisdom and power, namely folly and impossibility, because every virtue finds its occasion in those opposites by which it is challenged.

3. We shall keep this pronouncement in mind as something that really settles the issue in advance, but we will all the same discuss the 'folly' and 'impossibility' of being remade by water. Since this form of matter has been granted a function of such great dignity, I think the importance of the liquid element needs investigation. It proves to be very great indeed – and from the very beginning. For it is one

---

* Reading *aliquo* (with Evans) rather than *aliquando*.
† Omitting *si* (with Evans, and with C. Mohrmann in *Vigiliae Christianae* 5 [1951], 49).

of those elements which, before the world was set in order, were at rest with God in still unfinished form. 'In the beginning', it says, 'he made the heaven and the earth: but the earth was invisible and without order, and there was darkness over the deep, and the Spirit of God was carried upon the waters' [Gen. 1 : 1–2]. In the first place, then, there is the age of the waters for you to revere – the fact that water is a primaeval substance; then there is their high honour – the fact that they were the seat of God's Spirit, no doubt because they were more acceptable to him at that time than any of the other elements. For the darkness was totally without form, as yet lacking the adornment of stars; the deep was grim; the earth was unprepared; the sky was unshapen. Only the liquid, a material always perfect, cheerful, simple and naturally pure, provided a vehicle worthy of God. Then what of the fact that the waters had a kind of regulative function in God's ordering of the world? It was by dividing the waters that he achieved the suspension of the firmament of heaven in the midst; and it was by gathering the waters together that he produced the expanse of dry land. Then when the elements had been arranged to form the world and inhabitants were being given to it, the waters were the first to receive the command to bring forth living things. Liquid was the first to produce things that would live. So then there should be no surprise that in baptism the waters already know how to give life. Was not even the task of fashioning man himself accomplished with the aid of waters? Matter was taken up from the earth; but it was only workable through being moist and spongy – no doubt because when the waters were gathered together into their own place four days previously the moisture left behind had turned it to mud.

If I were to go on and recount all or even most of what could be said about the importance of this element – the greatness of its power or value, the number of its qualities, of its functions, and of its uses to the world – I fear I would appear to have composed a panegyric on water rather than an explanation of baptism; though, were I to do so, it would serve to show more fully that there is no ground for doubting that God has brought into service in his own sacraments the same material which he has employed in all his acts and dealings, and that the material which directs our earthly life makes provision for our heavenly life as well.

4. But for this purpose I need to take only the initial instance in which the meaning of baptism is to be seen – the Spirit who even then by his actual position was a prefigurement of baptism. For the Spirit who was carried upon the waters from the beginning was to remain upon them as an animating power. Something holy was in

fact carried upon something holy – or rather that which did the carrying received holiness from that which was carried upon it. For any material put underneath another is bound to acquire the character of that which is on top of it; this applies particularly to corporeal matter acquiring the character of the spiritual since the very fine nature of spiritual substance enables it to penetrate and inhere in other substances without difficulty.* Thus the nature of the waters, having received holiness from that which was holy, itself took on the ability to sanctify.

No one should object: 'But surely we are not baptized with the very same waters which were there at the beginning?' Admittedly they are not the very same – yet they are the same in the sense in which sameness refers to unity of genus and allows for variety of species. Whatever has become an attribute of the genus overflows into the species as well. So it makes no difference whether baptism takes place in the sea or in a pond, in a river or in a fountain, in a cistern or in a tub; there is no difference between those whom John baptized in Jordan and those whom Peter baptized in the Tiber – unless it is being suggested that the eunuch whom Philip baptized in water that they happened to find on their journey received a greater or lesser measure of salvation.

In view of this ancient privilege at its source, water of whatever sort acquires the mysterious power of conveying sanctity when God is invoked. Immediately the Spirit comes down from heaven, rests upon the waters and sanctifies them from within himself. By being thus sanctified they absorb the power of sanctifying. Although the imagery of the basic action is appropriate – as we are fouled by sin like dirt, so we are washed clean by water – yet sin does not show up on the flesh; no one carries the stains of idolatry, adultery or embezzlement on his skin. Men of this kind are dirty in their spirit, which is where sin begins; for the spirit is the master and the flesh the servant. Yet each of these imparts guilt to the other: the spirit by its exercise of authority, the flesh by its rendering of service. So in waters that have received their healing properties by angelic intervention, the spirit receives bodily washing and the flesh spiritual cleansing.

5. 'But', you will say, 'the nations who are strangers to all understanding of spiritual things ascribe power of equivalent efficacy to their idols.' In doing so they deceive themselves, for their waters are barren. In some sacred rites a bath is the means by which they become initiates of some Isis or other or of Mithras. Even their gods

---

* Tertullian, in line with Stoic thought, regarded spirit not as something wholly immaterial but as an extremely refined form of matter.

themselves are carried in procession for ceremonial washings. Water is carried round and sprinkled as a ritual purification of their country villas, their town houses, their temples and even whole cities. Mass baptisms take place at the Apollinarian and Pelusian games, which are performed in the confidence that they will lead to rebirth and release from their broken oaths. To take another case, in ancient times those who had defiled themselves by the taking of human life used purifying water as their means of expiation. Because water has the natural property of cleansing,* they invite an idol to preside over their purification; how much more truly will they be purified by water when they use it under the authority of the God who endowed it with all its natural properties. If they think that water gains healing properties from use in religion, what religion can have greater power than acknowledgement of the living God?

Here too we observe the devil's zeal in rivalling the ways of God, in that he too practises baptism among his people. What sort of similarity is there? The unclean cleanses; the destroyer liberates; the condemned acquits! Then he must be undoing his own handiwork by washing away the sins that he himself inspires! I set this down as evidence against those who reject faith because they give no credence to the ways of God but do give credence to his rival's attempts to copy them.

Then are there not other cases where, without any sacred rite, unclean spirits settle on waters in imitation of the way the divine Spirit was carried upon the waters at the beginning? As examples one can cite various shady springs, and unfrequented streams, pools at the baths, conduits or storage-tanks in private homes, and wells which are said to spirit men away – no doubt by the force of some malignant spirit. Where people have been drowned or driven out of their mind or terrified by water we use such words as 'pulled under', 'lymphatic' and 'hydrophobic'. Why mention all this? So that no one should find it too hard to believe that God's holy angel should have a hand in controlling the waters for the purpose of man's salvation when an unholy angel of the evil one often does things to that same element for the purpose of man's destruction.

If the idea of angelic intervention having an effect on water seems strange, there is a precedent from the past pointing forward to it. An angel used to act in that way and disturb the waters of the pool of Bethsaida [see John 5: 4].† People who were ill watched for the disturbance and the first one to get down into the waters was free of

---

* Reading *abluendi* (with Evans) rather than *adlegendi*.
† This verse is a gloss on the original text of John. Tertullian is the earliest witness to it.

his complaint after that washing. This bodily healing was a prophetic type of spiritual healing to come, on the general principle that physical things function as anticipatory types of spiritual things.

The general advance of God's grace has enlarged the role of the waters and the angel. They used to remedy bodily defects; now they heal the spirit. They used to produce health for this temporal world; now they restore man eternally. They used to free one man once a year; now they save whole nations every day. Death is destroyed by the washing away of sins; the removal of the guilt brings with it the removal of the punishment also. So man is being restored to God; he who was originally in God's image is being reinstated in his likeness (the image is to be found in man as created; the likeness in man as eternal); he receives again that spirit of God which he had earlier been given by God's breathing on him, but which he had subsequently lost through sin.

6. It is not that we actually receive the Holy Spirit in the water; rather in the water we are cleansed by the ministry of an angel and made ready for the Holy Spirit. Here too there was a type in advance. As John was the Lord's forerunner making ready his way before him, so the angel who presides over baptism makes the way straight for the Holy Spirit who is to come after him. This he does by that abrogation of sins which faith secures when sealed in the Father and the Son and the Holy Spirit. Now if every word of God is to be established by three witnesses [see Matt. 18: 16], how much more does this apply to his gift. The benediction provides us with witnesses of our faith who are also sureties of our salvation. The number of the divine names in itself is sufficient to give confidence to our hope. But since it is under the auspices of the three that both the attestation of faith and the promise of salvation are pledged, there is a necessary addition – the mention of the Church. For where there are the three, namely the Father, the Son and the Holy Spirit, there is the Church which is a body of the three.*

7. Then we come up from the washing and are thoroughly anointed with an unction that has been blessed; this follows the ancient practice by which, ever since Aaron was anointed by Moses, it was customary to anoint men for the priesthood with oil from a

---

* Tertullian is referring to the triple confession of Father, Son and Holy Spirit that accompanied baptism. It is clear that the third article of the confession mentioned not only the Holy Spirit but also the Church. It is less clear what he means by calling the Church 'a (*or* the) body of the three (*or* of three)'. Perhaps he is thinking of the Church as the instrument of the divine triad (as the body is instrument of the soul). There may also be an allusion to Matt. 18: 20.

horn. That is why priests were called 'christs', from the word 'chrism' which means anointing. It is also the source from which the title came to be applied to the Lord, though (in his case) it had become a spiritual anointing; for he was anointed with the Spirit by God the Father, as we see in the book of Acts: 'They were gathered together in this city against thy holy Son whom thou didst anoint' [Acts 4: 27]. In our case too, though the unction is given physically its effect is spiritual, just as in baptism itself there is a physical action (namely our immersion in water) and a spiritual result (namely liberation from our sins).

8. Next follows imposition of the hand in blessing, calling on and inviting the Holy Spirit. It will be admitted that human ingenuity is able to summon spirit to combine with water, and by application of a man's hands over the result of their union to bring it to life with another spirit of outstanding clarity. Is it then not to be admitted that God by use of holy hands can play on an organ of his own a spiritual tune of the greatest sublimity? The practice also follows that ancient sacred act in which Jacob blessed his grandsons, Joseph's sons Ephraim and Manasseh, by interchanging the hands which he placed on their heads, thus making his hands cross one another in such a way as to make the shape of Christ* and thus even at that time to prefigure the blessing that would come in Christ [see Gen. 48: 14].

At this point that most holy Spirit willingly comes down from the Father on the bodies that have been cleansed and blessed. He comes to rest on the waters of baptism, recognizing in them, one might say, his original resting-place. When he came down on the Lord he did so in the form of a dove, to reveal the nature of the Holy Spirit by means of an animal of simplicity and innocence – for even physically the dove is without gall. That is also why it says, 'Be ye simple as doves' [Matt. 10: 16]. For this point too there is evidence in an earlier type. After the waters of the flood by which the ancient iniquity was washed away – the baptism of the world, if I may so call it – a dove was sent out of the ark as a herald to proclaim peace from the wrath of heaven to the earth and then returned to the ark with an olive-leaf (which is still used as a sign of peace by heathen nations). There is just the same pattern here, worked out at the spiritual level: the dove, which is the Holy Spirit, is sent out from heaven, where there is the Church which is depicted by the ark, and

---

* Tertullian, like Novatian in his treatment of the same incident (*De Trinitate 19*), appears to be thinking of the shape of the cross rather than that of X as the initial letter of Christ's name. But perhaps he had both in mind (compare 'that wood was Christ' in § 9 below).

flies down bringing God's peace to the earth, that is to our flesh as it comes up from the washing after the removal of its ancient sins. 'But', you may say, 'the world sinned again; so the analogy between baptism and the flood does not work out very well.' Yes, indeed, the world did sin again; that is why it is destined for fire. And so it is with the man who starts sinning again after baptism. So this too should be taken as a warning sign to us.

9. See how numerous are the arguments from nature, the provisions of grace, the customary observances and the types, preparations and prophecies, all of which have governed the religious use of water! First of all, when the people were set free from bondage in Egypt it was by passing through water that they escaped from the might of the king of Egypt and it was water which destroyed the king himself with all his forces. What type could be more clearly fulfilled in the sacred act of baptism? Nations are set free from this present world by means of water and they leave behind their former master, the devil, drowned in the water. Then water is cured from the bitterness which spoiled it to its proper and usable sweetness by the wood of Moses. That wood was Christ who from within himself cures its nature from the infection of poison and bitterness and makes it into the most salubrious of waters – namely the water of baptism. This is the water which flowed for the people from the rock that accompanied them, and since the rock is Christ it is plain that it is from the water which is in Christ that baptism receives its blessing.

In further corroboration of baptism see how great is the role of water in relation to God and his Christ. Christ was never without water. He himself was baptized with water; he inaugurates the exercise of his power with water when invited to a marriage; when talking he invites the thirsty to partake of his own everlasting water; when teaching about charity he approves among the works of love the offering of a cup of water to a neighbour; he refreshes his strength at a well-side; he walks on water; he crosses it at will; he uses water to do an act of service to his disciples. This witness to baptism continues right up to the passion. When he is handed over to the cross, water plays a part (witness Pilate's hands); and when he is pierced, water gushes out from his side (witness the soldier's spear).

37 Cyril of Jerusalem
On the Mysteries 2
[*SC* 126, 104–18]

Second Address on the Mysteries: Baptism

Lesson from the epistle to the Romans: *Do you not know that all of us who were baptized into Christ Jesus were baptized into his death . . . for you are not under law but under grace* [Rom. 6: 3–14].

1. In these daily addresses on the mysteries, this new recitation of new realities, there is value for you all, but especially for those of you who have undergone renewal from an old life to a new. So I must go on and give you the sequel to yesterday's address; this will enable you to learn the real meaning of those symbolic acts which you performed in the inner building.*

2. As soon as you had gone in, you stripped off your tunic; that was a picture of stripping off the old man with his deeds [Col. 3: 9]. Thus stripped you were naked; that was in imitation of Christ stripped naked on the cross and by that nakedness stripping himself of the principalities and powers and triumphing over them publicly on the tree [see Col. 2: 15]. Since the hostile powers had their hiding place in your members, you could not go on wearing that old tunic – I do not of course mean the literal tunic but the old man who is corrupted in his deceitful lusts [see Eph. 4: 22]. And may the soul who has once put him off never put him on again, but rather say in the words of the bride of Christ in the Song of Songs: 'I have put off my tunic; how shall I put it on?' [Song of Songs 5: 3]. Wonder of wonders! You were naked in the sight of all and were not ashamed; you bore the true likeness of Adam at the original creation, who was naked in Paradise and was not ashamed.

3. Then having stripped, you were anointed with exorcized oil, from the topmost hairs of your head right down to your feet. Thus you were given a share in the good olive-tree, Jesus Christ. For you were cut out from the wild olive-tree and grafted into the good one and given a share in the richness of the true olive [see Rom. 11: 17–24]. In other words the exorcized oil was a symbol of sharing in the richness of Christ; it is a power that dispels every trace of hostile influence. Just as insufflation by the faithful and invocation of the

---

* In the previous lecture Cyril has expounded the meaning of the preliminaries to baptism which took place in 'the outer building' of the baptistery, i.e. the renunciation of Satan and the confession of Christian faith.

name of God burns and drives away demons like a fierce flame, so too the invocation of God and prayer give power to the exorcized oil not only to burn up and destroy the vestiges of past sins but also to drive away all the invisible powers of the evil one.

4. After that you were led to the holy pool of divine baptism, as Christ was taken from the cross to the sepulchre which we see before us.* Each of you was asked whether he believed in the name of the Father and of the Son and of the Holy Spirit. You made that saving confession and three times went down into the water and rose up out of it again. This was another symbolic action, one which represented the three days' burial of Christ. For just as our Saviour spent three days and three nights in the heart of the earth [see Matt. 12: 40], so you too, the first time that you rose from the water, were imitating Christ's first day in the earth, and when you went down into it you were imitating his night there. At night one can no longer see, but by day one lives in the light. In the same way when you went down it was like night and you could see nothing; but when you came up again, it was like finding yourselves in the day. That one moment was your death and your birth; that saving water was both your grave and your mother. What Solomon declared in another context can be applied to you. He said: 'There is a time to give birth and a time to die' [Eccles. 3: 2]. But in your case it is the other way round – a time to die and a time to be born. One time has effected both; your birth coincided with your death.

5. What a strange and wonderful occurrence! We did not really die, we were not really buried; we were not really crucified and raised again. But though those imitative acts are figurative, the salvation is real. Christ was actually crucified, actually buried, really rose again. All these things he has given us freely, so that by imitatively sharing in his sufferings we may win salvation in reality. What surpassing love! Christ received in his undefiled hands the agony of the nails, and now through this imitative sharing he gives me salvation without any agony or pain.

6. No one should think that baptism consists only in the grace of the forgiveness of sins (which was all that John's baptism conferred) – or even only that and the grace of adoption as well. Rather we know full well that, in addition to being a source of cleansing from sins and of providing the gift of the Holy Spirit, it is also a representation of the sufferings of Christ. Paul's words which we have just heard make the point precisely: 'Do you not know that all of us who

---

* The post-baptismal lectures were delivered at the shrine which contained the holy sepulchre. On the buildings connected with this site see J. D. Wilkinson, *Egeria's Travels* (London, 1971), pp. 39–46.

were baptized into Christ Jesus were baptized into his death? Therefore through baptism we were buried together with him' [Rom. 6: 3–4]. These words were surely spoken to people who were clear in their minds that baptism provides forgiveness of sins and adoption as sons but not that it also conveys a share by imitation in the real sufferings of Christ.

7. To teach us that everything that Christ underwent for us men and for our salvation he suffered in reality and not in appearance and that we are given a share in his sufferings, Paul declares with absolute precision: 'For if we have been planted together with him in the likeness of his death, so we shall also be in the likeness of his resurrection' [Rom. 6: 5]. The words 'planted together' are well chosen. The true vine was planted here [see John 15: 1]* and we by sharing in the baptism of death are planted together with him. Pay careful attention to the apostle's words. He does not say 'if we have been planted together with him in his death' but 'in the likeness of his death'. In Christ's case it was a real death; his soul was parted from his body. It was also a real burial; his holy body was wrapped in a pure linen shroud. With him everything happened in reality. But in your case it was a likeness of death and of sufferings – yet your salvation is not a likeness but a reality.

8. Now that you have received this instruction, keep it well in mind, I pray you. Let me too (unworthy though I am) be able to say of you: 'I love you, because you always remember me and keep the traditions which I have delivered to you' [see 1 Cor. 11: 2]. The God, who has brought you from death to life, has the power to make you walk in newness of life [see Rom. 6: 4, 13], for his is the glory and the might now and for ever. Amen.

38 Irenaeus
Against the Heresies IV, 17.5–18.6
[*SC* 100, 590–615]

17.5. Our Lord commanded his disciples to offer to God the first-fruits of his own creation, not because God was in need of them, but to enable the disciples to bear fruit and show gratitude. He took a piece of creation – bread – and gave thanks, saying: 'This is my body.' Similarly with the cup, also a part of the creation to which we

---

* Cyril is referring to the crucifixion, when Christ, the 'true vine', was planted on Golgotha, a few yards from the spot on which Cyril was speaking.

belong – he declared that it was his blood, and taught that it was the new oblation of the new covenant. This oblation was handed on to the Church by the apostles, and she offers it throughout the world to the God who gives us our sustenance, as the first-fruits of his gifts under the new covenant.

One of the twelve prophets, Malachi, spoke of this beforehand: 'I have no pleasure in you, says the Lord Almighty, and I will not accept sacrifice at your hands. For from the rising of the sun to its setting my name is glorified among the nations; and in every place incense is offered to my name, and a pure sacrifice. For my name is great among the nations, says the Lord Almighty' [Mal. 1: 10–11]. By those words he clearly indicated that the first people would cease to make offerings to God, but that in every place a sacrifice would be offered to him, and that a pure one; and that his name would be glorified among the nations. [17.6] Now what name is there that is glorified among the nations but the name of our Lord, through whom the Father is glorified and man also is glorified? He has called it his own because it belongs to his own Son and because he himself bestowed it. If a king were to draw a likeness of his son, there would be two grounds on which he could reasonably speak of that likeness as his own; it is the likeness of his son, and he made it himself. It is the same with the name of Jesus Christ, which is glorified by the Church throughout the world. The Father has called it his own, both because it is the name of his own Son, and because he himself wrote it when he gave it to men for their salvation. So since the name of the Son belongs to the Father, and since in every place the Church makes offering to God Almighty through Jesus Christ, there are two good grounds for the saying: 'And in every place incense is offered to my name, and a pure sacrifice.' ('Incense', says John in the Apocalypse, 'is the prayers of the saints' [Rev. 5: 8].)

18.1. Accordingly it is the Church's offering, the offering that the Lord has taught us to make throughout the world, which is counted as a pure sacrifice before God and which is acceptable to him. He needs no sacrifice from us, but the offerer is himself glorified through his offering, if his gift is accepted. Through this gift we show the honour and devotion we are paying to the King. The Lord expressed his desire that we should offer it in all simplicity and innocence in the words: 'If you are offering your gift at the altar and you re-member that your brother has something against you, leave your gift before the altar and go; first be reconciled to your brother, and then come and offer your gift' [Matt. 5: 23–4]. So we are to offer to God the first-fruits of his own creation, as Moses says: 'You shall not appear before the Lord empty-handed' [Deut. 16: 16] – the purpose being that man should express his gratitude to God by means of the gifts that have been bestowed on him, and thereby receive the honour which comes from God.

18.2. Offerings, as a general class, have not been abolished. There were offerings then, and there are offerings now. The people of God had sacrifices and his Church has sacrifices. The only thing that has changed is the particular form of the offering; this is no longer made by slaves but by free men. The Lord is one and the same; but the offerings of slaves and the offerings of free men each have their own particular character. Thus even our offerings exhibit the distinctive marks of liberty; for with God nothing is otiose or meaningless. That is why, whereas the men of old consecrated a tenth part of their goods, those who have freedom put their entire property at the Lord's disposal. Joyfully and freely they give their lesser goods because of their hope of greater ones to come – like the poor widow who threw her whole livelihood into the treasury of God.

18.3. In the beginning God had regard for the gifts of Abel, because he offered them in simplicity and righteousness. But for the sacrifice of Cain he had no regard, because he was full of envy and malice and had division (*divisionem*) in his heart against his brother – as God said when reproving his secret thoughts: 'If you offer rightly, but do not share (*dividas*) rightly, have you not sinned? Be calm' [Gen. 4: 7 (LXX)]. God is not appeased by sacrifices. If anyone tries to make an offering that in appearance is pure and right and lawful, but in his soul does not share his fellowship rightly with his neighbour and has no fear of God, the outward rectitude of the sacrifice he is offering does not deceive God, since he is sinful within. Such a man will not be helped by his offering, but only by the abandonment of the evil he has conceived within himself. Otherwise some sin will use this hypocritical action to make a man his own murderer.

This too is why the Lord said: 'Woe to you, scribes and Pharisees, hypocrites! For you are like whitewashed tombs. From the outside the tomb looks beautiful, but inside it is full of dead men's bones and all uncleanness. So it is with you; from the outside you look to men as if you are righteous, but inside you are full of iniquity and hypocrisy' [Matt. 23: 27–8]. From the outside they seemed to be making their offerings rightly, but just like Cain, they were envious within. And so they murdered the righteous one, and rejected the advice of the Word, just as Cain had done. For when the Word said to Cain, 'Be calm', he did not obey. ('Being calm' must surely mean abandoning the impulse of the moment.) Similarly in this case he said, 'Blind Pharisees, clean the inside of the cup, that the outside also may be clean' [Matt. 23: 26], but they did not listen. 'Behold', says Jeremiah, 'your eyes and your heart are not good; but in your cupidity they are turned to the shedding of innocent blood and the doing of wickedness and murder' [Jer. 22: 17]. Isaiah too says: 'You have made a plan, but not through me; and agreements, but not through my Spirit' [Isa. 30: 1]. When men's inner will and desire is exposed to the light, God is seen to be blameless, for while he brings what is hidden to light, he himself does no evil; that is why when Cain did not calm himself, he said to him: 'He shall turn to you, and you shall rule over him' [Gen. 4: 7 (LXX)]. Similarly he said to Pilate: 'You would have no power against me if it were not given you from above' [John 19: 11]. For God always gives up the righteous to suffering, so that he may be tested by what he suffers and endures and so be accepted, while the evildoer will be condemned for what he has done and so be rejected.

So it is not sacrifices that sanctify a man; for God has no need of sacrifices. It is the purity of the offerer's disposition that sanctifies the sacrifice. It is this that constrains God to accept the sacrifice, as the gift of a friend. 'But the sinner', he says, 'who sacrifices a calf to me, is as one who kills a dog' [Isa. 66: 3].

18.4. Since the Church makes her offering in simplicity of heart, her gift is rightly regarded as a pure sacrifice before God, like that of which Paul spoke to the Philippians: 'I am filled, having received from Epaphroditus the gifts you sent, a fragrant offering, a sacrifice acceptable and pleasing to God' [Phil. 4: 18]. For an offering must be made to God. We must show ourselves grateful to the Creator in everything; and when we offer him the first-fruits of his own creation we must do it with a pure intention, in sincere faith, in firm hope and in fervent love. This offering, this pure offering, is presented to the Creator by the Church alone, as she offers him with thanksgiving a portion of his own creation.

The Jews do this no longer. Their hands are full of blood, for they would not receive the Word through whom offering is made to God. Neither do any of the heretical conventicles make the offering. Those of them who maintain that the Father is different from the Creator and yet offer him what belongs to this creation of ours, are making him out to be greedy and covetous of property that does not belong to him; whilst those who say that our world is the product of shortcoming, ignorance and passion and yet offer him the fruits of ignorance, passion and shortcoming, are sinning against their Father by offering him insults rather than thanks.*

* Irenaeus is alluding to the particular account of the origin of matter in Valentinian Gnosticism (*Against the Heresies* 1, 4, 1–2).

How can they hold that the eucharistized bread is the body of their Lord, and the cup his blood, unless they hold that he is the Son of the Creator of the world, that is, his Word, through whom wood bears fruit, springs gush out and the earth puts forth 'first the blade, then the ear, then the full grain in the ear' [Mark 4: 28].

18.5. Again, how can they say that the flesh goes to corruption and has no share in life, when it is nourished by the Lord's body and blood? They must either change their way of thinking, or stop offering the things we have been speaking of. Our way of thinking is in harmony with the eucharist, and conversely the eucharist confirms our thinking. We offer him what is his own, and thereby proclaim the harmonious fellowship and union of flesh and Spirit. When the bread, which comes from the earth, receives the invocation of God, it is no longer ordinary bread; it is eucharist – composed of two elements, one earthly and one heavenly. Similarly, when our bodies partake of the eucharist, they are no longer corruptible; they have the hope of resurrection.

18.6. So we make offering to him, not as if he were in need of it, but in order to give him thanks with the aid of his gifts and to sanctify the creation. God has no need of anything that is ours; we do have a need – to offer something to God. As Solomon says: 'He who is kind to the poor, lends to God' [Prov. 19: 17].* And this God, who needs nothing, accepts our good actions, in order to repay us with his own good gifts. As the Lord says: 'Come, O blessed of my Father, inherit the kingdom prepared for you; for I was hungry and you gave me food; I was thirsty and you gave me drink; I was a stranger and you welcomed me; naked, and you clothed me; sick and you visited me, in prison and you came to me' [Matt. 25: 34–6]. He asks for these things, not because he needs them, but for our sake, in order that we may not be unfruitful. Similarly the same Word commanded the people of God to make offerings, not because he needed them, but to teach them to serve God – just as it is his will that we too should unceasingly offer our gift at the altar.

* The verse continues: 'and he will repay him in accordance with his gift'.

39 Cyril of Jerusalem
On the Mysteries 4 and 5
[SC 126, 134–60, 168–74]

Fourth Address on the Mysteries: The Body and Blood of Christ

Lesson from the epistle to the Corinthians: *For I received from the Lord what I also delivered to you ... etc.* [1 Cor. 11: 23–5].

1. These words of the blessed Paul are in themselves sufficient to give you full assurance about the divine mysteries to which you have been admitted and by which you have been made of one body and one blood with Christ. Paul was here affirming 'that on the night that he was betrayed our Lord Jesus Christ took bread, and when he had given thanks broke it and gave it to his disciples saying: "Take, eat, this is my body." And he took the cup and gave thanks and said: "Take, drink, this is my blood." ' As therefore he himself has expressly said 'This is my body', who will dare to doubt it any longer? As he has specifically stated 'This is my blood', who will even voice a suspicion that it may not be his blood?

2. He once changed water into wine by a word of command at Cana of Galilee. Should we not believe him in his changing wine into blood? It was when he had been invited to an ordinary bodily marriage that he performed the wonderful miracle at Cana. Should we not be much more ready to acknowledge that to 'the sons of the bridechamber' [Matt. 9: 15] he has granted the enjoyment of his body and blood?

3. So let us have full assurance that we are partaking of Christ's body and blood. For in the figure of bread it is his body that is given to you and in the figure of wine it is his blood, so that by partaking of the body and blood of Christ you may become of one body and one blood with him. Thus we also become Christ-bearers, since his body and his blood are spread throughout our limbs. In words of the blessed Peter 'we are made sharers in the divine nature' [2 Pet. 1: 4].

4. In discussion with the Jews, Christ once said: 'Unless you eat my flesh and drink my blood, you have no life in yourselves' [John 6: 53]. Failing to understand his words spiritually, they were offended and drew back, thinking that the Saviour was urging them to cannibalism.

5. Then again in the old covenant there was the shewbread. But that, since it belonged to the old covenant, has come to an end. In the new covenant there are the bread of heaven and the cup of

salvation, which sanctify body and soul. For as bread corresponds to the body, so the Word is appropriate to the soul.

6. So do not think of them as mere bread and wine; in accordance with the Lord's declaration, they are body and blood. And if sense suggests otherwise, let faith confirm you. Do not judge the issue on the basis of taste, but on the basis of faith be assured beyond all doubt that you have been allowed to receive the body and blood of Christ.

7. The blessed David indicates the power of this mystery when he says: 'Thou hast prepared a table before me over against them that trouble me' [Ps. 23: 5]. What he means is something like this: 'Before your coming the demons prepared a table for men, defiled, polluted and filled with the power of the devil; but since your coming, Lord, you have prepared a table before me.' When he says to God, 'thou hast prepared a table before me', what else could he be meaning but that mystical and spiritual table which God has prepared for us 'over against' (in other words, contrary and in opposition to) the demons? This is surely the sense; for the one provided communion with demons while the other provides communion with God. 'Thou hast anointed my head with oil' [Ps. 23: 5]. He has used oil to anoint your head on the forehead (this refers to the seal you have received from God), that you may become what is engraved on the seal 'Holy to the Lord' [see Exod. 28: 36]. 'And your cup intoxicates me, like very strong drink' [Ps. 23: 5]. Here you see a cup spoken of – the one which Jesus took in his hands, gave thanks and said, 'This is my blood which is poured out for many for the remission of sins' [see Matt. 26: 28].

8. Solomon also is speaking indirectly of this grace when he says in Ecclesiastes: 'Come, eat your bread with joy' – spiritual bread. 'Come' – an invitation to salvation and blessing. 'And drink your wine with a merry heart' – spiritual wine. 'Let oil be poured over your head' – you see that he alludes too to the mystic chrism. 'And let your garments be always white, because the Lord is well pleased with your works' – now indeed the Lord is well pleased with your works [see Eccles. 9: 7–8]; but before you attained to grace your works were 'vanity of vanities' [Eccles. 1: 2]. But now that you have put off your old garments and put on spiritually white ones, you must be dressed in white all the time. By that we do not of course mean that you should always wear white garments but that you need to be clothed in that which is truly white and shining and spiritual, so that you can say in the words of the blessed Isaiah: 'Let my soul rejoice in the Lord, for he has put on me a garment of salvation and clothed me with a robe of gladness' [Isa. 61: 10]. *

* The newly baptized wore white robes during Easter week.

9. Now you have learnt and are fully convinced that that which appears to be bread is not bread even though it seems so to the taste, but the body of Christ, and that which appears to be wine is not wine, even though taste suggests it, but the blood of Christ. David spoke of this long ago in his Psalms: 'And bread strengthens man's heart, to make his face shine with oil' [Ps. 104: 15]. So strengthen your heart by partaking of it as spiritual food and make the face of your soul shine. Then with that face unveiled with a pure conscience may you come to reflect as in a mirror the glory of the Lord and proceed from glory to glory [see 2 Cor. 3: 18] in Christ Jesus our Lord, to whom be glory for ever and ever. Amen.

Fifth Address on the Mysteries

Lesson from the general epistle of Peter: *So put away all malice and guile and slander ... etc.* [see 1 Pet. 2: 1 ff.].

1. At our previous meetings you have, thanks to God's kindness, received instruction enough about baptism, anointing, and the communion of the body and blood of Christ.* We must now move on to our next subject, for our intention today is to put the crowning piece on to the edifice of your spiritual equipment.

2. You saw the deacon giving water to the priest to wash with, and to the elders encircling God's altar.† Of course he did not do this because of any physical dirt. That is not the point. Our bodies were not dirty when we entered the church at the outset. No, this washing is a symbol of our need to be clean from all sins and transgressions. Hands symbolize action; and in washing them it is clearly the purity and blamelessness of our actions that we are expressing. You must have heard the passage where David explains this mystery and says: 'I shall wash my hands among the innocent and go about your altar, O Lord' [Ps. 26: 6]. So the washing of the hands means that one has no sins to one's account.

3. The deacon then calls out: 'Receive one another and let us kiss one another.' You must not suppose that this is the usual kind of kiss which ordinary friends exchange when they meet in the street. This

---

* Baptism is the subject of the first two addresses on the mysteries, the second of which is translated on pp. 181–3 above. The anointing which followed baptism is the subject of the third address.

† The Greek word ἱερεύς ('priest') is used of both bishops and presbyters. It is the natural word to use of the celebrant, who in this case would be the bishop. The 'elders' are the presbyters who assist him.

kiss is different. By it souls are united with one another and receive a pledge of the mutual forgiveness of all wrong. So then, the kiss is a sign of the union of souls and of the expulsion of all remembrance of wrong. This is why Christ said: 'If you are offering your gift at the altar, and there remember that your brother has something against you, leave your offering on the altar, and go first and be reconciled with your brother, and then come and offer your gift' [Matt. 5: 23–4]. So the kiss means reconciliation, and is therefore holy, as was declared by the blessed Paul, 'Greet one another with a holy kiss' [Rom. 16: 16; 1 Cor. 16: 20], and by Peter, 'Greet one another with the kiss of love' [1 Pet. 5: 14].

4. After this the priest calls out: 'Lift up your hearts!' For at that most awesome moment we must indeed have our hearts on high with God and not below, occupied with the earth and earthly affairs. The priest is in effect commanding you all at this hour to lay aside the cares and concerns of your daily life, and to have your hearts in heaven with the merciful God. You then reply: 'We have them with the Lord.' By your answer you give your assent to what he has said. No one should be there who says with his lips, 'We have them with the Lord', while in his mind he is preoccupied with the concerns of every day. We ought indeed to remember God at all times; but if human weakness makes that impossible, one should try especially hard at this time.

5. Then the priest says: 'Let us give thanks to the Lord.' Truly we ought to give thanks, because he has called us, unworthy as we were, to receive so great a gift, because he has reconciled us, enemies though we were, and because he has bestowed on us the spirit of sonship. You then say: 'It is right and just.' In giving thanks we do what is right and just. But God has done not what is just, but what far surpasses justice, in treating us so kindly and in granting us such blessings.

6. After that we make mention of sky and earth and sea, of sun and moon and stars and of all creation, rational and irrational, visible and invisible. We recall angels and archangels, virtues, dominions, principalities, powers and thrones, and the many-faced Cherubim. In effect we bid them, in the words of David: 'Magnify the Lord with me' [Ps. 34: 3]. And we recall the Seraphim whom in the Holy Spirit Isaiah saw standing about the throne of God, with two wings covering their faces, with two their feet, and with two flying, and saying: 'Holy, holy, holy is the Lord of hosts!' [see Isa. 6: 2–3]. We repeat this doxology, which has come to us from the Seraphim, so as to join in song with the hosts of the world above.*

* Reading διὰ τοῦτο, not διὰ τό (which is presumably a misprint).

191

7. Having sanctified ourselves by these spiritual hymns, we call upon the merciful God to send his Holy Spirit on the elements we have set before him, that he may make the bread the body of Christ, and the wine the blood of Christ.* For whatever is touched by the Holy Spirit is sanctified and transformed.

8. Then, when the spiritual sacrifice, this worship without blood, has been completed, we call upon God in the presence of this atoning sacrifice for the peace of all the churches, for the stability of the world, for rulers, for armies and allies, for the sick and the afflicted; in a word, it is for all who need aid that we, who also need it ourselves, offer this sacrifice.

9. Then we recall those who have fallen asleep, and first of all the patriarchs, prophets, apostles and martyrs, that at their prayers and intercessions God may receive our petition. Then we pray for the holy fathers and bishops who have fallen asleep, and indeed for all who have fallen asleep before us. For we believe that those souls will receive most help for whom prayer is made in the presence of this holy and most awesome sacrifice.

10. May I use an example to persuade you of the truth of this? For I know that many people say, 'What use is it to a soul that leaves this world, whether in a state of sin or not, if it is remembered at this offering?' Well, if a king sends some people who have offended him into exile, and then their relations come with a garland they have woven and offer it to him on behalf of those undergoing sentence, surely he will grant them some remission of their punishment. It is the same when we offer our petitions to God on behalf of those who have fallen asleep, even if they are sinners. We weave no garland. We offer Christ, slain for our sins, to win the favour of the merciful God both for them and for ourselves.

11. After that, you say the prayer which the Saviour gave to his own disciples. With a pure conscience we call God Father, and say: 'Our Father, who art in heaven . . .'†

19. After that the priest says: 'What is holy for the holy!' Holy are the elements on which the Holy Spirit has descended; and holy

---

* Cyril ascribes the transformation of the elements to the invocation of the Holy Spirit. Ambrose, instructing the newly baptized in Milan in the late fourth century, ascribes the transformation to the priest's repetition of Christ's words 'This is my body . . .' and 'This is my blood . . .' (*De Sacramentis* 4, 14–23). This difference was to become a point of bitter dispute between East and West.

† There follows an exposition of each petition of the Lord's Prayer. Cyril refers the petition for bread to the bread of the Eucharist, the food of the soul, and not to ordinary bread.

too are you, on whom has been bestowed the Holy Spirit. The holy things and the holy people belong together. You then say: 'One is holy, one is Lord, Jesus Christ!' In truth only one is holy – that is, holy by nature. If we too are holy, it is not by nature but by participation, discipline and prayer.

20. After that you hear the cantor singing a sacred melody to summon you to share in the holy mysteries. His words are: 'O taste and see that the Lord is good!' [Ps. 34: 8]. It is not your bodily palate which is to be the judge of this, but unwavering faith. For in tasting it is not bread and wine that you taste, but the body and blood of Christ which they signify.

21. So when you approach, do not stretch out your arms or part your fingers. Make your left hand a throne for your right, which is about to receive your king. Cup your hand to receive the body of Christ and respond, 'Amen'. Carefully sanctify your eyes with a touch of the holy body and then consume it, taking care to lose none of it. For to lose any of it is like being deprived of part of one of your own limbs. Tell me, if you were given some gold dust, would you not guard it most carefully, and take care not to lose or be deprived of any of it? Now this is more precious than gold and precious stones. Are you not then going to take even more care not to drop a crumb of it?

22. Then, after partaking of Christ's body, you approach the cup of his blood. Do not stretch out your hands. Bow your head, say 'Amen' with adoration and reverence, and sanctify yourself by partaking of Christ's blood also. And while the moisture is still on your lips, touch them with your hands and sanctify your eyes, your forehead and all your senses. Then wait for the prayer and give thanks to God for counting you worthy of such mysteries.

23. Keep these traditions inviolate, and keep yourselves free from fault. Do not cut yourselves off from communion. Do not deprive yourselves, by the stain of sin, of these holy and spiritual mysteries.

'May the God of peace sanctify you wholly, and may your body and soul and spirit be kept whole at the coming of our Lord Jesus Christ' [1 Thess. 5: 23]; to whom be glory for ever and ever. Amen.

40 Gregory of Nyssa
Catechetical Oration 37
[Ed. J. H. Srawley (Cambridge, 1903), pp. 141–52]

Man has a two-fold nature, composed of both body and soul. Both must therefore play their part in joining those who would be saved to him who leads them to life. The soul is united with him by faith. That therefore provides the means by which the soul gets its salvation; union with life gives it a share in life. But the way in which the body comes to participate in its saviour and to be united with him is different. Those who have been deceived into taking a poison use another drug to counter its harmful effects. Moreover the antidote, just like the poison, must enter a man's system, so that its healing effect may be thereby spread throughout his whole body. Such was our case. We had eaten something that was disintegrating our nature. It follows, therefore, that we were in need of something to restore what had been disintegrated; we needed an antidote which would enter into us and so by its counteraction undo the harm already introduced into the body by the poison.*

And what is this remedy? It is that body which proved mightier than death and became the source of our life. For, as the apostle says, a little yeast makes the whole lump of dough like itself [see 1 Cor. 5: 6]. In the same way, when the body which God made immortal enters ours, it transforms it entirely and makes it like itself. It is just like mixing poison with something wholesome, where everything in the mixture is rendered as worthless as the poison. Similarly the entry of the immortal body into the body that receives it transforms it in its entirety into its own immortal nature.

Now nothing can enter the body unless it is assimilated into the system by eating and drinking. This then is the way – the way which accords with its nature – in which the body is bound to receive the power which gives it life. But since it is only that body in which God dwelt which has been given this life-giving power and since (as we have already shown) our body can become immortal only by sharing in immortality through participation in the incorruptible, we are bound to ask how that one body can be perpetually distributed throughout the world to so many thousands of the faithful, and yet be received in its entirety in the portion each gets, and still remain whole in itself. In consequence we must turn aside for a moment to a dis-

* Compare pp. 108–10 above.

cussion of the nature of the body, in order that our faith, in its concern for logical consistency, may have no doubts on this question.

As everyone knows, our bodily nature is not possessed of life in virtue of any subsistence of its own. It maintains itself and continues in existence by means of the power which enters it from outside itself. It is perpetually in motion, appropriating what it needs and disposing of what is superfluous. When a skin is full of a liquid and its contents leak out at the bottom, it fails to retain its shape around the bulk inside it unless new liquid comes in to replenish what is being emptied. The observer will recognize that the bulky shape of the skin is not a property of the object itself which he is looking at, but that it is the liquid flowing into it and occupying it which gives shape to the object which contains this bulk. In the same way the constitution of our body possesses nothing which we can recognize as a property of its own by which it can maintain itself. Rather its continued existence depends upon the power which comes into it from outside. This power is food, as we call it. It is not the same for all bodies that need nourishment; but each has been granted its appropriate food by him who has allotted its nature. Some animals live on roots which they dig up; others feed on grass; others again on flesh. Man's chief food is bread.

Moreover, for the maintenance and preservation of the body's moisture there is drink; not only water itself on its own, but often sweetened with wine to further the heat of the body. So when we look at those things, we are looking at what is potentially the bulk of our own body. In me they become blood and flesh; in each case the food is subjected to the transforming power which changes it into the form of the body.

After this analysis we must turn our attention back to the issues before us. We were inquiring how it is that Christ's one body can give life to the whole of mankind – to as many, that is, as have faith – and while being distributed to all, itself suffers no diminution. Perhaps we are close to the probable explanation.

All bodies owe their subsistence to nourishment, that is, to food and drink. Food includes bread, and drink includes water sweetened with wine. The Word of God, as we explained at the beginning,* although he is God and Word, was united with human nature. When he entered this body of ours, he did not make any innovation in the constitution of that human nature, but maintained his own body by the usual and appropriate means, providing for its continued subsistence by food and drink, his food being bread. What therefore is true of us – namely, as we have several times observed

* Gregory is referring to the earlier chapters of the *Catechetical Oration*.

already, that in looking at bread we are, in a way, looking at the human body, since that is what bread, by entering it, becomes – was equally true of him. The body in which God dwelt, by receiving the nourishment of bread, was in a sense identical with it, since, as we have said, the nourishment was changed into the nature of the body. What is recognized as a universal characteristic applied to his flesh too; his body too was maintained by bread. At the same time, by the indwelling of the divine Word that body was transmuted to the dignity of divinity.

We have good reason, then, to believe that now too the bread which is sanctified by the Word of God is transformed into the body of the divine Word. That body was virtually bread, and it was sanctified by the indwelling of the Word in the flesh. The means whereby the bread was changed in that body and converted into divine power operate precisely the same way now. In the former case, the grace of the Word sanctified the body which was constituted by bread and which, in a way, actually was bread. And in the latter case, similarly, the bread (as the apostle says) is sanctified by the Word of God and prayer [1 Tim. 4: 5]. The difference in the second case, however, is that it does not become the Word of God gradually by way of being eaten, but is immediately changed into the body by the Word – as the Word himself declared: 'This is my body' [Matt. 26: 26].

But all flesh is nourished by the element of moisture as well; for the earthy element in us could not continue to live unless combined with moisture. Just as we sustain the solid mass of the body by firm and solid food, so we supplement its moisture from what is akin to this. By entering into us it gets changed by the transforming power into blood – all the more readily if there is wine to give it the capacity of being turned into heat. This element too was used by the flesh in which God dwelt in order to maintain its existence. Now the reason why God, in his self-revelation, joined himself with our perishable nature was to divinize humanity, by union with deity. Accordingly in the dispensation of grace he implants himself by means of his flesh, constituted by wine and bread, in all believers. He fuses himself with the bodies of the faithful so that man, thus united with the immortal, may have a share in incorruption. This he confers by the power of the prayer of blessing whereby he changes the nature of the visible elements into that immortal body.

41 John Chrysostom
*Homilies on 1 Corinthians 24, 1–2 (on 1 Cor. 10:
16–17)*
[Ed. F. Field (Oxford, 1847), pp. 287–90]

*The cup of blessing which we bless, is it not a participation in the blood of
Christ?*

1. How is it, Paul, that you can speak like this? You are seeking
to stir your hearers to reverence; you are reminding them of the
awesome mysteries. Do you at that point speak of the fearful and
most awesome cup as a 'cup of blessing'? 'Yes', comes Paul's reply,
'and it is a term of deep significance. When I say blessing, I mean
thanksgiving, and when I say thanksgiving I am unfolding the whole
treasure of God's goodness and calling to mind his marvellous gifts.'
We too recite over the cup the unspeakable mercies of God and all
the benefits we enjoy from him, as we approach and partake of it;
we give thanks that he has delivered from error the whole race of
men, that those who were far off he has made near, and that those
who were without hope and without God in the world he has made
his own brothers and fellow-heirs. It is for these things and all his
other similar gifts that we give thanks, as we approach. So Paul is
saying to the Corinthians: 'Are you not contradicting yourselves
when you bless God for delivering you from idols and then go running back to their tables?'

'The cup of blessing which we bless, is it not a participation in the
blood of Christ?' Paul's words are thoroughly persuasive and awe-
inspiring. What he is saying is this: 'What is in the cup is what
flowed from Christ's side; that is what we share in.' He has called it
a cup of blessing, because when we have it in our hands we praise
Christ in wonder and astonishment at his unspeakable gift, by blessing him for pouring out this very cup to free us from error; and not
only for pouring it out but also for allowing us all to share in it. So
Christ is saying to us: 'If you want blood, do not make the altar of
idols red with the blood of irrational beasts; let it be my altar with
my blood.' What could be more awesome, what more profoundly
loving than that?

2. This is the way lovers behave. When they find those whom they
love getting tired of their own things and longing for what others
have to offer, they make gifts from their own possessions to draw
them away from those of others. Lovers express this kind of generosity
by means of money or clothes or possessions; no one ever does it with

blood. But that is how Christ showed his care and the warmth of his love for us. In the days of the old covenant, since men were at a much more imperfect stage, he was prepared to accept the blood which they offered to idols – with the aim of drawing them away from such things; and that is yet another example of his unspeakable love. But now he has provided in its place a far more awesome and glorious way of worship. He has changed the very sacrifice itself, and in place of the slaughter of irrational beasts, he has commanded us to offer up himself.

The bread which we break, is it not a participation in the body of Christ?
Why did he not use the word 'sharing'? He wanted to convey something more than that word implies and to stress the closeness of the union. Our participation is not a matter simply of having or get-ting a share; it is a matter of participation by union. For as that body is united to Christ, so we are also united to him by means of this bread.

Why did he add: 'which we break'? This is something which we actually see happening at the Eucharist, though it did not happen at the cross. Indeed there just the opposite was true. I quote: 'Not a bone of him shall be broken' [John 19: 36]. But what he did not undergo on the cross, that he does undergo in the oblation for the sake of each one of you. He allows himself to be broken up, so that he may fill all men.

The phrase which he uses, 'participation in the body', might suggest a distinction between that which participates and that in which it participates. But even this small distinction is not allowed to stand. Having said 'participation in the body', he then looks for another phrase to express an even greater closeness and so adds: *Because there is one bread, we who are many are one body.* In effect he is saying, 'Why do I speak of participation? We actually are that body.' What is the bread? The body of Christ. And what do those who receive a share of it become? The body of Christ – not many bodies, but one body. For as the loaf is composed of many grains united in such a way that the separate grains cannot be seen at all (they do exist, but the distinction between them cannot be observed when they are united); so are we joined to one another and to Christ. There is no question of your being fed from one body and your neighbour from another; everyone is fed from the same body. So Paul goes on: *For we all share in the one loaf.*

If then we are all fed from the same loaf and actually become the same body, why do we not all show the same love as well and become one in that respect too? For that was true of our forefathers in the old days. I quote: 'For the company of those who believed were of one

heart and one soul' [Acts 4: 32]. But now the exact opposite is true.
There are battles of every kind between Christians everywhere and
our behaviour to one another is more ferocious than that of wild
beasts. Christ united you to himself when you were removed from
him. Yet you do not deign to be united with appropriate closeness to
your brother; you, who have enjoyed the great benefits of love and
life from your master, separate yourself from your brother. Indeed
Christ's gift was not simply the giving of his body. Our original
fleshly nature, which had been fashioned from the dust, had been
killed by sin and had no life left. So he brought in, so to speak, the
new dough or leaven of his own flesh. His flesh was of the same
nature as ours but free of sin and full of life. This he has given to us
all to share, in order that we may feed on it. We are to be rid of the
old flesh, which is dead, and, by means of this table, are to be united
with the living and immortal flesh.

42 Augustine
Sermon 272
[PL 38, 1246–8]*

What you now see on God's altar, you also saw last night.† But you
have not yet learnt what it is, what it signifies, or how great is the
reality of which it comprises the sacrament. What you see is bread
and a cup; that is what your eyes tell you. But what your faith (as yet
uninstructed) insists is that the bread is the body of Christ and the
cup the blood of Christ. That can briefly be stated and it may be all
that faith needs. Yet faith does crave instruction. The prophet says:
'Unless you believe, you will not understand' [Isa. 7: 9]. So‡ you
can now say to me: 'You have told us so that we can believe; now
explain to us so that we can understand.'
   Perhaps the following argument has arisen in someone's mind:
'Our Lord Jesus Christ, we know, took flesh from the virgin Mary;
he was suckled as a baby, was reared, grew up, reached manhood,

---

* See also the critical edition of Fulgentius of Ruspe, *Ep. xii ad Ferrandum*,
  25 (*CCL* 91, 379–80). Fulgentius quotes all but the last paragraph of
  this sermon.
† Augustine is preaching to the newly baptized at the second mass of
  Easter, on Easter morning. He is speaking after the dismissal of all
  but the baptized, when the bread and wine already stand ready on the
  altar for the Eucharist. See F. van der Meer, *Augustine the Bishop*
  (London, 1961), pp. 371–3.
‡ Reading *ergo* (with Fulgentius) rather than *enim*.

underwent persecution by the Jews, was hung upon a cross, put to death on the cross, taken down from the cross; was buried, rose again on the third day, and on the day of his own choosing ascended into heaven. Thither he raised his body; thence he will come to judge the living and the dead; there he now is seated at the right hand of the Father. How then can the bread be his body and the cup (or rather the contents of the cup) be his blood?'

These things, my brothers, are called sacraments because there is a difference between their appearance and their true meaning. In appearance they have a physical form; in their true meaning they have a spiritual effect. If you want to understand what is meant by 'the body of Christ', you must attend to the words of the apostle: 'You are the body of Christ and his members' [1 Cor. 12: 27]. So then if you are the body of Christ and his members it is the mystery of yourselves that is placed on the Lord's table; it is the mystery of yourselves that you receive. It is to what you are that you make the response 'Amen', and in making that response you give your personal assent. You hear 'the body of Christ' and you answer 'Amen'. Be a member of Christ's body and make your 'Amen' true.

But why the bread? Here too, let us not use any arguments of our own but continue to listen to the apostle himself and to what he has said about the sacrament: 'One bread, one body are we, many that we are' [1 Cor. 10: 17]. Understand and rejoice: unity, truth, virtue, love. 'One bread.' Who is this one bread? The 'one body many that we are'. Remember that bread is not made from a single grain, but from many. When you were exorcized, that was a kind of grinding; when you were baptized, that was a kind of moistening; and when you received the fire of the Holy Spirit, that was a kind of baking. Be what you see and receive what you are. That is what the apostle said about the bread.

What about the meaning of the cup? He makes this clear enough even though he does not spell it out in so many words. To produce the bread that we see many grains are moistened into unity (the result is like what holy Scripture says of the faithful: 'they were of one soul and one heart towards God' [Acts 4: 32]). It is the same with the wine. Remember, my brothers, how wine is made. There are many grapes hanging on the vine, but the juice of the grapes is mixed up together in unity. In this the Lord Christ was giving us a picture of ourselves. He wanted us to belong to him; at his table he consecrated the mystery of our peace and of our unity. He who receives the mystery of unity but does not keep the bond of peace, receives not a mystery that will profit him but a testimony that will witness against him.

Augustine

Let us turn to the Lord, to God the Father almighty, and with pure hearts let us offer true thanks to him as fully as our weakness will allow. With all our powers let us implore him that in his matchless kindness he will graciously deign to hear our prayers; that by his power he will drive the enemy far away from our actions and our thoughts, that he will increase our faith, direct our minds, grant us spiritual thoughts and bring us in the end to his own blessedness through Jesus Christ his Son. Amen.

9 Christian Living

From earliest times Christians reflected on the implications of their faith for their day-to-day lives. But Clement of Alexandria was the first Christian writer to give any extended attention to questions of ethics. His work *The Rich Man's Salvation* is interesting not only for its treatment of a perennial dilemma – that is, whether the imperatives of the gospel are to be taken in an absolute sense or not – but also for its evidence that by the beginning of the third century there were enough prosperous Christians to call for discussion of the particular injunction to sell all.

Hippolytus of Rome, a younger contemporary of Clement, gives us a picture of what was expected of the piety of the ordinary Christian of his time – though it can be questioned how far his words are prescription rather than description. Cyprian reveals the deeply Jewish character of the piety of the African church of this period: almsgiving is a good work which atones for sin.

The passages from Basil and Chrysostom, both from the latter half of the fourth century, come from a different world. Basil is prescribing the regime for a solitary, Chrysostom for the education of a young gentleman. Both writers are self-consciously Christian, yet both are much more deeply imbued than they realize with the educational and cultural heritage of the classical world. Among the characteristics of this tradition are the emphasis on the imitation of noble example, the stress on self-mastery and detachment, and the desire on no account to be vulgar.

43 Clement of Alexandria
The Rich Man's Salvation 11–17
[*GCS* 17, 166–70]

11. What was it that turned him* to flight and made him desert his teacher, and give up his entreaty, his hope, his life and his past labour?

'Sell what belongs to you' [Matt. 19: 21]. But what is the meaning of this? It is not, as some hastily take it to be, a command that he should throw away the property that belongs to him and renounce his wealth. What he is told to banish from his soul are his beliefs about wealth, his attachment to it, his excessive desire for it, his diseased excitement over it and his anxious cares – those thorns of earthly existence which choke the seed of true life. There is nothing marvellous or enviable about having no money, unless true life be the reason for it. Otherwise it would be people with nothing at all, the destitutes who beg for daily bread in abject poverty by the roadside, even though they are 'ignorant' of God and 'of God's righteousness' [Rom. 10: 3], who would be the most blessed of men, the dearest to God, the only possessors of eternal life, solely in virtue of their complete lack of any ways or means of livelihood and of their want of the smallest necessities. Again, there is nothing new in renouncing one's riches and giving them in charity to the poor or to one's fatherland. Many men did this before the Saviour's coming, some to have leisure for the pursuit of dead wisdom, others to gain empty fame and notoriety – men like Anaxagoras, Democritus and Crates.

12. Why then does he give this command which failed to bring salvation to men of old as if it were something new, peculiarly divine and uniquely life-giving? If there is something exceptional that the new creation, the Son of God, discloses and teaches, then it cannot be the outward action that he is commanding; others have done that. It must be something else that is being signified through it – something greater, more divine and more perfect. It is the soul and the disposition which are to be stripped of the passions that lie concealed in them; all that is alien must be excised and expelled from the mind. This is something distinctive for the believer to learn, and something worthy to be the teaching of the Saviour.

Men of old did give up their possessions and abandon them entirely

---

* I.e. the young man of Matt. 19: 16–22 and parallels.

in their contempt for outward things, but I would judge that they actually exacerbated the passion of their souls. They became arrogant, boastful, vain, and contemptuous of other men, as if they had achieved something superhuman. How then could the Saviour have given to those who would live for ever advice that would be ruinously injurious in respect of the life that he promises?

And there is another point. It is possible for a man to unburden himself of his wealth and to remain none the less sunk in habitual desire and hankering for it. He has given up the use of it and then finds himself both needing and longing for what he has thrown away; so he has the double affliction of absence of support and presence of regret. For when someone lacks the necessities of life he cannot possibly fail to be broken in spirit; he will have no time for higher things, since his efforts will be directed to providing for his wants however and whenever he can.

13. How much better are the possibilities of the opposite condition, in which one not only possesses enough not to have to worry about possessions oneself, but can also aid others as one ought. How much opportunity would men still have for sharing their goods, if no one had any? Would not this precept prove to be in open and direct contradiction with many other noble precepts of the Lord? 'Make friends for yourselves by means of the mammon of unrighteousness, so that when it fails, they may receive you into the eternal habitations' [Luke 16: 9]. 'Get for yourselves treasure in heaven, where neither moth nor rust consume nor thieves break in' [Matt. 6: 20]. How could anyone feed the hungry, give drink to the thirsty, cover the naked or welcome the homeless (and those who fail to do so are threatened with fire and outer darkness) if no one possessed any of those things himself [see Matt. 25: 35–43]? The Lord himself was a guest of Zacchaeus, Levi and Matthew, rich tax-collectors, and never told them to give up their wealth. No, after commanding the just and forbidding the unjust use of it, he says, 'Today salvation has come to this house!' [Luke 19: 9]. So what he is doing is to commend the use of wealth, though with the addition of the injunction to share it by giving drink to the thirsty, and bread to the hungry, welcoming the homeless and clothing the naked. If it is impossible to satisfy these wants except with wealth, and he also commands us to renounce wealth, then what the Lord would be doing is telling us to give and not to give the very same things, to feed and not to feed, to welcome and to reject, to share and not to share. And that is utterly illogical.

14. We must not then fling away the wealth which is of help to our neighbours as well as to ourselves. These things are called 'possessions' because they are possessed, and 'wealth' (χρήματα) be-

cause they are useful (χρήσιμα) and provided by God for the use (χρῆσις) of men. They lie at our disposal like materials or like instruments which can be well used by those who know how to. An instrument, if you use it with skill, will produce a skilful effect. If you lack the skill, it gets the benefit of your incapacity, but is not itself responsible.

Wealth is an instrument of this kind. You can use it justly; then it will serve justice. If it is used unjustly, it will be the servant of injustice. For its nature is to serve, not to rule. That which is in itself incapable of good or evil is not responsible and must not be treated as if it were so; that which is capable of using wealth well or badly on the basis of its own choices is for that reason responsible. This is the human mind, which possesses both independent judgement and the power of free choice about the management of what has been given it. So what is to be destroyed is not one's possessions but the passions of the soul, which hinder the right use of one's belongings. By thus becoming good and noble, a man will be enabled to make good use of his possessions. So 'renouncing all that one has' [see Luke 14: 33] and 'selling one's belongings' [see Matt. 19: 21] are to be understood in this way – as spoken with reference to the passions of the soul.

15. I could put the matter thus. Some things are internal to the soul, and others external. The latter, if the soul uses them well, appear to be good; if badly, then bad. So when the Lord commands us to dispose of what belongs to us, is he forbidding those belongings after whose removal our passions still remain? Or is he rather forbidding those after whose removal even our outward possessions become useful? The one who renounces his worldly wealth can still be rich in passions, even when his material resources are gone. For his disposition does its own work, choking and stifling his reason, inflaming him with its habitual desires. So he gains nothing by being poor in possessions, while being rich in passions. The things he has rejected are not things that needed to be rejected, but things neither good nor bad. He has deprived himself of things that could be of service to him, and at the same time, by his want of outward things, has set fire to the stuff of evil within him. We must then renounce the belongings that are harmful, not those which can actually be of profit to us if we know their right use. Things used with prudence, moderation and piety are of profit; things that do damage must be rejected. Externals, however, do no harm.

Thus the Lord allows us the use of external things. What he tells us to put away is not the means of livelihood, but the things that make bad use of them. Those, as we have seen, are the infirmities and passions of the soul.

16. A wealth of those things brings death whenever it is present; its removal brings salvation. This is the wealth of which the soul must be purified, that is, impoverished and stripped bare. Only then can one hear the Saviour's call, 'Come, follow me' [Mark 10: 21]. Then he himself becomes the way for the pure in heart; but an impure soul is impervious to the grace of God – an impure soul being one that is wealthy in desires and groaning with a multitude of worldly affections.

Imagine a man who holds his possessions, his gold, silver and houses, as gifts from God; who serves the God who gave them by using them for the welfare of mankind; who knows that he possesses them for his brothers' sakes rather than his own; who is superior to and not the slave of his possessions; who does not go around with his possessions in his heart or let them determine the horizons of his life; who is always engaged on some fine and holy work; and who, if he comes to be deprived of them, can bear their loss as cheerfully as their abundance. Such a man is the one whom the Lord calls 'blessed' and 'poor in spirit'. He is the one who is fit to be an inheritor of the kingdom of heaven [see Matt. 5: 3; also Mark 10: 17]; he is not the rich man who cannot obtain life.

17. Contrast with him the man who has his money in his soul, who carries in his heart not the Spirit of God but gold or land; who is endlessly extending his possessions and always looking out for more; whose gaze is fixed downwards, who is trapped in the snares of the world; who is earth and to earth shall return [see Gen. 3: 19]. How can such a man set his desires or his thoughts on the kingdom of heaven, who carries about with him not a heart, but an estate or a mine? Is he not certain to be found among those things on which he has fixed his choice?* 'For where a man's mind is, there will his treasure be also' [see Matt. 6: 21].†

* A reference to an uncanonical saying (explicitly attributed by Justin to Jesus) which Clement quotes in full elsewhere in this work (40, 2): 'In whatsoever things I find you, in the same I will judge you.' See J. Jeremias, *Unknown Sayings of Jesus* (1964²), pp. 83–7.
† Clement habitually quotes and alludes to this saying in this form.

44 Hippolytus
*Apostolic Tradition 41–2**
[Ed. B. Botte (Münster, 1963), pp. 88–101]

41. All the faithful, men and women, on rising from sleep in the morning should wash their hands and pray to God before they undertake any sort of work; then they may proceed to their work.

But if any instruction in the Word is to be given, everyone should choose to go there in the conviction that it is God he is hearing in the person of the one giving the instruction. The man who prays in the church will be enabled to avoid the evil of that day. The god-fearing man should regard it as a serious loss if he does not go to the place where instruction is given, especially if he can read.† If a teacher is to be there, none of you should be late at the church, the place where teaching is given. The one who speaks will be endowed with the ability to say things of help to each person. You will hear things you did not know and you will be benefited by the things the Holy Spirit will give you by means of the person giving the instruction. Thus your faith will be strengthened through what you hear. You will also be told there what you ought to do at home. So everyone should be punctilious in going to church, the place where the Holy Spirit abounds.

On days when there is no instruction and everyone is at home, one should take a holy book and read as much of it as is likely to be of help.

If you are at home pray and give praises to God at the third hour. If you are somewhere else at that time pray to God in your heart; for that is the hour at which Christ was seen to be fastened to the tree. For this reason the law in the old dispensation also prescribed the continual offering of the shewbread as a type of the body and blood of Christ. The sacrifice of the lamb, an irrational animal, is also a type of the sacrifice of the perfect lamb. For Christ is the shepherd and also the bread which comes down from heaven.

Similarly pray at the sixth hour too. For when Christ had been fastened to the wood of the cross, the day was cut off and there came a great darkness. So at that hour people should pray powerfully, imitating the cry of him who prayed and turned the whole creation to darkness for the unbelieving Jews.

---

* Paragraphs 35–7 in the edition of G. Dix (London, 1968²).
† Public reading is probably intended. But the context is obscure both in text and meaning.

One should also offer extended prayer and blessing at the ninth hour in imitation of the way the souls of the just bless God who does not lie but who remembered his saints and sent his Word to enlighten them. For at that hour Christ was pierced in the side, poured forth water and blood, and made light shine on the remainder of the day as he brought it to its evening. Thus at the moment when he was about to fall asleep he created the start of a new day and thus supplied an image of his resurrection.

Pray before your body takes rest on your bed.

At midnight get up, wash your hands with water and pray. And if your wife is there too, the two of you should pray together. But if she is not yet a believer, go off into another room to pray and then go back to your bed again. Do not be reluctant to pray; the man who has been joined in matrimony is not defiled. For 'those who have been washed do not need to wash again, since they are clean' [see John 13: 10]. Sign yourself with the moistness of your breath and catch your spittle in your hand and your whole body will be purified right down to your feet; for the gift of breath or spirit and the moistening of cleansing water, when they come from the foundation of a believing heart, sanctify the man of faith. So it is essential to pray at this hour.

Moreover those elders who handed this tradition on to us taught it us on the ground that at that hour every creature is quiet for a moment to praise the Lord; stars, trees and waters stand still for an instant, and the whole host of ministering angels join with the souls of just men to praise God at that hour. So all believers should be sure to pray at that hour.

The Lord also provides evidence in support of this in his saying: 'Behold a cry goes up at midnight "Behold, the bridegroom comes; rise to meet him." ' And a little later he says, 'Keep awake therefore, for you do not know at what hour he comes' [see Matt. 25: 6, 13].

In the same way we should arise at cock-crow. For it was at that hour, when the cock was crowing, that the children of Israel denied Christ. But we have come to know him through faith and look forward to the day with hope of eternal light at the resurrection of the dead.

So all the faithful should act in this way; you should hold these things in your memory, instruct one another and give a lead to the catechumens. You will be free of the possibility of temptation and ruin as long as you remember Christ at all times.

42. If you are tempted, make the sign on your forehead reverently.*

* For the use of the sign of the cross at this period, see also the evidence of Tertullian (p. 136).

For this sign of the passion is a known and tested weapon against the devil, provided you use it in faith – that is, as long as you do not use it to be seen by men but know what you are doing when you employ it as a shield. When the adversary sees the power that comes from your heart, how it is the inner (that is the rational) man giving clear and outward expression of his inner likeness to the Word, then he flees from the spirit that is in you. It was to symbolize this through the paschal lamb that was killed that Moses sprinkled its blood on the lintel and anointed the doorposts. His act depicts the faith in the perfect Lamb which we now enjoy. So by signing our forehead and eyes with the hand let us avoid him who is seeking to destroy us.

45 Cyprian
On Works and Alms, 1–5
[*CSEL* 3, 373–6]

1. Many and great are the blessings, dear brothers, which have been and are being ever bestowed on us for our salvation by the boundless mercy of God the Father and Christ. The Father sent the Son to restore us by saving us and giving us life. The Son was content to be sent and to be called Son of Man in order to make us sons of God; he humbled himself to exalt a people who were prostrate; he was wounded to heal our wounds; he became a slave to bring to liberty those who were slaves; he underwent death that he might procure immortality for mortals. Such is the measure and the extent of the gifts of the divine love.

But God's providence and God's mercy are not yet fully told. In the plan of our salvation there is provision of still greater care for the preservation of man after his redemption. When by his coming the Lord had healed those wounds which Adam had suffered and had cured the ancient serpent's bite, he gave a law to man thus healed and commanded him to sin no more lest a worse thing befall him [see John 5: 14]. This command to be free from sin puts us in a critical position. The weakness and folly of human frailty would have been at a loss, had not the divine love come to our aid once more and by showing us works of justice and mercy provided a way of preserving our salvation – namely that by almsgiving we can wash away whatever subsequent defilement we may incur.

2. In Scripture the Holy Spirit says: 'By almsgiving and by faith sins are purged' [Prov. 16: 6]. This cannot possibly refer to sins committed before our redemption, for they are purged by the blood of

Christ and by sanctification. Again the Spirit says: 'As water extinguishes fire, so does almsgiving extinguish sin' [Ecclus. 3: 30]. This proves the same point: as the saving waters of baptism extinguish the fires of Gehenna, so almsgiving and good works quench the flame of our sins. Just as remission of sins is given once for all in baptism, so unremitting and ceaseless service fulfils a role similar to that of baptism by bestowing once again the mercy of God.

This is also taught by the Lord in the gospel. When his disciples were commented on for eating without first washing their hands, he replied: 'He who made the inside, made the outside also. But give alms and behold all things are clean to you' [Luke 11: 40–1]. Thereby he plainly teaches that it is not hands that need washing but the heart, that it is internal rather than external defilement that needs to be removed, that the man who has cleansed the inside has cleansed the outside too and that the man who has purified his mind has as good as purified skin and body too. He then goes on to show how we can be clean and purified and says that alms must be given. The merciful one tells us to do acts of mercy, and, because he wants to preserve those whom he has redeemed at so great a cost, he teaches us how we can be cleansed once more if we become defiled after receiving the grace of baptism.

3. Let us therefore, my dear brothers, acknowledge this health-giving gift of the divine mercy for the purifying and purging of our sins and, as we can never be without some wound of conscience, let us use these spiritual remedies to heal our wounds. No one should boast of having a pure and immaculate heart, and so come to rely on his own sinlessness and to think he has no need to apply this medicine to his wounds. It is written, 'Who can boast that he has a clean heart or who can boast that he is pure from sin?' [Prov. 20: 9]. Again, John affirms in his epistle: 'If we say that we have no sin, we deceive ourselves and the truth is not in us' [1 John 1: 8]. No one, then, can be without sin and anyone who claims to be faultless is either proud or foolish. How vital, therefore, how gracious is the divine mercy, which, recognizing that those who have been healed cannot remain wholly free of subsequent wounds, has provided saving remedies for curing and healing them anew.

4. In conclusion, my dear brothers, the divine admonition never rests, is never silent; in the holy Scriptures, both old and new, the people of God at all times and in all places are stirred up to works of mercy; everyone who is being prepared for the hope of the kingdom of heaven is commanded by the voice and counsel of the Holy Spirit to give alms. To Isaiah God gives the command: 'Cry aloud; spare not. Lift up your voice like a trumpet; declare to my people their

transgressions and to the house of Jacob their sins' [Isa. 58: 1]. First of all he orders that their transgressions be brought up against them and sets forth their sins with the full force of his indignation; he then says that neither prayer, supplication or fasting can make satisfaction for their sins; that not even if they cover themselves in sackcloth and ashes will they be able to assuage God's wrath; finally in the last section he shows it is only by almsgiving that God can be placated. That latter section reads: 'Share your bread with the hungry and bring the homeless poor into your house. When you see the naked, clothe him; and do not neglect the household of your own family. Then shall your light break forth in due season and your garments* shall arise quickly; your righteousness will go before you and the glory of God will encompass you. Then you shall call and God will hear you; while you are still speaking, he will say: "Here I am"' [Isa. 58: 7–9].

5. Thus the remedy by which God is to be propitiated is given in the words of God himself; divine instruction teaches the sinner what he has to do. God is to be satisfied by good works; sins are to be purged by the merits of acts of mercy.

46   Basil
Letter 2
[Ed. Y. Courtonne (Paris, 1957–66), 1, 5–13]

1. I recognized your letter, just as one recognizes one's friends' children from their obvious likeness to their parents. You say that the nature of our surroundings will not go far to persuade you to share our life here until you have heard something about how we spend our time. It was truly characteristic of you to think this, for you count everything on earth as nothing in comparison with the promised bliss which is in store for us.

What I myself do, night and day, in this remote spot, I am ashamed to write. I have abandoned my life in the town as the occasion of endless troubles; but I have not managed to get rid of myself. I am like people who, because they are unused to travelling by sea, become ill and seasick. They complain of the size of the ship, because it rolls so much. If they then transfer to some smaller vessel they find that they are distressed and seasick everywhere; for their

---

* Cyprian's Latin (*vestimenta*) is dependent on a Greek text reading ἱμάτια in place of ἰάματα.

discomfort and sickness go with them. My condition is something like that. Because I carry my internal disorders around with me, I am everywhere beset by similar discomforts. So I have not got much benefit from the solitude here. However, what I ought to have done, and what would have enabled me to keep close to the steps of him who has led the way to salvation (for he has said, 'If anyone will come after me, he must deny himself and take up his cross and follow me' [Matt. 16: 24]) is this.

2. We must strive for quietness of mind. The eye is unable to see an object clearly if it is continually wandering about from side to side or glancing up and down; the gaze must be firmly fixed on the object one is looking at if one is to see it clearly. In the same way man's mind is incapable of attending clearly to the truth if it is distracted by a host of worldly cares. The man who is not yet yoked in the bonds of marriage is harassed by violent desires, unruly impulses and disastrous infatuations. He who is already yoked to a partner is attended by another horde of anxieties. If he is childless, he longs for children. If he has them, there is the worry of bringing them up. He must guard his wife, look after his household, manage his servants. He loses money on contracts, has disputes with his neighbours, gets entangled in litigation. There are the risks of business and the wearing labour of farming. Every day brings its own darkness to the soul. The nights take up the worries of the day and delude the mind with vain thoughts of the very same things.

The one escape from all this is complete separation from the world. Withdrawal from the world does not mean leaving it physically; it does mean ridding the soul of all concern for the physical. One must live without city or home; one must have nothing of one's own – no friends, no possessions, no livelihood, no business, no company; one must renounce human learning and prepare the heart to receive the impressions of divine instruction. Preparation of the heart consists in the unlearning of those teachings, born of bad habit, which already possess it. It is as impossible to write on a wax tablet without first erasing whatever is already written on it, as it is to instruct the soul in the things of God without first removing its habitual and preconceived notions.

What is of most help in this respect is solitude. Solitude stills our passions and gives reason the opportunity to cut them right out of the soul. Wild animals are easily brought under control if they are stroked. Similarly desire and anger, fear and sorrow, the wild beasts of the soul, are more easily brought under the control of reason if they are stilled by quietness and not stirred up by repeated provocation. So the place to be chosen must be like ours here, well away from human company, to ensure that nothing external can interrupt the continuity of the disciplined life.

Disciplined piety feeds the soul on holy thoughts. What can be more blessed than to imitate on earth the chorus of the angels; to begin the opening day with prayer, honouring the Creator with hymns and songs; and when the sun is up to turn to work, always accompanied by prayer, and to season one's labours with singing? Cheerfulness and freedom from sorrow are the gifts which the soul receives from the singing of hymns.

Quiet then is the beginning of the soul's purification; the tongue not discussing the affairs of men; the eyes not looking around at beauty of complexion or figure; the ear not letting the attention of the soul grow slack through listening to songs designed for mere pleasure or – what is worst for the condition of the soul – to the words of wits and buffoons. The mind which does not dissipate itself on what is external or let itself be dispersed in the world by means of the senses, will return to itself, and of itself will ascend to meditate on God. Surrounded and illumined by the light of that beauty, the soul forgets its own nature. It is not dragged down by concern for food or worry about clothing. Indeed, it keeps holiday from all earthly cares, transferring all its energy to the acquisition of those good things which are eternal. Its concern is the achievement of temperance and courage, justice and prudence, and of all the other virtues, ranged under these general heads, which prompt the zealous man to perform as he should the various duties of life.

3. The chief road to discovery of duty is the study of the inspired Scriptures. In them are to be found not only precepts for conduct. They also contain the lives of blessed men, put into writing and handed down to us, as living pictures of godly living for the imitation of their good deeds. So if a man applies himself to whatever aspect he feels himself to be deficient in, he will find that the Scriptures are like a public dispensary: each will discover the appropriate medicine for his own infirmity. He who seeks temperance will keep reading the story of Joseph. From him he will learn chaste conduct, finding him not only continent in the face of pleasure but habitually inclined to virtue. Courage he will learn from Job, who remained steadfast, his nobility of soul unimpaired, when the circumstances of his life were reversed and he found himself, in a moment of time, poor instead of rich, childless instead of blessed with fine children. More than that, he was not even provoked when his friends, who had come to console him, attacked him and aggravated his sorrows. Again, suppose that someone wants to know how one man can combine gentleness and a passionate spirit, so as to be passionate against sin and gentle

towards men. For him there is David – noble in the exploits of war, gentle and calm in his treatment of his enemies. Such too was Moses, who rose in great passion against those who sinned against God, but endured with a gentle spirit the accusations that were made against himself. The man who wants to make himself perfect in every kind of virtue must act in all these cases like a painter who, in copying one picture from another, keeps looking at his model in his determination to transfer its character to his own work.* He must look intently on the lives of the saints, like living and moving statues, and make their goodness his own by imitation.

4. Prayers after reading find the soul stirred by longing for God and so fresher and more vigorous. Prayer is good when it imprints in the soul a clear conception of God. This is in fact the indwelling of God – to have God established in oneself by means of the memory. Thus we become God's temple, when no earthly concerns interrupt the continuity of this memory, no unexpected emotions disturb the mind, and the worshipper escapes from everything to retire to God. Driving out all that invites us to vice, he devotes his time to the practices that lead to virtue.

5. The first thing to strive for in conversation is not to act boorishly. Ask questions without contentiousness and give answers without display. If someone who is talking to you is saying something profitable, do not interrupt him. When you introduce your own ideas, be free of any desire to do it with ostentation. Be measured in speaking and listening, unashamed to learn and ready to teach. If your words are somebody else's, you must not conceal their origin, like poor women passing off bastards as their own children, but you should have the good feeling to acknowledge their true parent. The voice should be pitched neither too high nor too low: neither so quiet as to be inaudible nor so forced as to be vulgar. One should first reflect on what one is going to say, and then give it utterance. One should be courteous when addressed, and easy in conversation. Do not use witticisms to try to achieve an agreeable effect, but be kindly and gentle in addressing people. Never be harsh, even when rebuke is necessary. For if you are the first to abase yourself and be humble, the man who needs your help will find it easier to accept it. The way in which the prophet rebuked David will often prove useful to us. He did not pronounce the sentence of condemnation on David's sin in his own person. Instead he used an imaginary character and made David the judge of his own sin. So David first pronounced judgement on himself. After that he could no longer

* This image can be traced back to Plato. See, for example, *Republic* 501B.

find fault with the man who had exposed him [see 2 Sam. 12: 1–15].

6. Together with a humble and submissive spirit go grave and downcast eyes, a neglected appearance, unkempt hair and dirty clothing. The appearance which mourners take pains to cultivate should be ours as a matter of course. The tunic should be fastened close to the body by a belt. The belt should not be above the waist – which is effeminate. Nor should it be slack, letting the tunic hang loosely – which is slovenly. One's walk should not be leisurely – revealing a laxity of mind. Nor should one strut about noisily, so as to exhibit an impulsiveness of character. The only object of clothing is to be a sufficient covering for the body for both winter and summer. Do not go after bright colours, or fine, soft materials. To be concerned about the colour of one's clothes is on the same level as women beautifying themselves by colouring their cheeks or dyeing their hair. The tunic ought to be thick enough to need no other garment to help keep the wearer warm. One's footwear should be cheap but adequate for its purpose. In a word, what we must attend to in dress is that it should meet our needs.

So with food. Bread will meet the needs of a man in good health and water will satisfy his thirst. In addition, there are the various vegetable dishes which help maintain the body's strength for the performance of its necessary functions. In eating there should be no exhibition of savage gluttony; we must always be calm, quiet and self-controlled with respect to our pleasures. Not even at table may our minds be idle and not occupied with God. The very nature of our food and the constitution of the body that receives it give us occasion for praising him. What a variety there is in the forms of nourishment, each adapted to the needs of particular bodies, provided by the ruler of the universe! There should be prayers before meals, that we may be worthy of God's bounties, both those which he is giving us now and those which he has in store for the future. Prayer after meals should express thanks for gifts received and petition for those which are promised. One hour should be appointed for food, the same regularly each day. Then, of the twenty-four hours of the day, this one alone will be spent on the body. During the remainder the ascetic should be wholly occupied in mental exercise.

Sleep should be light and easily shaken off, as naturally follows from a well-regulated habit of life. It should be deliberately broken by meditation on high matters. To let one's limbs be so relaxed that one is overcome by deep torpor and so open to unbefitting fantasies – to sleep in this way is a state of daily death. Midnight must take the place of dawn for the religious ascetic, when the silence of night gives most leisure to the soul, and when neither eye nor ear can furnish the heart with harmful sights or sounds. The mind is then alone by itself to commune with God, to correct itself by the recollection of past sins, to give itself rules for the avoidance of evil, and to seek God's aid for the fulfilment of all that it is striving for.

47 John Chrysostom
On Vainglory and the Upbringing of Children, 64–90
[*SC* 188, 162–96] *

64. Now that the gates are all in order, we must enter the city itself and draw up and enact laws for it.† But first we must acquaint ourselves thoroughly with the houses and chambers where its citizens live, the idle as well as the vigorous.

65. The spirited element, we are told, has its seat in the breast; in fact, in the heart. The seat of the appetite is the liver; of the reason, the brain. The spirited element has its virtues and its vices, its virtues being restraint and equability, its vices rashness and ill temper. The virtue of the appetite is restraint, its vice licentiousness. The virtue of the reason is prudence, its vice is folly. So let us take care that these virtues are brought to birth in their respective places and that they bear citizens like themselves, and not bad ones. For these conditions of the soul are like mothers to our thoughts.

66. We begin with the dominant part of the soul: the spirited element. We must neither excise it completely from a boy, nor allow it to be employed unchecked. We must train boys from their earliest years to be patient when they themselves are wronged, but when they see another being wronged, to act courageously and defend the victim with appropriate means.

67. But how shall we achieve this? They must get training with their slaves. They must be patient when slighted, keep their tempers

* The text has been compared with that of B. K. Exarchos (Munich, 1955).
† The idea that the soul of the individual is a microcosm of society is a commonplace of the classical tradition. The particular notion that the soul consists of three elements (the spirited, the appetitive and the rational) goes back to Plato. Chrysostom combines it with another idea, which is likewise found both in pagan and in Christian authors, that if the soul is a city, the senses are the gates through which the soul receives its perceptions of the outside world. In the preceding chapters Chrysostom has spoken about the training of the senses. Now he turns to the soul itself.

when disobeyed, and carefully examine their own faults against others. In such matters the father must at all times be master, stern and unbending when the rules are broken; but when they are kept, he will be kind and gentle and will give the child plenty of rewards. That is how God rules the world, by the fear of hell and the promise of the kingdom. We must treat our own children in the same way.

68. They should be surrounded by people who will provoke them, to give them training and practice at home in putting up with adversity. In a wrestling-school athletes practise with friends before they take part in actual contests, so that through doing well with them they may prove invincible when they meet real opponents. In the same way a boy must be trained at home. Often it should be his father or his brother who acts as his special tormentor; but everyone should try his hardest to get the better of him. Or somebody should stand up to him and defend himself at wrestling, to give him practice at that. The servants too should provoke him continually, with or without justification, to teach him always to keep his temper. For if his father provokes him, that is no great test; for his father's status overpowers his soul and does not allow of any resistance. But those of his own age, slaves and free, should treat him in this way, to teach him to be of an even temper in their company.

69. There is a further point. It is this. When he is angry, remind him of his own weaknesses. If he is vexed with a slave, is he himself without fault? And how would he himself have behaved in the same situation? If you see him striking a slave, punish him; likewise, if he treats him with insolence. He need be neither soft nor harsh in order to be both manly and gentle. He will often need the resources of his spirit, for instance if he ever has children or becomes the master of slaves himself. The spirited element is always of help to us, the only exception being if we use it in self-defence. That is why Paul never used this faculty on his own behalf, but only on behalf of others who had been wronged. Moses, too, when he saw a brother being wronged, was angry – and in a most noble manner – although he was the meekest of all men. But when he himself was attacked, he did not defend himself but fled.

The boy should hear these stories. When we are still fitting out the gates, simpler stories are required. But when we have entered* and are training the citizens, it is time for profounder tales like these. So let this be his first law, never to defend himself when insulted or ill used, but never to allow anyone else to receive such treatment.

70. The father will be much better at teaching these things if he

---

* Reading εἰσελθόντες (with Exarchos) rather than εἰσελθόντας.

keeps himself in training. He should set about his own self-improvement if for no other reason than so as not to spoil his own example.

So the boy must learn to be despised and treated with contempt. He is to make no demands of the servants on the ground of his freedom, but must for the most part attend to his own needs. The only help that the slaves are to give is in services that he cannot perform for himself. A free man for instance cannot cook. It would be wrong for him to abandon the tasks appropriate to a free man to attend to tasks like that. But if his feet need washing, a slave must never do it; he must do it for himself. Thus you will make the free man considerate towards his servants and greatly loved by them. No one must give him his cloak; nor must he expect anyone else to attend to him in the bath. All these things he must do for himself. This will make him robust, unpretentious and courteous.

71. You must also teach him the facts about human society, and about the difference between slave and free. Say to him, 'My child, formerly, in the days of our ancestors, there were no slaves. It was sin that introduced slavery. A son insulted his father, and the penalty he paid was to become the slave of his brothers [see Gen. 9: 20–5]. * So take care not to be a slave of your slaves. If you get angry as they do, if you act exactly like them, if you are no more virtuous than they, then you will be no more honoured than they. So strive to become and to remain their master, not by means of your position as master, but by means of your behaviour. Otherwise, though you are free, you will turn out to be their slave. Do you not see how many fathers have disowned their children, and introduced slaves in their place? Take care that nothing like that happens to you. I neither wish it nor desire it. The choice is yours.'

72. In this way make his spirit gentle. Tell him to treat his servants like brothers, and teach him the facts about human society. Repeat the words of Job to him: 'If I have despised the cause of my manservant or maidservant when they contended against me, what shall I do if the Lord afflicts me? And if he visits me, how shall I answer him? As I was made in the womb, were not they made also? Were we not made in the same womb?' [Job 31: 13–15 (LXX)]. And again: 'If my maidservants did not often say, "Who will give us of his meat that we may be filled?" For I am too kind' [Job 31: 31 (LXX)].

73. Do you think Paul silly for thinking that a man who does not know how to rule his own household is also unfit to rule the church [see 1 Tim. 3: 5]? So say to the boy: 'If you see that one of your

* See also pp. 241–2 below for a fuller development of the same idea by Augustine.

pencils or pens has been lost or broken by your servant, don't be angry or abusive, but be understanding and readily soothed.' In this way small losses will teach him to bear * big ones. (Or it might be the strap or the brass clasp on his writing tablet that is broken.) Children take such losses very badly. They would sooner lose their lives than let such an injury go unpunished. So this is a point at which you must soften the roughness of his spirit. Believe me, a boy who is easy and even-tempered about these things will readily endure any loss once he is a man. So if a boy has a writing tablet made of nice wood, really clean and unstained, with brass clasps on it, and silver pencils and other such things that appeal to children, and the servant who attends him loses or breaks it; then, if he does not get angry, he has already displayed the marks of a most philosophical character. Don't buy him a new one straight away; that would put an end to his distress. But when you observe that he does not miss it any more and has got over his distress, then you can heal the blow.

74. We are not discussing trifles; what we are discussing is how to govern the whole world. Teach him also to give precedence, if he has a younger brother; and if he has not, to give it to his servant. This too is a sign of a philosophical character.

75. Calm his spirit in this way, and the thoughts which come to birth will be of an even temper. If he is without inordinate attachments, if he can bear loss, if he wants no looking after, if he does not resent the honours paid to others, what will make him angry in the future?

76. It is now time to turn to the appetite. The restraint and the mischief involved are both of a two-fold character. He must neither prostitute himself nor go fornicating with girls. The medical profession says that it is from the age of fifteen that this appetite attacks most sharply. How are we to tie this wild beast down? What are we to do? What bridle can we put on it? I know none, except that of hell-fire.

77. First we must keep him away from shameful sights and sounds. A free-born boy should never enter a theatre. If he hankers for its pleasures, we should point out any of his peers who keep away from it, and restrain him by the spirit of rivalry. Nothing, absolutely nothing, is as effective as rivalry. We should always act in this way, but particularly if he is of a competitive nature. This is much more effective than fear, promises or anything else.

78. Then we must think of other pleasures which will not harm him. Take him to visit holy men.† Provide him with recreation. Give

---

* Reading οἴσει (with Exarchos) for οἴσῃ.

† Chrysostom is thinking of the solitaries who lived in the hills near Antioch.

him plenty of presents to help his soul patiently to endure this deprivation. In place of such sights introduce him to pleasant stories, to the countryside and to fine buildings. Further, we must overcome their threat by saying to him, 'My son, spectacles like that, the sight of naked women uttering lewd words – they are not for free men. Promise that you will hear and say nothing improper, and you may go. But it is quite impossible to hear nothing shameful there. What goes on there is unfit for your eyes.' As we say this we must kiss and embrace him; we must hold him close to us to show him our affection. By all these means we must mould him.

79. What next? As I said before, never let a girl come near him or wait on him, but only a servant of advanced years, an old woman. Guide conversation towards the kingdom of God and towards men of old, pagans or believers, who were illustrious for their self-restraint. We must fill his ears continually with talk of them. If we have servants who are of sober conduct, we should use them as examples, saying how absurd it is that a servant should exhibit this restraint, while a free man is his inferior in conduct.

There is another remedy. It is this: he must learn to fast, if not at all times, then at least on two days in the week, on Wednesdays and Fridays. He should also go to church.

His father should take him in the evening, when the theatre ends, and point to the spectators as they come out. He should scoff at the old men for becoming so much more foolish than the young, and at the young ones for being burned up with desire. And he should ask the boy: 'What have they all got out of it? Nothing but shame, reproach and damnation.' Abstention from all these sights and sounds makes no small contribution towards the acquisition of self-restraint.

80. There is something else: he must be taught to pray with great fervour and contrition. Don't tell me that a boy cannot manage this. Of course he can if he is sharp-sighted and wide awake. There are plenty of examples among men of old, such as Daniel and Joseph. Don't make objections about Joseph's seventeen years, but consider why it was that he won his father's love more even than his elder brothers. Was not Jacob also young? And Jeremiah too? And Daniel, was he not twelve years old? Was not Solomon also twelve when he prayed that marvellous prayer? Was not Samuel still young when he instructed his own teacher? So let us not despair. It is the man who is too young in soul who will not undertake this, not the man who is young in years. So train the boy to pray with great contrition and to keep vigils as far as he is able. In short, let the character of a saintly man be stamped on the boy. If he endeavours not to

swear, if he gives no injuries when he receives them, if he refrains from slander and hatred, and if he fasts and prays – all those things will help him to gain self-restraint.

81. If you are bringing him up for a life in the world, give him a bride soon; do not wait for him to be involved in military or public life.* First train his soul; only then start thinking about external glory. Or do you think it is only a small contribution to a marriage that those who are joined in it should both be virgins? It will contribute a great deal, not only to the self-restraint of the young man, but also to that of his wife. Is it not then that their love will be wholly pure? Above all, is it not then that God will be more gracious and will fill † their marriage with countless blessings, seeing that they are coming together as he has ordained? See that ‡ he keeps his love in the forefront of his mind; if he is held fast by this longing, he will spurn every other woman.

82. You must praise the girl for her beauty, her decorum and all her other qualities, and then you must add: 'If she hears that you live in an easy-going fashion, she will find it intolerable to marry you.' That will make him realize that ultimate things are at stake, and he will think hard. When the holy patriarch was cheated of his betrothed, he was persuaded by his love for her to serve another seven years – that is, fourteen years in all. How much more should we! Tell him: 'The bride's whole family, her father and mother, her servants, relations and friends, are all concerned about how you behave and they will all tell her about it.' Bind him with this chain, a chain that will ensure his restraint. So, even if he cannot be married from earliest manhood, let him be betrothed from the start, and let him do his best to show that he is of good character. This will suffice to ward off all vice.

83. There is something else that will help maintain his self-restraint. He should frequently see the leader of the church § and often be praised by him. His father should take pride in this in the presence of all who hear. Girls when they see him should regard him with reverence. On top of this, the stories that he hears, the fear of his father as well as his promises, together with the reward laid up for him by God and all the blessings which the virtuous are to enjoy – all these things will make him truly secure.

---

  * Omitting καὶ τότε, whose appearance in the *SC* text at this point appears to be a mistaken intrusion from the next sentence. The *SC* translation omits the words.

  † Reading ἐμπλήσει (with Exarchos and *SC* translation) for ἐμπλήσεις.

  ‡ Reading ποίει for ποιεῖ (with *SC* translation).

  § Chrysostom means the bishop.

84. You should also speak of the reputations to be won in the army and in public affairs. Furthermore, constantly express contempt for licence and praise for self-restraint. Together, these things will be sufficient to keep the boy's soul in check. So we shall see the birth of thoughts that are honourable.

85. We must move on. We come now to the supreme element, the one that controls everything else. I mean of course prudence or understanding. Here a great deal of work is needed, to make him wise and to banish all folly. Here especially philosophy has its great and wonderful function of bringing him to a knowledge of God, of all that awaits us hereafter, of hell and of the kingdom. 'The fear of the Lord is the beginning of wisdom' [Ps. 111: 10].

86. This quality of understanding must be implanted in him and it must be thoroughly trained, that he may acquire an understanding of human affairs, of wealth, reputation and power, and that he may come to despise these things and aspire to what is highest. We should keep him in mind of this advice: 'My son, fear God alone and beside him fear none other.'

87. These principles will make him a man of prudence and charm; for there is nothing as productive of folly as these passions. The fear of God and a proper evaluation of human affairs suffice to produce wisdom. For the crown of wisdom is this: not to be excited by childish things. He must be taught to think nothing of money, nothing of human reputation, nothing of power, nothing of death and nothing of this present life. Then he will be wise. If we can bring him to the bridal chamber with a training like this, think what a gift he will be to his bride.

88. At his wedding there must be neither flutes, harps, nor dancing. It would be quite outrageous thus to dishonour such a bridegroom. But let us invite Christ; for the bridegroom will now be worthy of him. Let us invite his disciples as well.* All will be well with him. He in his turn will learn to train his own children like this, and they theirs. The result will be a golden chain.

89. We should also make him engage in public affairs as far as he is able and as far as they do not involve him in sin. If he serves in the army, he must learn to avoid dishonest gain. So too if he acts in defence of the victims of injustice,† or in any other circumstance.

90. A mother must also learn to train her daughter on these principles. She must lead her away from extravagance, personal adornment and every other mark of the harlot. This must be her rule at all

---

* Chrysostom means that the clergy should be invited; see Matt. 10: 40 and John 2: 2.

† Chrysostom is thinking of the profession of advocacy.

points. Boy and girl alike must be kept from luxury and drunkenness. This is of the greatest importance for the development of self-restraint. For boys are troubled by desire, and girls by love of finery and excitement. All these things must be restrained.

Thus we shall succeed in pleasing God by rearing such athletes for him that we and our children together will be able to attain to the good things promised by God to those who love him, by the grace and kindness of our Lord Jesus Christ; to whom with the Father and the Holy Spirit be glory, might and honour, now and always, world without end. Amen.

10 Church and Society

Until the conversion of Constantine Christian attitudes to secular authority ran along lines inherited from Judaism. Secular authority was ordained by God for the government of the world; kings and rulers were to be respected and prayed for. At the same time no respect could be paid or prayer addressed to the gods of pagan society.

The first three passages of this section come from this early period and make these points. Irenaeus makes the general point that secular authority falls under the providence of the one God. The passages from Tertullian and Origen clearly reflect the hostility that Christians experienced in society. Tertullian writes against a background of actual persecution and Origen seeks to answer the charge of the pagan Celsus that Christians were guilty of an irresponsible abdication of their responsibilities to society.

Eusebius, in an oration delivered in Constantine's own presence in 335, writes in the new situation that followed the emperor's conversion. He draws on the language of Hellenistic writers on monarchy to produce a picture of the emperor that goes far beyond the traditional Christian respect for his office: Constantine is God's viceregent on earth. It is a picture of monarchy that leaves little room for any polarity of Church and state.

The last two passages come from Augustine, writing some eighty years later. The first is part of a public letter to a military commander, Boniface, justifying the suppression of Donatism. Augustine does not argue from any theory of church and state, but from the duty incumbent on Boniface and the emperors, as Catholic Christians, to enable the Church to discharge her pastoral function towards her erring children.

The City of God is not a treatise on church and state. It is an extended reflection on the relation between the two communities, heavenly and earthly, which run through history. In Book XIX, written towards the end of his life, Augustine is concerned with the proper ends of these two communities. In the course of this passage he illuminates many of the issues raised in the preceding passages of this section.

48 Irenaeus
Against the Heresies V, 24, 1–3
[*SC* 153, 294–304]

1. The devil lied at the beginning, and he was lying again at the end when he said, 'All these things have been delivered to me, and I give them to whom I will' [Luke 4: 6]. It is not the devil who has fixed the bounds of the kingdoms of this world, but God. For 'the king's heart is in the hand of God' [Prov. 21: 1]. Through Solomon the Word also says: 'By me kings reign and rulers exercise justice; by me princes are raised up and by me monarchs govern the earth' [Prov. 8: 15–16]. Moreover Paul the apostle speaks to the same effect: 'Be subject to all the higher powers; for there is no power except from God. Those that exist have been instituted by God' [Rom. 13: 1]. And later on he says of them: 'He does not bear the sword in vain; he is the minister of God to execute his wrath on the evildoer' [Rom. 13: 4]. Some people are rash enough to expound this passage as speaking of angelic powers and invisible rulers; but Paul is not talking about them but about human powers. This is clear from his going on to say: 'For the same reason you also pay taxes, since they are God's ministers, serving for this very purpose' [Rom. 13: 6]. The Lord himself confirmed this by not doing what the devil tried to persuade him to do, but giving instructions that the tribute-money was to be paid to the tax-collectors for himself and for Peter, his reason being that 'they are God's ministers, serving for this very purpose'.

2. By departing from God, men reached such a pitch of savagery that they came to treat even blood-relations as enemies and to practise all kinds of violence, murder and greed without any sense of fear. Since they knew no fear of God, God imposed on them a human fear. The aim was that by being subjected to the authority of men and educated by human laws, they might achieve some measure of justice and exercise restraint towards one another through fear of the sword so clearly held before them. This is what the apostle means when he says: 'He does not bear the sword in vain; he is the minister of God to execute his wrath on the evildoer.' For the magistrates themselves the laws provide a cloak of righteousness. As long as they act justly and in accordance with the laws, they will not be interrogated about what they do; but if ever they do anything to subvert justice, if they act unjustly, illegally or tyrannically, they too will perish for their actions. God's just judgement falls equally on all men, and never fails.

So then earthly authority has been established by God for the benefit of the nations. It has not been established by the devil, who is never at peace himself and has no wish to see the nations living in peace. God's purpose is that men should fear this authority and so not consume one another as fish do; his intention is that the imposition of laws should hold in check the great wickedness to be found among the nations. It is in this sense that they 'are God's ministers'.

3. If then those who demand taxes of us 'are God's ministers, serving for this very purpose', and if 'the powers that exist have been instituted by God', it is clear that the devil is lying when he says: 'All these things have been delivered to me, and I give them to whom I will.' It is by God's decree that men are born and it is by that same God's decree that rulers are set up – rulers appropriate to the people to be ruled over by them at that particular time. Thus some rulers are given by God with a view to the improvement and benefit of their subjects and the preservation of justice; others are given with a view to producing fear, punishment and reproof; yet others are given with a view to displaying mockery, insult and pride – in each case in accordance with the deserts of the subjects. Thus, as we have already said, God's just judgement falls equally on all men.

49 Tertullian
To Scapula 1–2
[*CCL* 2, 1127–8]

1. For us, the things that we suffer at the hands of ignorant men are not a source of great fear or dread. When we joined this sect we plainly undertook to accept the conditions this involved. So we come to these contests as men who have already hired themselves out for them. Our hope is to attain the promises of God; our fear is lest we should have to undergo the punishments with which he threatens those who live otherwise. When you turn on us with your utmost ferocity we are quite ready to do battle with you; indeed we enter the fray of our own accord. We find more cause for joy in condemnation than in acquittal. So it is not fear for ourselves that makes us send you this pamphlet, but fear for you and for all our enemies, or I should rather say, our friends, since it is the teaching of our faith that we are to love even our enemies and pray for those who persecute us [see Matt. 5: 44]. Here lies the perfection and distinctiveness of Christian goodness. Ordinary goodness is different; for all men

love their friends but only Christians love their enemies. We are moved with sorrow at your ignorance and with pity for the errors of men's ways, and, as we look to the future, we see signs of impending disasters every day. In such circumstances we have no choice but to take the initiative and lay before you those things which you refuse to listen to openly and publicly.

2. We worship the one God. He it is whom you all know by the light of nature. His is the lightning and thunder at which you tremble. His is the bounty at which you rejoice. There are others whom you regard as gods; we know them to be demons. Nevertheless it is a basic human right that everyone should be free to worship according to his own convictions. No one is either harmed or helped by another man's religion. It is no part of the practice of religion to compel others to the practice of religion. Religion must be practised freely, not by coercion; even animals for sacrifice must be offered with a willing heart. So even if you compel us to sacrifice, you will not be providing your gods with any worthwhile service. They will not want sacrifices from unwilling offerers – unless they are perverse, which God is not. In fact the true God gives all that is his as freely to the irreligious as to his own; furthermore he has established an eternal judgement to distinguish the grateful from the ungrateful. Yet it is us whom you regard as sacrilegious, even though you have never found us guilty of theft – let alone of sacrilege. Those who actually rob temples are people who swear by the gods and worship them; in spite of not being Christians, they are still found guilty of sacrilege! It would take too long to describe the other ways in which all the gods are ridiculed and despised by their own worshippers.

Another charge against us concerns treason with respect to the person of the Emperor. Yet Christians have never been found among the followers of Albinus or Niger or Cassius.* Those who have actually been found in practice to be enemies of the Emperor are the very same people who only a day before had been swearing by his genius, had been solemnly offering sacrifices for his safety, and not infrequently had been condemning Christians as well. A Christian is an enemy to no man – certainly not to the Emperor, for he knows that it is by his God that the Emperor has been appointed. He is bound therefore to love him, to revere him, to honour him and to desire the safety not only of the Emperor but of the whole Roman empire as long as the world endures – for as long as the world

* Clodius Albinus and Pescennius Niger were Septimius Severus' unsuccessful rivals for power in the period of civil war which followed the death of Pertinax in 193. Avidius Cassius was an unsuccessful claimant to the throne in 175, during the reign of Marcus Aurelius.

endures, so also will the Roman empire. So then we do 'worship' the Emperor in such manner as is both permissible to us and beneficial to him, namely as a man second only to God. All that he is he has received from God, and it is God alone whom he ranks below. This surely is what the Emperor himself will desire. He ranks above all else; it is the true God alone whom he ranks below. This means that he is above even the gods themselves and they come within his sovereignty. So also we 'offer sacrifices' for the safety of the Emperor, but we do so to our God – and his – and we do it in the way that God has ordained, namely by the offering simply of prayers. (For God, being the creator of the whole Universe, is in no need of smells or of blood. That is the fodder of petty demons. We do not merely despise these demons; we subdue them; we put them to daily disgrace; we drive them out of people, as multitudes can testify.) So then our prayers for the safety of the Emperor are all the more real as we offer them to the one who is able to grant them.

Our religion teaches a divine patience and it is on this basis that we conduct our lives. You can see this clearly enough from the fact that although we are such a large company of men (almost a majority in fact of every city) yet we live out our lives quietly and temperately; we are probably better known individually than as a corporate entity, since the only way we can be distinguished is by the way we get rid of our former vices. Far be it from us to react with indignation when we suffer things which in fact we welcome or in any way to plot the vengeance at our own hands which we confidently await from God.

50 Origen
Against Celsus VIII, 73–5
[*GCS* 3, 290–2]
Translation by H. Chadwick (Cambridge, 1953), pp. 509–10: revised.

73. Then Celsus next exhorts us to *help the emperor with all our power, and cooperate with him in what is right, and fight for him, and be fellow-soldiers if he presses for this, and fellow-generals with him.* We may reply to this that at appropriate times we render to the emperors divine help, if I may so say, by taking up even the whole armour of God [see Eph. 6: 11]. And this we do in obedience to the apostolic utterance which says: 'I exhort you, therefore, first to make prayers, supplications, intercessions, and thanksgivings for all men, for em-

perors, and all that are in authority' [1 Tim. 2: 1–2]. Indeed, the more pious a man is, the more effective he is in helping the emperors – more so than the soldiers who go out into the lines and kill all the enemy troops that they can.

We would also say this to those who are alien to our faith and ask us to fight for the community and to kill men: that it is also your opinion that the priests of certain images and wardens of the temples of the gods, as you think them to be, should keep their right hand undefiled for the sake of the sacrifices, that they may offer the customary sacrifices to those who you say are gods with hands unstained by blood and pure from murders. And in fact when war comes you do not enlist the priests. If, then, this is reasonable, how much more reasonable is it that, while others fight, Christians also should be fighting as priests and worshippers of God, keeping their right hands pure and by their prayers to God striving for those who fight in a righteous cause and for the emperor who reigns righteously, in order that everything which is opposed and hostile to those who act rightly may be destroyed? Moreover, we who by our prayers destroy all demons which stir up wars, violate oaths, and disturb the peace, are of more help to the emperors than those who seem to be doing the fighting. We who offer prayers with righteousness, together with ascetic practices and exercises which teach us to despise pleasures and not to be led by them, are cooperating in the tasks of the community. Even more do we fight on behalf of the emperor. And though we do not become fellow-soldiers with him, even if he presses for this, yet we are fighting for him and composing a special army of piety through our intercessions to God.

74. If Celsus wishes us to be generals for our country, let him realize that we do this too; but we do not do so with a view to being seen by men and to being proud about it. Our prayers are made in secret in the mind itself, and are sent up as from priests on behalf of the people in our country. Christians do more good to their countries than the rest of mankind, since they educate the citizens and teach them to be devoted to God, the guardian of their city; and they take those who have lived good lives in the most insignificant cities up to a divine and heavenly city. To them it could be said: You were faithful in a very insignificant city [see Luke 16: 10; 19: 17]; come also to the great city where 'God stands in the congregation of the gods and judges between gods in the midst', and numbers you even with them, if you no longer 'die like a man' and do not 'fall like one of the princes' [Ps. 82: 1, 7].

75. Celsus exhorts us also to *accept public office in our country if it is necessary to do this for the sake of the preservation of the laws and of piety.*

But we know of the existence in each city of another sort of country, created by the Word of God. And we call upon those who are competent to take office, who are sound in doctrine and life, to rule over the churches. We do not accept those who love power. But we put pressure on those who on account of their great humility are reluctant hastily to take upon themselves the common responsibility of the Church of God. And those who rule us well are those who have had to be forced to take office, being constrained by the great King who, we are convinced, is the Son of God, the divine Word. And if those who are chosen as rulers in the Church rule well over God's country (I mean the Church), or if they rule in accordance with the commands of God, they do not on this account defile any of the appointed civic laws.

If Christians do avoid these responsibilities, it is not with the motive of shirking the public services of life. But they keep themselves for a more divine and necessary service in the Church of God for the sake of the salvation of men. Here it is both necessary and right for them to be leaders and to be concerned about all men, both those who are within the Church, that they may live better every day, and those who appear to be outside it, that they may become familiar with the sacred words and acts of worship; and that, offering a true worship to God in this way and instructing as many as possible, they may become absorbed in the word of God and the divine law, and so be united to the supreme God through the Son of God, the Word, Wisdom, Truth, and Righteousness, who unites to Him every one who has been persuaded to live according to God's will in all things.

51 Eusebius
Oration in Honour of Constantine on the Thirtieth Anniversary of his Reign 1–3
[*GCS* 7, 196, 198–202]

1. This is the festival of our great king. Let us, the royal children, rejoice in it, inspired and instructed by our sacred theme. The leader of our feast is the great king himself. In saying 'the great king' I mean him who is truly great. The king who is present with us will not be offended but will rather join in applauding this expression of piety, for I refer to Him who is beyond the universe, the highest of all, the supremely exalted, the supremely great, the thrones of whose kingdom are the vaults of heaven and the earth the footstool of his

feet. None can worthily conceive him; the light about him flashes with beams of ineffable brightness, so that none may approach the vision of his godhead. Him the hosts of heaven surround and the supernal powers attend; him they acknowledge as their master, their lord and their king ... [*Eusebius continues to describe the praises of the created order. The passage concludes as follows.*] To him, its great king, the whole universe itself gives concerted praise. To him the heavens above, and the choirs beyond the vaults of heaven, give honour. Hosts of angels sing his ineffable praises. Spirits who spring from incorporeal light adore the parent of their being. The timeless ages which were before this heaven and this earth, and still yet other and infinite ages of ages, antecedent to all visible existence, acknowledge him as their sole and supreme sovereign and lord. To him too he who is over all, before all, and after all, the pre-existent only-begotten Word makes propitiation for the salvation of all. He is the great high-priest of the great God; he is older than all time and all ages; he supremely and solely is dedicated to the honour of the Father. His glory is that of supreme ruler of the universe and viceroy of the Father's kingdom; for He is that light transcending all things which surrounds the Father and stands as both mediator and barrier between the being of created things and the unbegun and uncreated – that light which, streaming down from the godhead that is without end or beginning, goes forth to illuminate all things, both the realm above the heavens and all that is under heaven, with the radiance of a wisdom brighter than the sun in splendour. He then must be ruler of this whole universe – the Word of God, whose presence is all-pervasive, over all things, through all things, and in all things both visible and invisible.* From him and through him the king who is dear to God receives an image of the kingdom that is above and so in imitation of that greater king himself guides and directs the course of everything on earth.

2. The only-begotten Word of God continues sharing in his Father's rule from ages without beginning to infinite and endless ages. So too the one who is dear to him, sustained by royal aid emanating from on high and strong in the power of his sacred title, has been exercising an earthly rule for long periods of years. Again, the saviour of the universe is bringing the whole heaven and earth and the kingdom that is above into a condition worthy of his father. So too the one dear to him directs those who come under his control on earth to the only-begotten saving Word and makes them fit for his kingdom. The one saviour of the universe, like a good shepherd

* For a fuller development of Eusebius' understanding of the Word, see pp. 47–52 above.

keeping wild beasts far from his flock, drives away by his divine and invincible might the rebellious powers which used to fly about in the air above the earth and harass the souls of men. So too the one dear to him is adorned by him from on high with the trophies of victory over his enemies; by the rule of war he masters the open enemies of the truth and brings them to a right mind.

The Word who is before the world, the saviour of the universe, imparts seeds of reason and salvation to his disciples, making them rational and giving them an understanding of the Father's kingdom. So too the one dear to him is a kind of spokesman of the divine Word, who summons every race of mankind to a knowledge of the Almighty; he calls aloud in the hearing of all and proclaims in clear tones to everyone on earth the laws of true piety. The saviour of the universe opens wide the heavenly gates of the Father's kingdom to all who are travelling from this world to the other. And he in his turn, emulating the divine example, removes every stain of godless error from his earthly kingdom; he invites within in his royal palaces bands of holy and pious men, firmly resolved to save without loss of a single life that whole company whose helmsman and governor he is.

And now, in celebrating this festival, when the all-sovereign God has granted him the honour of reigning for these three decades, he, alone of all those who have yet ruled the Roman empire, keeps it not as the ancients did, in honour of earth spirits, of seducing demonic apparitions or of any other of the deceptions or fooleries of godless men; rather, fully conscious of the good things bestowed on him, it is to the one who has thus honoured him that he pays his thank-offering. Nor does he follow the ancients in defiling his royal palaces with blood and gore or in appeasing the earth spirits with smoke and fire and the whole burnt offerings of animal sacrifice. Instead he offers to the king of the universe the sacrifice which is dear and pleasing to him, namely his own royal soul and godly spirit. For this is the only appropriate sacrifice – the acceptable sacrifice which our king has been taught to offer not with fire or blood but with purified mind and understanding. With true conviction of soul he holds fast to the ways of piety; with exalted mind he utters the praises of God; with royal deeds he imitates the divine benevolence. So, wholly devoted to God, he presents to him the great offering of his own self, the first-fruits of the world which has been entrusted to him. This is the first and greatest sacrifice he makes; then, like a good shepherd he offers, not 'a splendid sacrifice of first-born lambs',* but the souls

* Homer, *Iliad* 4, 102.

of the spiritual lambs within his care, whom he leads to the knowledge and worship of God.

3. Rejoicing in such an offering, gladly welcoming the proffered
gift and delighting in the priest who makes so solemn and noble a
sacrifice, God has given to him further long periods of kingly rule,
adding to his favours in response to the worship given to him. With
his sovereign freedom God has granted him the celebration of a
multitude of festivals, and at each ten-yearly celebration has chosen
one of his sons to have a share in the imperial throne, thereby, as it
were, giving an increase of time to a healthy and flourishing plant.
First of all, to mark the first ten years of his imperial rule he appointed the son who bears his own name to a share in his royal office,
to mark the second decade he appointed the next in age, and
similarly the third to mark the decade which we are now celebrating.
And now as the fourth period begins its course and his allotted time
extends still further into the future, he plans to expand his royal
authority still further by ungrudging association of his family with
himself.* By this appointment of Caesars he is fulfilling the oracles of
the holy prophets, who long ago declared 'the saints of the most high
will receive the kingdom' [Dan. 7: 18]. So God himself the all-
sovereign grants to his beloved king increase alike of time and
children and has made his rule over the nations of the world fresh
and vigorous, like a plant that is putting forth its shoots. He it is who
is granting him this festival, establishing him as victor over all his
enemies and foes and providing in him an example of true piety for
all the inhabitants of the world. As for our emperor, just as the sun
gives light to those who dwell in the very furthest parts by means of
the rays that stream out from it into the distance, so he assigns his
sons to the corners of the globe as lamps and torches bearing the
light of which he is the source – to us whose home is in the east he
gives a son worthy of himself, and to other races yet others of his
children. These noble Caesars he has harnessed, as it were, under a
single yoke as the four horses of his royal chariot. He himself directs
and guides from on high with the reins of an inspired harmony and
concord. At one and the same time he traverses the whole world
under the sun; he himself is present to all; he himself oversees all.

The kingdom with which he is invested is an image of the heavenly
one. He looks up to see the archetypal pattern and guides those

---

* Constantine II was appointed Caesar in 317, Constantius II in 323,
and Constans in 333. Their cousin Dalmatius was appointed Caesar
in 335. Eusebius does not mention Constantine's eldest son Crispus,
appointed Caesar in 317 and executed in mysterious circumstances
in 326.

whom he rules below in accordance with that pattern. The example of monarchical rule there is a source of strength to him. This is something granted to man alone of the creatures of the earth by the universal King. The basic principle of kingly authority is the establishment of a single source of authority to which everything is subject. Monarchy is superior to every other constitution and form of government. For polyarchy, where everyone competes on equal terms, is really anarchy and discord. This is why there is one God, not two three or even more. Polytheism is strictly atheism. There is one king, and his Word and royal law are one. That Word is not something expressed in phrases or syllables, not something that takes a period of time to write down with a pen; he is the living and existent divine Word dispensing to all those under him and after him the kingdom of his Father. The heavenly hosts surround him, the myriads of God's ministering angels, the great company of the supernal armies and of the invisible spirits of the lower heavens who play their part in maintaining the order of the whole world. And at the head of all these is the royal Word as a viceroy of the great king. The inspired voices of the sacred writers have honoured him with countless titles – captain of the host, great high-priest, prophet of the Father, angel of great counsel, effulgence of paternal light, only-begotten son. He who begat him made him to be living word, law, wisdom, the full complement of every good and gave him to all who are subject to his kingdom as a gift embodying the greatest goods. He pervades all things and reaches to every place. He unfolds God's favours bountifully to all, including even the rational creation on this earth. On them he has bestowed a copy of kingly authority, in that he has furnished the soul of man, made after his own image, with divine powers. From that same source the soul receives as an outcome of divine emanation its participation in the other virtues also. For he only is wise who is also the only God. He alone is essentially good; he alone is truly powerful, he is the begetter of righteousness, the Father of Word and wisdom, the source of light and life, the dispenser of truth and virtue; so too he is the author of kingship itself and of all rule and authority.

52 Augustine
Letter 185, 19–24
[*CSEL* 57, 17–23]

19. Those who object to just laws being instituted against their own impieties claim that the apostles never required such measures from the kings of the earth. But they fail to consider that that was a different age and that one must always act in accordance with the conditions of one's own age. Then there was no emperor who was a believer in Christ and therefore in a position to serve him by bringing forward laws in support of piety and against impiety. That age was the one which fulfilled the prophetic saying: 'Why did the nations rage and the peoples plot vain things? The kings of the earth stood up and the princes took counsel together against the Lord and against his Christ' [Ps. 2: 1–2]. The time had not yet come to which the same psalm refers a little later: 'And now, O kings, be wise; be instructed you who judge the earth. Serve the Lord with fear and exult in him with trembling' [Ps. 2: 10–11]. How can kings serve the Lord with fear except by prohibiting and punishing with conscientious strictness actions that are contrary to the commands of the Lord? A king serves him in one way as a man and in another way as a king. He serves him as a man by living a faithful life; but he also serves him as a king by decreeing with appropriate vigour laws which enjoin just acts and prohibit the opposite. That was how Hezekiah served the Lord, by destroying the groves, the idols' temples and the high places, which had been set up in contravention of the commands of God. That was how Josiah also served him, by acting in the same way. That was how the king of Nineveh served him, by compelling the whole city to appease the Lord. That was how Darius served him, by giving Daniel authority to smash the idol and by throwing his enemies to the lions. That was how Nebuchadnezzar (whom I referred to earlier) served him, by prohibiting with a fearsome law anyone holding office in his kingdom from blaspheming God. Therefore kings serve the Lord in their capacity as kings when they do things in his service which only kings are in a position to do.

20. In the times of the apostles, then, kings did not yet serve the Lord; they were still plotting vain things against him and his Christ, so that the prophetic predictions might be completely fulfilled. At that time, therefore, there was no possibility of laws prohibiting impiety – they were more likely to enforce it. The succession of ages was running its course with Jews killing Christian preachers (thinking

they were doing God service thereby, as Christ had foretold [see John 16: 2]), the nations raging against the Christians and the endurance of the martyrs vanquishing them all. It was after that that the saying began to be fulfilled: 'All kings of the earth will worship him and all nations will serve him' [Ps. 72: 11]. So who in his right mind would say to a king: 'Do not worry if anyone hinders or attacks the Church of your Lord within your kingdom; do not let it concern you whether anyone chooses to be religious or sacrilegious'? One would never dream of saying to him: 'Do not let it concern you whether anyone in your kingdom chooses to be virtuous or not.' Free-will is God's gift to mankind, so why should adultery be punished by law and sacrilege permitted? Is it of less importance that a soul keep faith with God than that a woman keep faith with her husband? Even if offences committed through ignorance rather than contempt for religion should be judged more lightly, that does not mean that they should be overlooked.

21. No one will doubt for a moment that it is better for men to be led to the worship of God by instruction than for them to be forced to it by the fear of punishment threatened or the pain of punishment inflicted. But because the former method is the better way, it does not follow that the second method (for those who are not in the first category) should be disregarded altogether. There are many people for whom it has been of value, as we have learned and are still learning by experience. At first they are compelled by fear or pain; later they can be taught or can live out in practice what they had earlier learnt only in words. The opinion of a secular author has been quoted against me on this point: 'I believe it is better to restrain children by their sense of decency and by kindness rather than by fear.'* That is perfectly true. But if those whom love directs are the better, those whom fear corrects are the majority. To reply in the words of the same author, there is another quotation: 'You do not know how to act rightly unless you are compelled by fear of harm.'†

Holy Scripture says about the better group: 'There is no fear in love, but perfect love casts out fear' [1 John 4: 18]. And about the inferior and more numerous group: 'An obstinate servant will not be corrected by words: for even if he should understand, he will not obey' [Prov. 29: 19]. When it says that he is not going to be corrected by words, it does not direct that he should be abandoned. Rather it tacitly tells us how he is to be corrected. Otherwise it would not have said: 'Will not be corrected by words', but simply: 'Will not be corrected'. In another passage it speaks not only of a servant but of an undisciplined son as in need of correction with

* Terence, *Adelphi* 57–8.　　　† Terence, source unknown.

stripes – and to great profit too, 'If you beat him with the rod, you will save his soul from death' [Prov. 23: 14]. And elsewhere: 'He who spares the rod, hates his son' [Prov. 13: 24]. Admittedly the man who with true faith and real understanding declares with all the strength at his command, 'My soul is athirst for the living God; when shall I come and appear before the face of God?' [Ps. 42: 2], is in no need of the fear of hell, let alone of temporal punishments or imperial laws. For him it is so desirable a 'good to hold closely to God' [Ps. 73: 28] that he is not merely terrified of separation from that felicity as a great punishment; he can hardly even bear its delay. Most men, before they come to the point of saying as good sons, 'We have a longing to be gone and to be with Christ' [Phil. 1: 23], have at some earlier stage been recalled to the Lord by the lash of temporal scourging like wicked servants or some kind of dishonest runaway.

22. Who can love us more than Christ, who laid down his life for his sheep? Peter and the other apostles, it is true, he called simply by a word. But in the case of Paul (formerly Saul), who was later to be a great builder of the Church but was first its terrifying devastator, he used more than just a voice to stop him in his path; he prostrated him with an act of power, and in order to impel him from the mad grip of the darkness of infidelity into desiring the inward light of the heart, he first struck him with the outward blinding of his physical sight. If he had not had that punishment, he could not subsequently have been healed of it; if his sight had remained intact, Scripture would not have narrated how he could see nothing when he opened his eyes and how something like scales, by which his eyes had been closed, fell from them at the imposition of Ananias' hand for the restoration of his sight [see Acts 9: 18]. What is the good of that refrain people are so used to declaiming: 'There is freedom to believe or not to believe. On whom did Christ use force? Whom did he compel?' In the case of the apostle Paul they must acknowledge that Christ first compelled and then taught, first struck down and then consoled. It is a remarkable fact that the one who first came to the gospel under the compulsion of a physical punishment in fact laboured in the gospel more abundantly than all the others who were called by word alone. Fear played the greater part in driving him to love, and yet his perfect love cast out fear.

23. Why should not the Church compel lost sons to return, when those lost sons have compelled others to perish? There are cases too of people who were not compelled but only seduced; if they are recalled to the bosom of the Church by fearsome but health-giving laws, our holy mother will enfold them with special tenderness and

will rejoice over them more than over those whom she had never lost. It is surely a duty of pastoral care to seek out those sheep too, who were not stolen away by force but who were smoothly and quietly seduced, who wandered away from the flock and gradually fell into the possession of aliens, and to call them back to the Lord's sheepfold; and if they choose to resist, is it not right to use the threat or even the infliction of scourges to recall them? And if their numbers should increase by further births among those runaway and robber slaves, the Church has an even greater right, since she acknowledges the Lord's imprint among them and treats it with respect when we receive them into membership without rebaptizing them.* The sheep's error must be put right, so that the mark of the redeemer upon it be not marred. Suppose someone is stamped with the king's imprint by a deserter who had himself received that stamp and then both of them are pardoned; one of them returns to the army and the other begins to be in the army, in which he had never been before. In neither case is the imprint annulled; in both cases, surely, it is acknowledged and treated with appropriate respect because it is the king's. So since they cannot show that the direction in which they are being compelled is bad, they claim that they ought not to be compelled even in the direction of the good. But we have shown that Paul was compelled by Christ. In those cases, therefore, which merit compulsion the Church is imitating her Lord; in earlier days when she did not use compulsion she was waiting for the fulfilment of the prophetic prediction about the faith of kings and nations [see Ps. 72: 11].

24. An appropriate sense along these lines can also be given to the apostolic opinion expressed by Paul: 'Being ready to punish every disobedience, when your obedience has first been made complete' [2 Cor. 10: 6]. The Lord himself orders the guests to the great supper first to be invited and only later to be compelled. When the servants replied: 'Lord, what you commanded has been done and still there is room', he said, 'Go out to the highways and the hedges and whoever you find compel them to come in' [Luke 14: 21–3]. In the case of those who were first politely invited, we have obedience being first completed; in the case of those who are compelled, we have disobedience being coerced. For what is the significance of the 'Compel them to come in', following after the initial 'Invite them' and the reply 'What you commanded has been done'? If he had intended this to be understood of those who need to be compelled by awe of miracles, it would have been directed to those who were called first, for it was among them that many divine miracles were done. This was particularly true of the Jews, of whom it was said, 'Jews seek

* See pp. 163–6 above.

after signs' [1 Cor. 1: 22], though miracles of that kind were also used to commend the gospel among the gentiles in apostolic times. So if it was compulsion of this kind that was being ordered, one would reasonably expect, as I have said, that it would be the first guests who would have been the ones to be compelled. So then it is the power which the Church has received as a gift from God at the appropriate time in virtue of the religion and the faith of kings which is compelling those who are in the highways and hedges (that is, the heretics and the schismatics) to come in. They should not be complaining that they are being compelled but taking note of the goal towards which they are being compelled. The Lord's banquet is the unity of the body of Christ, not only in the sacrament of the altar but also in the bond of peace. But of them we can say most emphatically that they never compel anybody to a good end; those whom they compel, they always compel to an evil goal.

53 Augustine
The City of God XIX, 14–17
[CCL 48, 680–5]

14. In the earthly city the use of temporal things is related entirely to the enjoyment of earthly peace; but in the heavenly city it is related to the enjoyment of eternal peace.

If we were irrational animals, all we would desire would be the ordered adjustment of the parts of the body and the quieting of the appetites – in other words bodily ease and a sufficiency of pleasure so that the peace of the body might contribute to the peace of the soul. For absence of bodily peace is a hindrance to the peace of even the irrational soul, since it means it cannot achieve the quieting of the appetites. Both together contribute to that peace which belongs to the inter-relation of soul and body – namely an ordered life and good health. When animals flee from pain, they show how they love the peace of the body; when they pursue pleasure to satisfy the needs of the appetites, they show how they love the peace of the soul. Similarly when they flee from death they give a good indication of how much they love that peace which unites body and soul with each other.

But man has a rational soul and therefore subordinates all that he has in common with the brute creation to the peace of this rational soul. He reflects with the mind and acts in accordance with that reflection, so that there may be that ordered harmony between his thought and his action which we have called the peace of the rational soul. With this end in view he should avoid molestation by pain, distraction by desire and dissolution by death. Then he can gain some useful knowledge whereby he may regulate his life and his habits.

But because of the frailty of the human mind, his very zeal for knowledge may lead him into dangerous error. Therefore he needs divine instruction, which he may follow with certitude, and divine help, that he may follow it freely. But as long as he is in this mortal body, he is in exile from the Lord; he walks by faith and not by sight [see 2 Cor. 5: 6–7]; and for that reason he relates all these forms of peace – of the body, of the soul, and of body and soul together – to that peace which mortal man has with the immortal God, so that he exhibits the well-ordered obedience of faith to the eternal law.

Now God our instructor teaches us that there are two principal commandments, namely love of God and love of neighbour. Man thus finds that there are three things he is to love – God, himself and his neighbour. There is nothing wrong in the man who loves God loving himself. This means that he should take care that his neighbour too should love God, since he is commanded to love his neighbour as himself. This applies to his wife, his children, the members of his household and as many other people as possible. And he in his turn should want to receive the same help from his neighbour in this matter if he should happen to need it. Then, as far as it lies with him, he will enjoy human peace with all men – namely that ordered harmony, whose rule is first to harm no one and then to do good to anyone one can.

His first care is for those who specially belong to him, whether by the ties of nature or by the ordering of human society; with them he has the readiest opportunity for the exercise of that care. That is why the apostle says: 'The man who does not provide for his own, and especially for the members of his household, denies the faith and is worse than an unbeliever' [1 Tim. 5: 8]. This then is the basis of domestic peace, which is the ordered harmony of authority and obedience among people who live together. For those who exercise care also exercise authority; husband over wife, parents over children, masters over slaves. And those for whom that care is exercised practise obedience: wives to husbands, children to parents, slaves to masters. But in the home of a just man who lives by faith [see Hab. 2: 4] and is still in exile from that heavenly city, even those who exercise authority are really serving those over whom they appear to be exercising authority. For they exercise authority not from a desire to lord it over others but from a sense of duty to care for them, not out of pride in being the head but out of compassion which leads them to provide for others.

15. This is prescribed by the order of nature; this is how man has been created by God. 'Let him rule over the fishes of the sea, the birds of the air and all the creeping things which creep on the earth' [Gen. 1: 26]. Man being rational and made in God's image was intended to rule only over irrational beings. God did not intend man to rule over man, but man to rule over the beasts. So the first righteous men were shepherds in charge of beasts rather than kings in command of men. God was thereby indicating what was called for by the order of creation and what was demanded by the entail of sin. The condition of slavery is to be understood as something justly imposed on man as sinner. Thus we do not find the word 'slave' anywhere in Scripture, before its use by righteous Noah in punishing his son's sin [see Gen. 9: 25]. It was guilt, not nature, that gave rise to this term.

The equivalent word in Latin is thought to be derived from the way in which those who by usage of war were liable to be put to death were sometimes preserved by their conquerors and were reduced to a state of servitude, the name being taken from the fact of their having been preserved.* In this case too we have to do with the outcome of sin. For even in a just war, the cause of conflict is the sin of the opposing side. And every victory (even when it is the wicked who are victorious) is a divine judgement designed to humble the conquered for the correction or the punishment of their sins. A witness to this is that man of God, Daniel; in captivity he confessed both his own sins and those of his people and averred in godly sorrow that they were the cause of that captivity.

The first cause of slavery, therefore, is sin; that is why man is subjected to man in the state of slavery. This does not happen apart from the judgement of God, with whom is no injustice and who knows how to apportion varying punishments in accordance with the differing deserts of those who do wrong.

The heavenly Lord declares: 'Everyone who commits sin is the slave of sin' [John 8: 34]. That is why when, as often happens, religious men are slaves of unjust masters, their masters are not free. 'For whatever a man is overcome by, to that he is enslaved' [2 Pet. 2: 19]. And it is better to be the slave of a man than the slave of lust. For lust is a most savage master and one that devastates the hearts of men; this is true, to give only one example, of the lust for mastery itself. But in the peaceful order of human society, where one group of men is subjected to another, slaves are benefited by humility and masters are harmed by pride. By nature, as God first created man, no one is the slave, either of man or of sin. But slavery is ordained as a form of punishment by that law which enjoins the preservation of

* Augustine plays on the words *servus* (slave) and *servare* (preserve).

the natural order and prevents its disturbance. Had that law never been broken, there would have been no need for its enforcement by the punitive measure of slavery. So the apostle instructs slaves to be subject to their masters and to serve them wholeheartedly. Thereby, if they cannot get freedom from their masters, they can make their slavery into a kind of freedom, by performing this service not in deceitfulness and fear but in faithfulness and love, until injustice passes away and all domination and human power are brought to nothing and God is all in all.

16. Our righteous forefathers, then, did have slaves. In their ordering of domestic peace, they made a distinction, where temporal goods were concerned, between the position of their children and that of their slaves. But in respect of the worship of God on whom we look for eternal goods, they provided with equal love for every member of their household. This is so much in accord with the order of nature that it has both given rise to the name 'pater familias', or 'father of the family', and caused it to be used so widely that even unjust masters like to be called by it. Those who are really 'fathers of the family' show a concern for every member of their household, just like their concern for their own children, when it comes to the worship of God and the winning of his favour. Their longing and desire is to reach that heavenly household, where mortals will no longer be required to exercise authority, since they will no longer be required to show concern for those who are already enjoying the bliss of that immortality. But until that goal is reached, fathers bear a heavier load as masters than slaves do as servants.

If any member of the household opposes this domestic peace, he is dealt with by reprimand or whipping or any other fair and legitimate form of punishment, to the extent that human society allows. This is done for the good of the man being dealt with, with the aim of reintegrating him into that peace from which he had broken away. It is not an act of kindness to help a man achieve some good which involves his losing something better; and in the same way it is not a harmless act to spare someone and thereby to let him sink into some worse evil. To do no harm one must not only not inflict evil on anyone; one must also restrain people from sin and punish sin when committed, so that the sinner himself may be corrected by what he undergoes and others deterred by his example.

A man's household should be the starting point or basic element of the state. Now every starting point is related to some appropriate end and every element is related to the unity of that whole of which it is an element. So it clearly follows that domestic peace is related to the peace of the city – in other words the ordered harmony of authority and obedience among those who live together is related to the ordered harmony of authority and obedience among the members of the city. So the father of the family must take the rules by which he runs his household from the law of the city so that the household may be in harmony with the peace of the city.

17. The households of those whose lives are not based on faith try to find earthly peace in the affairs of this temporal life and the rewards it offers; but the households of those whose lives are based on faith long for those eternal things which are promised in the future and act like exiles in the use they make of temporal and earthly things; their aim is not to be captivated or distracted by them from the road that leads to God but to use them both in order to endure the burdens of this corruptible body which weighs down the soul and to keep those burdens to a minimum. So both kinds of people and both kinds of household alike make use of the necessities of this mortal life, but each has his own very different purpose for which he makes use of them.

The earthly city, whose life is not based on faith, seeks earthly peace and in doing so establishes a fixed harmony of its citizens in authority and obedience so as to provide a kind of orderly alignment of human wills in things pertaining to this mortal life. But the heavenly city – or rather that part of it which lives by faith as an exile in the midst of this mortality – has also to make use of that earthly peace until the mortality for which such peace is needed itself passes away. And so as long as it lives the captive life of an exile in the midst of the earthly city, it accepts the promise of future redemption and sees the gift of the spirit as a kind of pledge of it; and at the same time it does not hesitate to obey the laws of the earthly city which control the arrangements needed for the maintenance of our mortal life. Thus as it is a common mortality that the two cities share, harmony is preserved between them in those things which relate to that mortality.

But some of those whom the earthly city has regarded as its wise men are people of whom the divine teaching disapproves. There are those who were led either by their own imaginations or by the deception of demons to believe that there were many gods whose favour must be secured in human affairs and that different matters were somehow or other under the charge of different deities – for example, the body coming under one and the mind another; and, within the body itself, the head coming under one, the neck under another and so on for each part of the body; similarly within the mind, native ability coming under one, learning under another, the element of passion under another and that of desire under another yet again;

and in matters affecting human life cattle under one, and corn, wine, oil, woods, coinage, navigation, wars and victories, marriage, birth and fertility and so on – each under different gods. But the heavenly city knew that there is only one God to be worshipped; it was their faithful and pious conviction that he alone is to be served with that measure of service which the Greeks call λατρεία and which is properly bestowed on none but God. This meant that the heavenly city could not share religious laws with the earthly city; on that issue it had to dissent, and so to antagonize those who thought differently. It had to put up with their anger, their hatred and the violence of their persecutions – though the passions of its adversaries have been kept in check, sometimes by fear at the numbers involved and at all times by the providence of God.

So this heavenly city while living its life of exile on the earth calls out people from every race to be its citizens and builds up a society of exiles within every nation. It is not worried about the diversity of their customs, laws and institutions which serve to produce or to maintain earthly peace. It does not abrogate or annul them but rather preserves and complies with them; for whatever the diversities of law and custom among the various nations, they are all directed to the single and identical goal of earthly peace. Its only condition is that there shall be no interference with the religion which teaches us the worship of the one, supreme and true God.

So during its time of exile here the heavenly city makes use of earthly peace; it also maintains and seeks to promote agreement between the wills of men in all matters relating to man's mortal nature, so far as that can be done without violation of piety and religion. But it relates this earthly peace to heavenly peace, for that is peace in the fullest sense, that is, the only thing which the rational creation at least should think of or speak of as peace, consisting as it does in the perfectly ordered and perfectly harmonious society of those who enjoy God and one another in God. When we arrive there life will no longer be mortal life but life complete and real, and the body will no longer be an animal body whose corruptibility weighs down the soul but a spiritual body free of all want and subject to the will in every part. The heavenly city possesses this peace even while it lives in exile and by faith. It lives a life of righteousness based on this faith when it refers every good action it performs, whether towards God or neighbour (for the life of the city is certainly a social one),* to the acquisition of this heavenly peace.

* Augustine is referring to the dictum of the philosophers, of which he has already expressed his warm approval (*City of God* xix, 5), that the life of the wise man must be social.

11 Final Goal

One of the continuing debates of the patristic period was between those who took the biblical prophecies about the end of the present world and the coming of the next as literal predictions and those who took them more or less figuratively. The passage in which Dionysius of Alexandria discussed the interpretation of the Revelation of John (see pp. 145–51 above) provides an example of such controversy in the third century.

The passages in this section all come from the fourth and early fifth centuries. Rufinus provides a conventional and fairly literal exposition of belief in the resurrection of the flesh, and Chrysostom a harsh and uncompromising presentation of belief in the everlasting punishment of the wicked.

Gregory of Nyssa presents a very different picture. In a passage, the presuppositions for which are to be found in his deeply Platonizing view of evil and of the fall (see pp. 101–12 above), he expresses the belief that ultimately all mankind will be united with the divine and evil will be utterly annihilated. All punishment after death is remedial in intent, and the remedy will be effective. The fact that Gregory's views clearly owed much to Origen became a posthumous embarrassment to his memory when Origen's universalism, along with much else of his most characteristic teaching, came to be condemned as heretical.

Predictions of the imminent end of the world have been another recurrent source of dispute throughout Christian history. In 418 Augustine received a letter from a Dalmatian bishop, Hesychius, who saw in the spread of the faith throughout the Roman empire a sign of the imminence of the end. Augustine replies in the letter of which we print a part by pointing to the ambiguity of all signs of the end – there have been earthquakes and eclipses before – and to the fact that humanity is larger than the Roman empire.

We conclude with the last chapter of *The City of God*, written in Augustine's old age. Every line of it carries resonances of the themes that run through the rest of his work. The goal of man's life lies in that rest in which alone his restless heart will find its peace – that rest in God himself in which the vision, the love and the praise of God will all be one.

54 Rufinus
Commentary on the Apostles' Creed 39–45*
[*CCL* 20, 175–81]
(Translation of J. N. D. Kelly (Westminster, Maryland and London, 1955), pp. 78–86, revised)

39. The final clause, proclaiming as it does the *resurrection of the flesh*, rounds off the sum of all perfection with succinctness and brevity. Even so, the Church's faith has to meet attacks on this point from heretics as well as pagans. Valentinus, for example, denies the resurrection of the flesh altogether; so does Manes, as I have already pointed out. Such people have refused to listen to the prophet Isaiah's words: 'The dead shall rise again, and they who are in their graves shall be raised' [Isa. 26: 19]; or to the affirmation of the most wise Daniel: 'For then they who are in the dust of the earth shall rise again, some to everlasting life, but others to reproach and everlasting confusion' [Dan. 12: 2]. Even from the gospels, which they appear to regard as authoritative, they ought to have learned what our Lord and Saviour said when he was instructing the Sadducees: 'But that the dead rise again, have you not read how he says to Moses in the bush, "The God of Abraham, the God of Isaac, the God of Jacob"? But he is not the God of the dead, but of the living' [Matt. 22: 31–2; Mark 12: 26–7]. In the same context, in what went before, he disclosed the nature and glory of the resurrection in the statement: 'But in the resurrection of the dead they shall neither marry nor be married, but shall be as angels of God' [Matt. 22: 30]. Thus the power of the resurrection bestows the condition of angels on men. As a result, those who have been raised from the earth dwell no longer on the earth with brute beasts, but in heaven with angels, their purer fashion of life having fitted them for this privilege. This applies only to those individuals whose flesh, as the fellow-servant of their souls, has even in this world been tamed by chastity, and so brought into obedience to the Holy Spirit. Thus cleansing the flesh from every stain of vice and allowing it to be transformed into spiritual glory by the power of sanctification,

* Paragraphs 41–7 in the traditional text (*PL* 21, 378A–386A).

they have been counted worthy to have it admitted to the society o angels.

40. But unbelievers exclaim in protest: 'Human flesh rots and disintegrates, or else is changed into dust: it is sometimes sucked under the sea and dispersed in the waves. How then can it be collected together and fashioned into a whole again, so that a man's body is formed afresh out of it?' First, we may make a provisional reply to them in the words of Paul: 'Senseless man, what you sow is not brought to life, unless it first dies. And wheat you sow is not the body that shall be, but a bare grain of wheat or of some other kind of seed. But God gives it a body as he wills' [1 Cor. 15: 36–8]. Can you not then believe that that transformation which you observe taking place annually in the seeds you scatter on the earth will be accomplished in your flesh, which like seed is sown in the ground according to God's law? Why, I ask you, should you take such a restricted, feeble view of the divine power as to think it impossible for the dust out of which each individual's flesh is composed, once it is dispersed, to be collected together and restored to its original form? You observe the ingenuity of mere mortals discovering veins of metal buried deep in the earth, and the expert's eye noticing gold where the inexperienced man's assumes nothing but earth. Shall we not concede to man's creator at least the powers that man, his creature, can attain? Human skill discovers that there are distinct veins of gold and silver, another quite different vein of copper and still further ones of iron and lead – all concealed in what outwardly looks like earth. What right have we then to presume that, however widely dispersed the particles composing each individual's flesh may appear to be, the divine power will be incapable of finding and distinguishing them?

41. However, let us try to suggest reasons drawn from nature which may be of help to minds that are weak in faith. Let us imagine a man jumbling seeds of different sorts together and sowing them indiscriminately or just scattering them on the ground. Is it not the case that the natural constitution of every one of these seeds, wherever it may fall, will ensure the development of the appropriate shoot of its species at the proper season, followed by the fresh growth of a stalk of its own shape and structure? It is the same with the substance of each individual's flesh. However strangely and widely it is dispersed, it possesses its own natural constitution, and that an immortal one. For it will be the flesh of an immortal soul, when God commands spring to start smiling on the bodies that have been planted like seed in the earth. Its natural constitution will gather together from the earth everything that belongs to its substance

and will restore the identical structure which death previously destroyed. The result is that each soul has restored to it, not a composite or alien body, but the actual one it formerly possessed. That is why it becomes possible, in return for the struggles of the present life, for the flesh which has lived morally to be crowned along with its soul, and for the immoral flesh to be punished. That is why my church, in its teaching of the creed, makes an addition which shows care and foresight.* Where the form which others hand down is *the resurrection of the flesh*, she has *the resurrection of this flesh*. The word *this*, of course, refers to the flesh actually touched by the man making this confession, when he marks his forehead with the sign of the cross. The idea is that each of the faithful should realize that, if only he keeps his flesh clean from sin, it will be a vessel of honour, useful to the Lord and serviceable for every good work, whereas if he allows it to be sullied by sin, it will be a vessel of wrath fitted for destruction.

As for the splendour of the resurrection and the greatness of God's promises, anyone who desires fuller information will find allusions to it in almost all the sacred books. I shall mention a few of them at this point, simply by way of recalling them to your mind: they can form the conclusion of the treatise you asked me to write. The apostle Paul, for example, supports the claim that the dead will rise again with arguments like the following: 'But if there is no resurrection of the dead, then Christ himself has not risen again. And if Christ has not risen again, our preaching is vain; your faith, likewise, is empty' [1 Cor. 15: 13–14]. A few verses later he says: 'But now Christ has risen from the dead, the beginning of those who are asleep. For by a man came death, and by a man the resurrection of the dead. For as in Adam all die, so also in Christ all shall be made alive. But every one in his own order: the beginning, Christ; then those who are Christ's, who are at his coming. Afterwards the end' [1 Cor. 15: 20–4]. In what follows he adds: 'Behold, I tell you a mystery. We shall all indeed rise again, but we shall not all be changed' (or as we read in some copies, 'We shall indeed not all sleep, but we shall all be changed'), 'in a moment, in the twinkling of an eye, at the last trumpet: for the trumpet shall sound, and the dead shall rise again incorruptible. And we shall be changed' [1 Cor. 15: 51–2]. He wrote to the Thessalonians too in just the same sense: 'And I will not have you ignorant, brethren, concerning those who are asleep, that you should not be sorrowful even as others who have no hope. For if we believe that Jesus died and rose again, even

* Rufinus is referring to the creed of Aquileia, where he was baptized.

so God will through Jesus bring with him those who have fallen asleep. For this we say to you by the word of the Lord, that we who are alive, who are left at the coming of the Lord, shall not precede those who have slept. For the Lord himself shall come down from heaven with a cry of command, with the voice of an archangel, and with the trumpet of God; and the dead who are in Christ shall rise first. Then we who are alive, who are left, shall be taken up together with them in the clouds to meet Christ, into the air. And so we shall be always with the Lord' [1 Thess. 4: 13–17].

42. You must not assume, however, that Paul is the sole mouthpiece of these truths, as if his message were a novelty. Listen to the prophet Ezekiel's prediction, uttered long ago under the inspiration of the Holy Spirit: 'Behold, I will open your sepulchres, and will bring you out of your sepulchres' [Ezek. 37: 12]. Listen also to Job, who is throughout so rich in mystical language, unmistakably foretelling the resurrection of the dead: 'A tree has hope. For if it is cut down, it will bear buds again, and its shoots never fail. But if it grows old, its root is in the earth. And if its trunk be dead in the rock, at the scent of water it will flourish again, and it will put forth foliage like a young plant. But a man, if he should die, has he departed? And a mortal man, if he should fall, shall he then be no more?' [Job 14: 7–10]. Is it not clear that the intention of these words is, as it were, to shame men into agreement? 'Is mankind then so stupid', he is saying, 'that they can see the trunk of a felled tree shooting up again from the earth, and a dead log showing signs of renewed life, and yet cannot imagine something happening to them analogous to what happens to logs and trees?' For proof that the sentence, 'But mortal man, when he falls, shall he not rise again?' [Job 14: 12] is to be taken as a question, consult the verses which follow. He straightway adds: 'For if a man dies, he shall live' [Job 14: 14]. A moment later he remarks: 'I shall await until I be made again' [Job 14: 14]. Elsewhere he makes the same point: 'He shall raise again upon the earth my skin, which now drinks its fill of these things' [Job 19: 25–6].

43. Thus much, then, in demonstration of the belief we profess in the creed, *the resurrection of this flesh*. As for *this*, you observe how well its addition harmonizes with all my citations from Holy Scripture. What else, for example, is Job emphasizing in the passage I explained above, when he says: 'He will raise again my skin, which now drinks its fill of these things', that is to say, which has to put up with these sufferings? Is he not pointing in the plainest way to the resurrection of *this* flesh – the flesh, I mean, which in this world has to endure the anguish of tribulation and trial? Or take the

apostle's statement: 'For this corruptible must put on incorruption, and this mortal must put on immortality' [1 Cor. 15: 53]. Does it not suggest that he is somehow touching his own body and placing his finger upon it? *This* body, he is saying, which is now corruptible, will, through the grace of resurrection, become incorruptible, and *this* frame, which is now mortal, will be clothed with immortal capacities. Hence, just as 'Christ, rising from the dead, dies now no more: death shall no more have dominion over him' [Rom. 6: 9], so those who rise again in Christ will be no longer subject to either corruption or death, not because they will have discarded their flesh, but because its status and character will have been altered. It will be a real body, therefore, which will rise from the dead incorruptible and immortal; and this applies to the just and to sinners alike. In the case of the just it will be to enable them to abide for ever with Christ; in the case of sinners, so that they may discharge, without undergoing destruction, the penalties which are their due.

44. The just, I repeat, abide for ever with Christ the Lord. The proof of this I provided in a previous chapter when I quoted the apostle's statement: 'Then we who are alive, who are left, shall together with them be taken up in the clouds to meet Christ, into the air. And so we shall be always with the Lord' [1 Thess. 4: 17]. There is no need for astonishment that, as a result of their resurrection, the flesh of the saints is to be so gloriously transformed as to be suspended in the clouds and carried along in the air to meet God. The apostle himself, explaining the benefits God bestows on those who love him, remarks: 'Who will transform the body of our lowness, conformably to the body of the Son of his glory' [Phil. 3: 21]. So there is no absurdity in the suggestion that the bodies of the saints will be raised up on the clouds into the air, seeing it is stated that they are to be refashioned on the model of Christ's body, which is set on the right hand of God. The apostle brings out this point too, with reference either to himself or to others of like status or merit, when he says: 'For he has raised us up together with Christ, and has made us sit alongside him in the heavenly places' [Eph. 2: 6]. Since then we have been promised that these and countless similar blessings will attend the resurrection of the just, we should not find it difficult to credit the predictions made by the prophets, to the effect that 'The just shall shine as the sun' and 'as the brightness of the firmament, in the kingdom of God' [Matt. 13: 43; Wisdom 3: 7; Dan. 12: 3]. For will anyone find it difficult to believe that they will possess the brightness of the sun, and will be adorned with the splendour of the stars and the firmament, seeing that the life and

companionship of God's angels is being prepared for them in heaven and seeing that we are told they are to be refashioned on the model of the glory of Christ's body? It is this glory, promised them by the Saviour's own voice, which the blessed apostle had in mind when he said: 'It is sown a natural body: it will rise a spiritual body' [1 Cor. 15: 44]. For if it is true, as it assuredly is, that God's mercy is going to unite just men and saints, one and all, in fellowship with the angels, he will with equal certainty change their bodies too into the glory of a spiritual body.

45. You should not, however, draw the conclusion that what is here promised runs counter to the body's natural constitution. It is our belief, founded on Scripture, that God took 'the slime of the earth' when he made man, and that the nature of our body is constituted by the transformation, at God's command, of earth into flesh [see Gen. 2: 7]. If so, why should you think it absurd or contradictory that, just as we hold earth to have been promoted so as to form animal body, in exactly the same way we should believe animal body to be promoted so as to form spiritual body?

You will find all these testimonies to the resurrection of the just, and a host of others like them, in sacred Scripture. But sinners too, as I explained above, will have the state of incorruption and immortality granted to them at the resurrection. Just as this state serves to the perpetuation of the glory of the just, so too it prolongs the confusion and punishment of sinners. That prophetic utterance to which I referred a few moments ago makes this perfectly clear in the words: 'And many shall rise again from the dust of the earth, some to everlasting life, but others to confusion and everlasting reproach' [Dan. 12: 2].

55 John Chrysostom
Homilies on 1 Corinthians 9, 1–3 (on 1 Cor. 3: 12–15)
[Ed. F. Field (Oxford, 1847), pp. 100–6]

If anyone builds on this foundation with gold, silver, precious stones, wood, hay, stubble – each man's work will become manifest. For the day will disclose it, because it will be revealed with fire and the fire will test what sort of work each one has done. If any man's work survives, which he has built, he will receive a reward. If any man's work is burnt up, he will suffer loss. But he himself will be saved, yet only as through fire.

1. The subject now before us is one of no small importance. It is an issue of the highest significance and one of universal concern – namely whether the fires of hell have an end.

They have no end. Christ has shown this by declaring that 'their fire shall not be quenched and their worm shall not die' [Mark 9: 48; see Isa. 66: 24]. I know that those words make you shudder. But what can I do about it? God orders us to teach these things unceasingly. His word is 'Command this people' [Exod. 19: 10 (?)]. We who have been appointed to a ministry of the word have to make ourselves a burden to our hearers; that is not a matter of our own choice, it is something laid upon us. Yet we need not be a burden if you so choose. For 'if you do what is good, do not fear' [see Rom. 13: 3]. So it is open to you not merely to hear us without hostility but actually to listen with pleasure.

Well, then, hell-fire has no end; Christ has made that clear. Paul also shows punishment to be unending when he says that sinners 'will suffer eternal destruction' [2 Thess. 1: 9]; he also says, 'Do not be deceived; neither fornicators nor adulterers nor effeminates shall inherit the kingdom of God' [1 Cor. 6: 9–10]; and to the Hebrews, 'Strive for peace with all men and for the holiness without which no one will see the Lord' [Heb. 12: 14]. And to those who said, 'In your name we did many mighty works', Christ replies, 'Depart from me, I do not know you, you evil doers' [Matt. 7: 22–3]. The virgins who were shut out never got in at any later time, and of those who failed to minister to him he says, 'They will go away into eternal punishment' [Matt. 25: 46].

Do not say to me, 'How is the balance of justice preserved if the punishment has no end?' When God does something, obey his demand and do not submit what has been said to human reasoning. In any case is it not in fact just that one who has received countless good things from the very beginning, has then done things deserving punishment, and has not reformed in response either to threats or to kindness, should be punished? If it is justice you are after, we ought all on the score of justice to have perished at the very outset. Indeed even that would have fallen short of the measure of mere justice. Even that fate, if we had suffered it, would have contained some kindness. For if a man insults someone who never did him any wrong, it is a matter of justice that he be punished. But what if he insults his benefactor, who without having received any favour from him in the first place, has done countless things for him – in this case the one who was the sole source of his existence, who is God, who endowed him with a soul, who gave him countless other gifts and purposed to bring him to heaven? If after so many favours, he not only insults him but insults him daily by his conduct, can there be any question of deserving pardon?

Do you not see how he punished Adam for a single sin? 'Yes', you will say, 'but he had given him paradise and made him the recipient of very great kindness.' And I reply that it is not at all the same thing for a man in the tranquil possession of security to commit a sin and for a man in the midst of affliction to do so. The really terrible thing is that you sin when you are not in paradise but set amidst the countless evils of this present life, and that all this misery has not made you any more sensible. It is like a man who continues his criminal behaviour in prison. Moreover you have the promise of something even greater than paradise. He has not given it to you yet, so as not to make you soft at a time when there is a struggle to be fought, but neither has he been silent about it, lest you be cast down by all your labours.

Adam committed one sin, and brought on total death. We commit a thousand sins every day. If by committing a single sin he brought such terrible evil on himself and introduced death into the world, what should we, who live continually in sin, expect to suffer – we who in place of paradise have the expectation of heaven? This is a burdensome message; it does upset the man who hears it. I know, because I feel it myself. I am disturbed by it; it makes me quake. The clearer the proofs I find of this message of hell, the more I tremble and melt with fear. But I have to proclaim it so that we may not fall into hell. What you received was not paradise or trees and plants, but heaven and the good things in the heavens. He who had received the lesser gift was punished and no consideration exempted him; we have been given a greater calling and we sin more. Are we not bound to suffer things beyond all remedy?

Consider how long our race has been subject to death on account of a single sin. More than five thousand years have passed and the death due to a single sin has not yet been ended. In Adam's case we cannot say that he had heard prophets or that he had seen others being punished for their sins so that he might reasonably have been afraid and learnt prudence if only from the example of others. He was the first and at that time the only one; yet he was still punished. But you cannot claim any of these things. You have had numerous examples, but you only grow worse; you have been granted the great gift of the Spirit, but you go on producing not one or two or three but countless sins. Do not think that because the sins are committed in one brief moment the punishment therefore will also be a matter of a moment. You can see how it is often the case that men who have committed a single theft or a single act of adultery

which has been done in a brief moment of time have had to spend
all their lives in prison or in the mines, continually battling with
hunger and every kind of death. No one lets them off, or says that
since the crime was committed in a brief moment the punishment
should match the crime in the length of time it lasts.

2. 'People do act like that', you may say, 'but they are men,
whereas God is loving towards mankind.' Yes, but even the men
who act in this way do not do so out of cruelty but out of love to
mankind. So since God is loving to mankind he too will deal with
sin in this way. 'As great as is his mercy, so great is also his reproof'
[Ecclus. 16: 12]. So when you speak of God as loving towards mankind, you are actually supplying me with a further reason for punishment, in the fact that the one against whom we sin is such as this.
That is the point of Paul's words: 'It is a fearful thing to fall into
the hands of the living God' [Heb. 10: 31]. I ask you to bear with
these words of fire. Perhaps, yes, perhaps, they may bring you some
consolation. What man can punish as God has been known to
punish? He caused a flood and the total destruction of the human
race; a little later he rained fire from on high and utterly destroyed
them all. What human retribution can compare with that? Do you
not recognize that even this case of punishment is virtually endless?
Four thousand years have passed and the punishment of the
Sodomites is still in full force. As his loving kindness is great, so also
is his punishment.

Again if God had given you commandments that were burdensome or impossible to fulfil, someone might possibly have pleaded the
difficulty of the laws. But if they are easy of fulfilment, what excuse
can we offer when even so we fail to keep them? You cannot fast
or practise celibacy, you say. But you could if you so wished, and
those who have succeeded in doing so are our accusers. Nevertheless
God has not required such strict standards of us; he has not made
these things a matter of command or law. He has left them to the
free choice of the hearer. You can surely show self-control within
marriage and abstain from drunkenness. Then you will argue that
you cannot give away all your possessions. But you could – and
those who in fact do so are proof of it. Yet here again this is not something that God has laid on us. His command is that you should not
be grasping and that you should provide for the needy out of what
you have. And if anyone says, 'I cannot be content with my wife
alone', he is self-deceived and his claim is false. Those who live in
chastity without any wife are his accusers. Do not say you cannot
help cursing or swearing. It is doing these things that is burdensome,
not refraining from them. What possible excuse have we for failing

to keep laws as light and as easy as these? We have none whatsoever.

All this goes to show clearly that God's punishment is unending. But some people think that Paul's words contradict this. So we must bring them out into the open and see carefully what they mean. Paul says: 'If any man's work survives which he has built, he will receive a reward. If any man's work is burned up, he will suffer loss.' Then he goes on, 'But he himself will be saved, yet only as through fire.'

What are we to say to this? We must begin by considering what the various things are – the foundation, the gold, the precious stones, the hay and the stubble.

Paul himself reveals explicitly that the foundation is Christ. 'No other foundation can any one lay than that which is laid, which', he says, 'is Christ Jesus.' But the building seems to me to indicate actions. Some people say that this too* has to do with teachers and learners and with corrupt heresies. But this does not fit the sense of the passage. If this were the meaning, why should the building be destroyed but the builder be saved even if through fire? Surely it would be the one responsible who should suffer the destruction, whereas in this case it will be the one who has been built who receives the severer sentence. If the teacher were responsible for the evil, he ought to receive the severer sentence. So what could be meant by 'he will be saved'? And if he were not responsible, but the learners had become what they did become through their own waywardness, then the teacher having built well ought not to receive any sentence at all or undergo any loss. So what could be meant by 'he will suffer loss'?

So the passage must be about actions. Paul goes on a little later to deal with the man who had committed fornication [see 1 Cor. 5]; and here he is preparing the ground well in advance. He was very good at dealing with one topic in such a way as to prepare the ground for the topic to which he planned to move on next. For example when he is rebuking those who did not wait for one another at meals, he prepared the ground for his treatment of the mysteries. So here it is, because he is pressing ahead to the issue of the fornicator that, while still dealing with the foundation, he adds: 'Do you not know that you are God's temple and that God's spirit dwells in you? If anyone destroys God's temple, God will destroy him' [1 Cor. 3: 16–17]. This was intended to strike fear into the soul of the fornicator beforehand.

* See Chrysostom's discussion of 1 Cor. 3: 10–11 in *Homily* 8. He distinguishes the foundation, which is a matter of true or false teaching, from what is built on it.

If anyone builds on this foundation with gold, silver, precious stones, wood, hay or stubble. After faith there is need of building up. So in another place he says, 'Build one another up with these words' [see I Thess. 4: 18; 5: 11]. Both the skilled workman and the learner contribute to this building. That is why he says: 'Let each man take care how he builds.'

3. If these sayings referred to faith, the passage would not make sense. For in respect of faith everyone is necessarily equal since there is but one faith; whereas in quality of life it is not possible for everyone to be the same. Faith is not smaller in one case and better in another; it is the same for everyone who really believes. But as far as manner of life is concerned some are more serious, others more easy-going; some are stricter, others less so; some have great achievements to their credit, others smaller ones; some have been guilty of serious sins, others of lesser ones. That is why he speaks of gold, silver, precious stones, wood, hay and stubble.

Each man's work will become manifest. It is conduct of which he is speaking here. 'If any man's work survives, which he has built, he will receive a reward; if any man's work is burned up, he will suffer loss.' If this had been intended to refer to learners and teachers, the teachers would not have had to suffer loss if the learners did not listen to them. What he says is, 'Each man will receive his own reward according to his own labour' – labour, not result. What would happen if the hearers paid no attention? Here you have still further proof that the passage is concerned with deeds.

What he is saying is this. If any one has a correct faith but leads an evil life, his faith will not provide him with exemption from punishment. His work will be burnt up. The phrase 'will be burnt up' means will not stand up to the force of the fire. If a man with golden armour were to pass through a river of fire, he would come out all the brighter, whereas if a man with hay were to go through it he would not merely get no benefit from doing so but would actually destroy himself. It is the same with our deeds. The passage is not concerned with the burning up of material substances; it is intended to heighten men's fear and show that the man who lives a life of evil is utterly devoid of protection. So he says, 'he will suffer loss' – that is one punishment. Then 'he himself will be saved, yet as through fire' – that is a second punishment. What it means is this. He will not himself be destroyed, like his works, by passing into nothingness. He will remain in the fire.

'Yet he calls this "being saved"', you say. That is why he adds 'as through fire'. We often talk of things which are not immediately burned up and turned to ashes as being 'saved' or 'preserved' in the fire. So when you hear the word 'fire', do not start thinking of the things that are burned as being annihilated. And do not be surprised that such punishment is called 'being saved'. Paul often uses a euphemistic name for an evil thing and vice versa. 'Captivity' is the name for an evil thing, but Paul uses it of a good thing when he speaks of 'bringing every thought into captivity to the obedience of Christ' [2 Cor. 10: 5]. Or, the other way round, he says, 'Sin reigned' [Rom. 5: 21], where 'reign' is a euphemistic word to use. So here, 'he will be saved' is an indirect indication of the intensity of the punishment. It is as if he were saying: 'he himself will go on being punished for ever'.

56 Gregory of Nyssa
Sermon on 1 Corinthians 15: 28, §§32–44
[Ed. J. K. Downing, pp. 20–7]*

32. My plan is as follows. First of all I shall expound the sense of the passage in my own words. Then I shall add the actual words of the apostle which are in accord with the sense which I shall by then have expounded.

33. So I begin by asking what is the truth that the divine apostle intends to convey in this passage? It is this. In due course evil will pass over into non-existence; it will disappear utterly from the realm of existence. Divine and uncompounded goodness will encompass within itself every rational nature; no single being created by God will fail to achieve the kingdom of God. The evil that is now present in everything will be consumed like base metal melted by the purifying flame. Then everything which derives from God will be as it was in the beginning before it had ever received an admixture of evil. †

34. The way in which this will happen is as follows. In our mortal and perishable nature, says Paul, there has appeared the pure and uncompounded divinity of the only-begotten. Human nature as a whole has thus received an admixture of the divine. The manhood of Christ is a kind of first-fruits of this common man, and by it humanity as a whole has been grafted on to divinity.

---

* 'The Treatise of Gregory of Nyssa In *Illud: Tunc et Ipse Filius*, A Critical Text with Prolegomena' (Harvard dissertation). See *Harvard Studies in Classical Philology*, LVIII–LIX (1948), 221–3. The traditional text is found in *PG* 44, 1313A–1316D.

† Compare pp. 101–12 above.

35. Evil was totally abolished in him who 'knew no sin', as the prophet says, 'neither was any guile found in his mouth' [Isa. 53: 9]. Along with sin was abolished in him also the death which follows from it (for death has no other origin than sin). So the abolition of evil and the dissolution of death began with him. From this there followed a kind of sequentially ordered pattern.

36. In a pattern of this kind some members are further away from the prime member, in accordance with their declension from the good; others are found to be closer to it – each in accordance with its own deserts and powers. So in this case: we begin with the human element in Christ. As the recipient of divinity within himself, this man became the first-fruits of our nature. He also became the first-fruits of those who slept and first-begotten from the dead, loosing the pangs of death.

37. This man, who was wholly separated from sin, who has destroyed the power of death in himself and overthrown its rule, authority and might, comes first. After him comes a man like Paul who imitated Christ to the full in his separation from evil; a person of that kind will follow behind the first-fruits at the advent. [38] Then (just to take an example) might come perhaps Timothy, who imitated his teacher to the best of his ability, or anyone else like him. So the sequence continues, the gradual declension from the good putting each man respectively behind those in front of him, until it reaches those in whom there is so much evil that it constitutes a greater proportion in them than the good.

39. In accordance with this same pattern the sequence, which leads from those least involved in evil to those who are most involved in it, produces an ordered structure of persons who are returning to the good. Then when the advance of the good has reached the furthest extremity of evil, evil will be thereby abolished. [40] And this is the ultimate goal of our hope, that nothing should be left in opposition to the good but that the divine life should permeate everything and abolish death from every being, the sin, from which as we have already said death secured its hold over men, having already been destroyed.

41. Now when every evil authority and rule has been abolished from among us and no passion dominates our nature any longer, it follows inevitably that with no other master over us everything will be subjected to the power which is over all. Subjection to God is total separation from evil. [42] When we all are free of evil in imitation of the first-fruits, then the whole mass of our nature will be commingled with the first-fruits and we shall become completely one body which accepts the lordship of the good and of that alone. So

the whole body of our human nature will be commingled with the divine and uncompounded nature; and therein will be achieved in us what is called the subjection of the Son – for the subjection which is established in his body is being rightly ascribed to him who makes this grace of subjection effective in us.

43. That, we believe, is the sense of Paul's teaching. Now we must quote the actual words of the apostle: *For as in Adam all die, so also in Christ shall all be made alive. But each in his own order; Christ the first fruits, then at his coming those who belong to Christ. Then comes the end when he delivers the kingdom to God the Father after destroying every rule and every authority and power. For he must reign until he has put all his enemies under his feet. The last enemy to be destroyed is death. 'For God has put all things in subjection under his feet.' But when it says, 'He has subjected all things', it is plain that this does not include the one who had subjected all things to him. When he has subjected all things to him, then the Son himself will also be subjected to him who has subjected all things to him, that God may be all in all* [1 Cor. 15: 22–8].

44. That last phrase, which speaks of God coming to be in all by becoming all to each, clearly portrays the non-existence of evil. Obviously God will be 'in all' only when no trace of evil is to be found in anything. For God cannot be in what is evil. So either he will not be 'in all' and some evil will be left in things, or, if we are to believe that he is 'in all', then that belief declares that there will be no evil. For God cannot be in what is evil.

57 Augustine
Letter 199, 46–54
[*CSEL* 57, 284–92]

46. I do not know whether one can discover anything more definite on this question (supposing one had the knowledge or ability to do so) than what I wrote in my previous letter – that the Lord's coming will take place when the whole world is filled with the gospel.* Your Reverence's opinion that this was already achieved by the apostles themselves is, I am sure on the basis of definite evidence, not true. Here in Africa there are innumerable barbarian tribes to whom the gospel has not yet been preached, as can be learned from the daily evidence of those who have been taken

* Compare *Letter* 197, 4.

prisoner and are now in slavery to the Romans. Admittedly, over the last few years it has happened in the case of some, but only very few and very occasionally; some of those who live on the Roman frontier and have been pacified have as a result had governors appointed by the Roman empire instead of having kings of their own – and these governors have begun to be Christians. But those in the interior who are untouched by Roman authority are totally unaffected by the Christian religion. At the same time one cannot possibly say that the promises of God have nothing to do with them.

47. What the Lord promised to the seed of Abraham was not the Romans but all nations; and he promised it with an oath. In accordance with this promise it has already happened that several nations who do not fall under Roman jurisdiction have accepted the gospel and joined the Church as she bears fruit and grows throughout the world [see Col. 1: 6]. She still has room for growth before the prophecy is fulfilled which was made about Christ as prefigured by Solomon: 'He shall rule from sea to sea and from the river to the ends of the world' [Ps. 72: 8]. 'From the river' means from the place where he was baptized, since that is where he began to preach the gospel. But 'from the sea to sea' means the whole world with its inhabitants, since it is entirely surrounded by the ocean. How else is the prophecy to be fulfilled: 'All the nations thou hast made shall come and worship before thee, O Lord' [Ps. 86: 9]? They will not come by leaving their homes but by believing in their homes. It was of those who believe that the Lord said: 'No one can come to me unless it is granted him by the Father' [John 6: 65]. And the prophet said: 'They shall worship him, each one in his own home, all the islands of the nations' [Zeph. 2: 11]. 'All the islands', he said, as if he were saying, 'even all the islands'. By this he is indicating that no land is left without the Church, in that no island is left without it. There are a number of islands even in the ocean; and some of these, so we have been told, have already accepted the gospel. Thus in some individual islands the words are being fulfilled: 'He shall rule from sea to sea.' For every island is surrounded by the sea, as the whole world is; the world is, in a sense, the largest island of all, in that it is surrounded by the ocean. In the West, we are told, the Church has reached the shores of the ocean. Whatever shores she has not yet reached, she certainly will reach in the process, of course, of bearing fruit and growing [see Col. 1: 6].

48. Since true prophecy cannot lie, it must be the case that all the nations that God has made will worship him. But how will they worship him unless they call on him? And, 'how will they call on him in whom they have not believed? And how will they believe in

him of whom they have not heard? And how will they hear without a preacher? And how will they preach unless they are sent?' [Rom. 10: 14–15]. He sends his messengers and gathers his elect from the four winds, that is, from the whole world. Accordingly, in nations where the Church does not yet exist, she must come into existence; but this does not mean that all who live in them must come to believe. The promise refers to 'all nations', not to all members of all nations; 'for not all have faith' [2 Thess. 3: 2]. Each nation believes in the persons of all who were chosen 'before the foundation of the world' [Eph. 1: 4]; in the persons of the rest it does not believe, and, indeed, hates those who do believe. How else will the saying be fulfilled: 'You will be hated by all nations for my name's sake' [Matt. 24: 9]? It can only be fulfilled if in all nations there are those who hate and those who are hated.

49. So how can this prophecy have been fulfilled by the apostles when, as we know for a fact, there are still nations in which its fulfilment is just beginning, as well as nations in which it has not yet begun? Consequently, when the Lord said: 'You shall be my witnesses in Jerusalem and in all Judaea and Samaria and to the end of the earth' [Acts 1: 8], he did not mean that those to whom he was then speaking were to fulfil such a task by themselves. It was like those other words, apparently addressed to them alone: 'Behold, I am with you always, to the close of the age' [Matt. 28: 20]. Everyone understands these words as a promise to the universal Church which is to last through succeeding generations, each born and dying in its turn, from now until the close of the age. Similarly, he was saying something which was not of concern to them at all, and yet said it as if it concerned them alone, when he uttered the words: 'When you see all these things, know that he is near, at the very gates' [Matt. 24: 33]. The people whom these words concern are those who will be in the flesh when all things are fulfilled. Surely this can even more easily be the case with an activity which to a large extent was to be performed by them, although it was also being kept for their successors.

50. But what of the words of the apostle: 'Have they not heard? "Their voice has gone out into all the earth and their words to the ends of the world"' [Rom. 10: 18; Ps. 19: 4]? Although he used the past tense, he was speaking of something future, not of something done and finished – just like the prophet whom he cites as a witness. The prophet said, not, 'Their voice will go out', but, 'has gone out into all the earth', although he was clearly speaking of something that had not yet happened. A similar instance is: 'They have pierced my hands and feet' [Ps. 22: 16] – something which we

know happened long afterwards. We are not to suppose that this way of speaking is confined to the prophets and does not extend to the apostles. This is clear from the words of the same apostle: 'Which is the Church of the living God, the pillar and foundation of the truth. And without doubt great is the mystery of godliness which has been revealed in the flesh, justified in the Spirit, seen by angels, preached among the nations, believed on in the world, and taken up in glory' [1 Tim. 3: 15–16]. Surely it is obvious that this last phrase has not been fulfilled even now, let alone at the time when the words were spoken. The time when the Church will be taken up in glory is when the words will be spoken: 'Come, O blessed of my Father, receive the kingdom' [Matt. 25: 34]. Nevertheless the apostle spoke of this as something that had already occurred, although he certainly knew that it lay in the future.

51. It is much less surprising that he used the present tense in that other passage of his which you also mention: 'Because of the hope which is laid up for you, of which you have heard before in the word of the truth of the gospel which has come to you, as indeed in all the world it is bearing fruit and growing' [Col. 1: 5–6]. He said this, although the gospel was not yet in possession of the whole world. But he said that it was bearing fruit and growing in the whole world in order to indicate how far it was to extend by bearing fruit and growing. We do not know when the Church, bearing fruit and growing, will fill the whole world completely from sea to sea. Therefore it is certain that we do not know when the end will be; for it certainly will not be before then.

52. May I tell you, as a holy man of God and as a sincere brother, what I feel about this question? Whether one believes that the Lord is coming sooner, or whether one believes that he is coming later than he actually will come, in either case there is an error to be avoided, as far as man can avoid it. It seems to me that a man is not in error when he knows that he does not know something, but only when he supposes that he knows something which he does not in fact know. So let us remove from the scene that wicked servant who says in his heart: 'My master is delaying his coming', and who then bullies his fellow-servants and spends his time feasting with drunkards [Matt. 24: 48–9]. There is no doubt that he hates his Lord's coming. Let us remove this wicked servant and set before our eyes three good servants who manage their Lord's household with diligence and sobriety, and who wait for his coming with a thirsty longing, a vigilant hope, and a faithful love. One of them thinks that he will come sooner, the second later, but the third admits his ignorance. Although all of them are in accord with the

gospel, in that they all love the Lord's appearing and wait for it
with longing and vigilance, let us see which of them is in closest
accord with it.

53. The first says: 'Let us watch and pray, because the Lord is
coming soon.' The second says: 'Let us watch and pray, because
this life is short and uncertain – although the Lord is coming later.'
The third says: 'Let us watch and pray, both because this life is
short and uncertain and because we do not know the time at which
the Lord is coming.' The gospel says: 'Take heed, watch and pray;
for you do not know when the time will be' [Mark 13: 33]. I ask
you, what do we hear the third man saying but what the gospel
says? All of them, in their longing for God's kingdom, wish the truth
to be what the first man's opinion holds it to be. The second disagrees with this opinion. The third disagrees with neither of them,
but admits that he does not know which of their utterances is true.

If the first man's prediction comes true, the second and third will
rejoice with him. For all of them love the Lord's appearing, and so
will rejoice because the object of their love has come sooner. But if
this does not occur and the second man's opinion looks more likely
to be true, there is reason to fear that those who had believed what
the first man said may become unsettled by the intervening delay
and may begin to suppose, not that the Lord will come later, but
that he will not come at all. You can see how many souls will perish
that way. But even if they have sufficient faith to turn to the predictions of the second man and to wait for the Lord with fidelity and
patience despite his delay, there will still be plenty of taunts, insults
and mockery from the enemies of the faith; and these will turn many
of the weak from their Christian faith by telling them that the
promise of the kingdom is as fallacious as was the promise that it
would come quickly. However, the faith of those who believe the
second man's assertion, that the Lord will come later, will not be
troubled at all if that assertion is proved false by his coming sooner.
Their experience will be that of unexpected joy.

54. So first there is the man who says that the Lord is coming
soon. What he is saying is more to be desired; but it is dangerous if
it is mistaken. He must hope that it is true, because it will be harmful
if it is not. Then there is the man who says that the Lord will come
later and who still believes in, hopes for and loves his coming. If
he is mistaken about the Lord's delay, he is fortunate in his mistake.
He will have more patience if he is right; more joy if he is not. Those,
therefore, who love the Lord's coming, will find greater pleasure
in listening to the first man, but greater security in believing the
second. The third man confesses his ignorance; he does not know

which view is true. He wishes for the first, and is resigned to the second; but on neither account is he in error, since he neither affirms nor denies either of them.

I ask you not to spurn me if I take this view myself. I love you for affirming what I long to be true; and the measure of my desire that you should be correct is to be seen in my love for what you promise as well as in my vision of the dangers, should you be mistaken. Forgive me if I have been burdensome to you. Because opportunity comes so seldom, it has given me great pleasure to speak with you at length, if only by correspondence.

58 Augustine
The City of God XXII, 30
[*CCL* 48, 862–6]

How great that felicity will be, where no evil will be present, no good will be absent, and nothing will distract from the praises of God, who will be all in all. I can conceive of no other activity where there will be neither weariness to make one desist nor lack to make one work. I also learn about this from the sacred song in which I read – or hear – the words: 'Blessed are they who dwell in thy house! They will be praising thee for ever and ever' [Ps. 84: 4]. All the members and organs of the incorruptible body, which we now see devoted to their various necessary functions, will contribute to God's praises. For then there will be no necessity, but only felicity, full and secure, serene and eternal. All those elements which make up the harmony of the body and which now elude our discernment (we discussed this earlier) will then be discerned in their distribution, internal and external, throughout the whole body. Delight at the intellectual beauty which will be revealed in them, as in other great marvels which will there be disclosed, will set our rational spirits on fire in praise of such a creator. What kind of movements such bodies will make, I shall not be so rash as to define; they are beyond my powers of conception. But whether in motion or at rest, they and their appearance will always be seemly; for nothing will be present that is not seemly. Where the spirit wills to be, there it is certain that the body will immediately be; and the spirit will never will anything that is not becoming to spirit and body alike.

True glory shall be there; no one will receive praise in error or in flattery. True honour shall be there; no one who is worthy will be denied it, and no one who is unworthy will be granted it; indeed no one unworthy will seek for it, since only the worthy will gain admittance there. True peace shall be there; no one will encounter opposition, either from outside or from within himself. God himself will be virtue's reward; for he who gives virtue has promised himself as its reward, the greatest and best there can possibly be. What else did he mean when he said through the prophet: 'I shall be their God and they shall be my people' [Lev. 26: 12] but: 'I shall be their satisfaction; I shall be all that men can virtuously desire – life, health, food, wealth, glory, honour, peace and every good thing'? This is also the true meaning of the words of the apostle: 'That God may be all in all' [1 Cor. 15: 28]. He himself will be the end of our desires, whom we shall see without end, love without satiety, and praise without wearying. This employment, this devotion and this activity will undoubtedly be shared by all, like eternal life itself.

But what of the degrees of honour and glory which will exist, corresponding with the degrees of merit that are to be rewarded? Who can conceive, let alone describe them? That such degrees will exist, there is no doubt. Yet that blessed city will find within itself this great good also, that no one who is superior will be envied by his inferior, just as now the archangels are not envied by the rest of the angels. No one will wish to be what he has not received, however closely he is bound in peaceful concord with him who has received. It will be like the body, in which the finger does not wish it were the eye, but both are included within the peaceful structure of the body as a whole. And so, along with the gift which each man will receive, some smaller, some greater, he will receive the additional gift of desiring no more than he has.

We are not to suppose that because sin will have lost its power to delight them, they will be without freedom of will. No, the will will be all the more free, because set free from delight in sin to an indefectible delight in not sinning. The first freedom of the will, which was given to man when he was first created upright, consisted in the capacity not to sin, but also in the capacity to sin. The last freedom of the will will be stronger, in that it will be incapable of sin. But this too will be a divine gift and not a natural capacity. For it is one thing to be God, another to participate in him. God is by nature incapable of sin, whilst he who participates in God has received his inability to sin as a gift from him. There were stages in the divine gift which had to be preserved. By the gift of the first freedom of the will, man was made capable of not sinning; by the last, incapable of sinning. The former was suited to the acquisition of merit, the latter to the reception of merit's reward. Because our nature, when capable of sin, did sin, grace yet greater was needed to set it free to attain to that freedom in which it cannot sin. Just as our first immortality, which Adam lost by sin, consisted in the ability not to die, and our last will consist in the inability to die, so our first freedom of the will consisted in the ability not to sin, and our last will consist in the inability to sin. Our will for piety and justice will be as indefeasible as our will for happiness now is. For though sin has lost us possession of both piety and happiness, the loss of happiness did not lose us the will to be happy. Surely the fact that God is unable to sin, does not mean that he lacks free will.

In that city then, there will be one free will and it will be one and indivisible in each and every one of its citizens. It will be freed from all evil, and filled with all good. Its enjoyment of the pleasures of eternity will never cease. It will forget all guilt; it will forget all punishment. But it will not so forget its liberation as to be ungrateful to him who gave it liberty. At the level of intellectual knowledge, it will remember the evils of its past; but at the level of what is experienced by the senses, it will forget them completely. An expert doctor, as far as professional knowledge goes, is acquainted with almost all bodily diseases; but as far as physical experience is concerned, he is ignorant of nearly all of them, not having suffered from them himself.

There are two ways of knowing evil things. In the one it is intellect that becomes aware of them, and in the other the senses that are affected by them; for it is clearly one thing to know all about vice through wise instruction, and another to know it through a depraved life of folly. In the same way there are two ways of forgetting evil things. One way of forgetting is that of the man who has learned and been instructed about it; the other is that of the man who has experienced and suffered it. The former forgets by neglecting what he has learned; the latter by escaping from his wretchedness. It is in this latter way that the saints will forget the evils of the past; they will escape them so completely that they will lose all sensation of them. But at the level of the intellect, which will be a powerful faculty within them, they will be clearly aware not only of the wretchedness of their own past, but also of the eternal wretchedness of the damned. If this were not so and they are to know nothing of their past misfortunes, how is it that, in the words of the psalm, 'they will sing of the mercies of the Lord for ever' [Ps. 89: 1]? Surely there will be no greater joy in that city than to sing that song to the glory of the grace of Christ, whose blood has given us our liberty.

There the words will be fulfilled: 'Be at rest and see that I am God' [Ps. 46: 10]. That will be the great sabbath that has no evening which God commended to us at the beginning of creation, where it says: 'And God rested on the seventh day from all his works which he had made, and God blessed the seventh day and sanctified it, because on it he rested from all his works, which God had begun to make' [Gen. 2: 2–3]. We ourselves shall be this seventh day when his blessing and sanctification has filled and remade us.

There we shall be at rest and see that he is God; which is what we ourselves wanted to be when we fell away from him through listening to the voice of the seducer: 'You shall be as gods' [Gen. 3: 5]. We abandoned the true God, who indeed made us to become gods – though not by deserting him but by coming to share in him. What have we done without him except be undone in his anger? But when he has remade us and has perfected us by grace still greater, then we shall have rest for ever and see that he is God. And we shall be filled with him when he himself shall be all in all.

All our good works, when we understand them to be his and not ours, are counted as ours when it comes to the gaining of that sabbath rest. For if we reckon them as our own, they are servile; whereas it is said of the sabbath: 'You shall do no servile work' [Deut. 5: 14]. That is why it is also said through the prophet Ezekiel: 'And I gave them my sabbaths as a sign between me and them, that they might know that it is I, the Lord, who sanctify them' [Ezek. 20: 12]. We shall have this knowledge in perfection when we have rest in perfection and when we see with perfection that he is God.

If the ages are counted like days in accordance with the divisions of history indicated in the Scriptures, it becomes still clearer that this sabbath rest is to be found at the seventh stage. The first age is the first day and lasts from Adam to the flood, the second from the flood to Abraham. They are found to be equal, not in length of time, but in having the same number of generations – ten each. There then follow, according to the calculations of the apostle Matthew, three ages up to the coming of Christ, each of them containing fourteen generations – one from Abraham to David, a second from David to the exile in Babylon, a third from the exile to the birth of Christ in the flesh [see Matt. 1: 1–17]. That makes a total of five ages. We are now in the sixth, which is not to be measured by any number of generations. For it has been said: 'It is not for you to know the times which the Father has put in his own power' [Acts 1: 7].

After this age, on the seventh day, God will rest by causing that seventh day, which we ourselves shall be, to rest in himself, who is God. It would take too long to discuss each of those ages in detail.

But this seventh day will be our sabbath, whose end will not be any evening, but the Lord's day, an eternal eighth day. For that day has been sanctified by the resurrection of Christ to prefigure the eternal rest not only of the spirit but also of the body.

There we shall rest and we shall see; we shall see and we shall love; we shall love and we shall praise. That is what shall be in the end without end. For what is our end but to arrive at the kingdom which has no end?

I think that I have now, by God's help, discharged my duty in completing this great task. Those who think I have written too little or too much, must forgive me. Those who are satisfied must not thank me, but join with me in giving thanks to God. Amen. Amen.